ABOUT THE AUTHOR

BETTY LEHAN HARRAGAN is an independent business
counselor specializing in the total integration of
women in the American work force. She writes a
monthly advice column in *Working Women*
magazine answering readers' ongoing job problems.
She travels extensively throughout the U.S. and
Canada addressing women's conferences on
employment issues. Her previous experience consists
of twenty-five years as a professional and executive
in private industry. She lives in New York City.

GAMES MOTHER NEVER TAUGHT YOU

BETTY LEHAN HARRAGAN

WARNER BOOKS

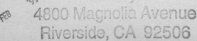
R

WARNER BOOKS EDITION

Copyright © 1977 by Betty Lehan Harragan
All rights reserved.

This Warner Books Edition is published by
arrangement with Rawson Associates, 115 Fifth
Avenue, New York, N.Y. 10003

Cover photograph by Superstock
Cover design by Anthony Russo

Warner Books, Inc.
1271 Avenue of the Americas
New York, N.Y. 10020

Visit our Web site at
http://warnerbooks.com

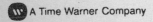 A Time Warner Company

Printed in the United States of America

First Warner Books Printing: May, 1978

Reissued: March, 1992

35   34   33

For my daughter Kathleen who will enter the workforce in the mid-1980's prepared to accept nothing less than fully vested citizenship in the American economy.

Acknowledgments

I could not have written this book without the hundreds of discussions over the years with other working women who were experiencing the same job problems that beset me repeatedly over a twenty-five-year working career. Many facets of their stories appear here though their names and identifiable industries have been changed. I am especially grateful to Elaine First Sharpe, founder and director of the Womanschool in New York, for her personal and professional faith in me and many thousands of today's rejuvenated business women.

Contents

PART
1
The Game, the Board, the Rules

CHAPTER
1

Working Is
a Game Women
Never Learned
to Play

* Ellena has a degree in art history which she partially financed by working at a steady part-time job weekends and summers in a factoring concern. The company was so impressed with her mathematical skills and grasp of economics that one of the executives asked her to join the firm permanently and learn the business under his guidance. She turned down the offer, considering the field too grubby and competitive because "all they thought about was money." She chose the clean, undemanding atmosphere of college teaching and is now out of work and in dire financial straits since the bottom dropped out of her occupational market.

* Eunice has a senior position in the auditing department of a multinational conglomerate, achieved after twenty years accumulating diversified experience in prestigious firms. She can't get excellent evaluations of her work because her immediate supervisor gets barely passing evaluations by his boss. Most of the time he can't even judge the quality of her work, but when he does give her glowing reports, nobody believes it because he has no credibility at upper levels.

* Harriet was an account executive at an expanding advertising–public relations agency where she devoted herself to building a tiny consumer product account into a major contributor to her agency's growth and income picture. She was rewarded with constant praise, merit raises, and complete autonomy on her account. After twenty-two years, the account was involved in a corporate takeover and left the agency. She was stunned beyond belief when she was unceremoniously fired by the agency she helped build and is too despondent to recoup her shattered self-esteem.

* Edna is a cum laude Harvard graduate who entered the management training program of a major bank along with nine men. In the second year of the program she found herself settled into a branch office handling personal checking accounts while the men were located in various sections of the commercial operations and had progressed several notches above her in status and salary. When she complained about being sidetracked, she was told there were two different training programs and since she hadn't specified either one, she was naturally funneled to the division where her ability to get along with female customers would be most useful.

* Suzanne is a research supervisor with an extraordinary grasp of interviewing, analytic, and validating techniques. She takes her work very seriously and follows reports right through to the final proofreading. She has attended assertiveness workshops and become an expert at persuasion tactics to gain the added help or deadline extensions needed to produce award-winning studies. Nevertheless her confidence and self-esteem are slowly diminishing as the choice projects in her area are assigned to other supervisors who regularly produce inferior or incomplete final reports.

* Francine has an impressive title, a fancy office, and an elegant engraved business card announcing her executive position in the human resources department of a Wall Street financial institution. When some two dozen female employees filed a class-action sex discrimination suit in federal court, she dismissed them as malcontents and incompetents, unqualified for promotion and disloyal to their employer. Not long afterward, her department was radically overhauled, and she expects to go next as she has no supporters, male or female.

These friends of mine are exceedingly accomplished working women who are suffering from traumatic experiences on their jobs. Their problems are having a disproportionate impact on their life plans, their feelings, and their future employment. Their situations are typical. I've heard almost the same story time and again from other equally competent, ambitious women. The tragedy is that *all* of these consequences could have been avoided, counteracted, or at least foreseen if the employees understood the game of corporate politics.

Like so many of their female cohorts in the male business world, they lack elementary conceptual knowledge about the working environment. What their mothers, teachers, husbands, friends, and employers have taught them—deliberately or unwittingly—has managed to distort their perspective, warp their judgment, pervert their trust, exploit their goodwill, distract their common sense, and divert their energy to helping everyone but themselves.

The past—good, bad, or indifferent—is gone. The present moment is the start of a new ball game for employees and employers alike. This time there's no reason for working women of any age to enter the action unprepared, ill-equipped, or uncertain of their position or opponents. The facts can set you free to determine your own fate in the corporate game plan.

Overview of the Master Game Board

For all practical purposes, the invasion of women in the corporate hierarchy has just begun.

When the octogenarian southern congressman Howard W. Smith of Virginia inserted his little "joke" into the highly charged debate over the Civil Rights Act of 1964, he accidentally incorporated "sex" into forms of discrimination prohibited by Title VII. Everyone expected that this innocuous gallantry would recede into the limbo of silly, obsolete laws that litter the federal and state statute books.

Unfortunately for the entrenched male power structure, a few perspicacious members of the discarded sex recognized the raw material for fashioning an innovative weapon in the seemingly hopeless struggle for female equality. Contrary to expectations, these farsighted pioneers began passing word of the secret cache to their historical enemies—other women. Simultaneously the feminist movement was being revived in myriad forms: radical, conservative, middle-of-the-road, loud, quiet, straight, gay, urban, suburban, political, personal, sophisticated, and naïve.

Within less than a decade after the act was passed, the emergence of women as a cohesive force began to threaten the very fabric of society, first in America but increasingly in the developed and undeveloped nations of the world. In the U.S., the first crack in the impenetrable male fortress was achieved through a series of government compliance guidelines and, since the early 1970s, a succession of landmark judicial decisions which established equal employment opportunity for women as a legitimate, enforceable premise. Now that the barbed-wire fence that used to exclude women from the battle-field has been breached, women are pouring into the fray.

Understandably, most of them are totally unprepared for the situations they will encounter. Worse yet, the vast majority are oblivious to the fact that they have stumbled onto a playing field where the rules of participation are rigidly enforced and the criteria for success are known to all but them. Clearly it is in the best interests of the entrenched power group to keep the new female players ignorant of the rules since uninformed recruits present little competition to the veterans and can be legally eliminated at very early stages of the game.

Women's assault on the bastions of corporate power must be deflected if men are to retain their traditional authority positions. Experienced warriors, trained since childhood or early manhood in the mightiest military machine of all time (World War II), are not to be easily vanquished by a guerrilla force of untrained female militia. Faced with this unexpected challenge, the strategists of business (including government bureaucracies and academic institutions, which are equally "in business" to maintain their male-dominated status quo) began drawing up long-range plans to dissipate the opposition.

The counteroffensive (also called the backlash) is well underway and the underlying strategy to block the progress of women is clearly visible to battle-scarred female veterans. They perceive the diversionary intent behind proclamations of "good intent" as an intentional ruse to confound many trusting women players who want to believe that their lifelong male protectors will continue to function in that same capacity. Women who count on "protectors" are inevitably in a weak and powerless position—precisely where their protectors want to keep them.

Other women players, inexperienced as they are in

following the more sophisticated moves, are easily distracted by pyrotechnic displays of concern and commitment to equal employment rights. They fail to see that the same old clerical, secretarial, and other "support" jobs that have been women's bailiwick are now simply renamed—and perhaps slightly better paid. It has been estimated that some 60 percent of the people in supervisory jobs today are women. Phenomenal progress, right? Not when you know that most of these women have already been labeled as lacking in management potential and are consequently locked in to minor supervisory positions for life.

The existing system is the game of business. The landscape which has been contoured out of a military-sports subsoil is the territory of play, the game board. The rules of the game are those firmly established generations ago by the male WASP founders whose descendants are still the star players. At this moment, not a single *rule* of the game has been challenged by Congress, the courts, or the commonweal, only the *custom* of applying the rules selectively in order to restrict the players. Obviously anyone who wants to join in the game must, perforce, subscribe to the standard rules of play. It does not follow that all players who meekly accede to the rules will win. Job success is a tantalizing prize to be sought, seized, and retained.

The real rules of the ongoing game are operating at full force, but what do most of the female rookies see? They are being deflected by:

—A blizzard of rhetoric and meaningless statistics to prove how fast women are progressing. (Public relations puffery is a tax-deductible business expense.)

24

—A proliferation of affirmative action programs aimed at finding "qualified" women who will be *given* great jobs.

—A plethora of new titles for certain women, including token elections to assorted boards of directors. (Is anything cheaper than a made-up word?)

—An added corporate entity called "EEO professionals" or "Affirmative Action Officers." (All carefully buried in the powerless personnel department.)

—A torrent of literature for ambitious women extolling the virtues of dead-end specialty occupations and the need for excessive formal education and academic degrees. (Most of these books bear the imprint of the business community: American Management Association, corporate personnel executives, or management consultants to big business clients.)

—Sudden concern for the rights of men whose individual constitutional rights are endangered by reverse discrimination. (Coupled with secret organizational funding of anti-ERA groups determined to withhold from women that same constitutional recognition which would be insured by the Equal Rights Amendment.)

This book is directed to the millions of women already in or preparing to enter the workforce with the express intention of reaching genuine policy-making levels. As later chapters will show, corporate privates or sergeants such as professional specialists or first-line supervisors have no chance whatsoever to change the system; that power resides solely in the hands of those in decision-making positions at the top of the pyramid, an exclusive group still totally dominated by white males.

It will take at least twenty years before significant numbers of women begin to reach the higher echelons of business, but they will all come from today's expeditionary forces of working women. It's important that volunteers in this force don't get deflected, distracted, or discouraged simply because they don't know the ground rules of what is essentially a childish and heretofore strictly a boys' game—playing corporate politics. When a participant knows what forces are controlling the moves of experienced players, she is in a position to outwit, outmaneuver, and outplay the opposition—and win.

The "X" Factor That Can Even the Odds

There are nearly 40 million women in the workforce in the United States today, and roughly half—almost 20 million—are employed full-time in nongovernment jobs. Concurrently, there are 56 million workforce men, almost 40 million of whom hold full-time nongovernment jobs. The ratio, surprisingly, is just a little over one to two.

Everything now being equal in the Land of Opportunity (that's what the employment laws say, don't they?), it should seem safe to predict that the future chief executives of America's four million major corporations will start turning up in a ratio of one woman to every two or three men. Yet the odds against a woman becoming chief executive officer of AT&T, General Electric, Xerox, IBM, First Boston Corporation, Bank of America, Pillsbury, Revlon, CBS, or Sears by the year 2000 are so astronomical that, in real terms, she has almost no hope. But we *know* that the reins of controls will inevitably pass into the hands of men who are working side by side today with female peers.

26

Why do knowledgeable people agree (and they do) that it's ridiculous to envision women at the top of the business pinnacle? Their reasons differ as widely as their perspectives. Women, of course, claim that it's sex discrimination, pure and simple. Businessmen are equally adamant that women "don't have what it takes" to get ahead in industry. Even when offered good opportunities (according to their bosses), women turn them down. Employers who insist they are looking to hire women for nonclerical positions say they're defeated because qualified women either do not exist or do not apply.

It is this endlessly repetitive adjective "qualified" that has absorbed my attention for the past five years. It crops up thousands of times—in every book or article about women and work and in every conversation on the subject with either employers or employees. It is a word used constantly and indiscriminately by everyone whose life is affected by the changing attitudes of women in business. "Qualified" turns out to be a magic word—like abracadabra it changes eggs into rabbits or makes coins disappear.

It's a word that can mean nothing or everything, depending on who's using it. Ardent feminists are quite convinced it is a contemporary euphemism for penis, and in a high proportion of cases they are absolutely right. There is no question that all established corporations discriminate against female employees in a thousand overt or subtle ways, both wittingly and unwittingly. To put it in more positive terms, business continues to follow its historical practice of discriminating *in favor of* white males for important jobs while welcoming the influx of women employees to fill the bottomless pit of support services.

Career counselors and vocational guidance people almost unanimously accept the employer definition which presumes a deficiency in women's ability. At any rate,

27

their plethora of advice is aimed at encouraging women to compensate for deficiencies by returning to school for additional college courses, different degrees, graduate degrees, or specialized education. At the other end of the spectrum, career guidance takes the form of ceaseless probing into the woman's personal attributes. Can she lead others? Can she make decisions? Is she willing to sacrifice her home for her job? Has she analyzed her patterns of success, her assertiveness, her reasons for working? No doubt these are valid considerations for women who do lack educational credentials or have ambivalent motivations, but they paint a romantic, idealistic picture of business qualifications. Men are not guided by such abstract watercolors of the terrain; they are supplied early in life with a realistic photograph.

Not to be outdone, corporate managements are also hard at work to remedy the alleged female shortcomings which prevent companies from hiring and promoting all the women they are so anxious to have on staff. As a rule, their approach takes one or more standard forms. They release official memos announcing that they are equal opportunity employers m/f and never think of such irrelevancies as sex when looking for qualified people; they set their head-hunters scouring the ranks of other corporations to find the rare woman who has achieved a minimal managerial level so they can hire her away for more money and acquire one visible female for their payroll; or (very popular) they set up scholarships and award grants to major universities to research those female faults which render them unqualified to fill male-dominated occupations.

And the women themselves? They seem to be increasingly bewildered at the vast discrepancy that exists between workday reality and proffered hopes or media hoopla. As the chasm of reality widens with each successive year, their frustration turns to anger, hostility, or utter discouragement. Especially so for those long-term working women who are aware that they and many other businesswomen are thoroughly educated, highly experienced, very competent, totally dedicated, strongly self-confident, and extremely ambitious. Even though they have all the publicized personal and professional qualifications, they still can't seem to bridge the gap that separates them from genuine job success on a par with men.

Clearly, there must be another factor in the equation for "qualified," a mathematical x that is withheld from women. I am convinced that there is, and the purpose of this book is to isolate that factor so that career women (any woman who works full-time for a lifetime has a career, whether she knows it or not) can begin to compute their future chances using the same number of component elements as their male colleagues and bosses.

In the course of talking to hundreds of working women in low and high jobs from many parts of the country over the past five years, I began to notice a strong undercurrent of similarity in job frustration stories. It had nothing to do with educational background because these women included engineers, lawyers, doctors, chemists, M.B.A.'s, C.P.A.'s (the supposed elite in business credentials), yet their job problems were no different from those of women with liberal arts B.A.'s who were working at secretarial jobs or at lowest level editorial, advertising, personnel, accounting, data processing, or sales work. Nor did the commonality of frustration relate to personality or self-assurance, since these women ran the gamut of age, life-style, family situation, meekness, aggressiveness, non-ambition, and fierce competition. There was no substantive difference whether the women worked in New York, Pittsburgh, Chicago, Des Moines, San Francisco, Los Angeles, Phoenix, Houston, New Orleans, Atlanta, or corporate suburban sprawls in between.

29

Such striking repetition of job difficulties could easily be dismissed as proof of traditional discrimination against women as a class. Since I don't for a moment discount the impact of cultural sexism and the undeniable fact that sex discrimination in employment is blatant and widespread, I was ready to agree. Gradually, however, I began to spot revealing glimpses in the stories which suggested that something else was also operating, an ingredient that went beyond sexism and offered a scheme to combat it.

"My boss is such a nice guy. I always liked him; we got along so well. He knew how much I wanted that promotion! I just can't understand why he voted against me."

"I liked that company. They're not perfect, but I think they're really trying to give women a chance and they have a pretty good grievance program so you can go to Personnel if you have a serious conflict with your boss. That's why I can't believe how they stuck up for him when they fired me. They know about his drinking problem."

"One of my good friends was finally made supervisor of our department—the first woman in history to get that job. I was so happy for her because I know how good she is and after all these years, she certainly deserved it. But now, well, things have changed. She's different. Ever since she got promoted, she's stuck up, acts cool and distant."

"When I got this job, I was thrilled. The work was interesting, exactly what I want to do. From the first day, I worked like crazy, about sixty hours a week, and

there is no question I am the best person in the depart-
ment—I'm really a top expert in my field. But you
know, they don't seem to appreciate it. I can't figure
it out. It's a weird situation; nobody seems to like
me."

Almost any working woman can add to these examples
from her own experience—situations at work, or reactions
of bosses, which are utterly incomprehensible given the
employee's knowledge of her company, her generally good
relationship with colleagues and superiors, her dedication
to long hours, hard work, and excellent performance.
Men, too, suffer disappointments during a long business
career, but their reactions are qualitatively different. As
a rule, they are not dumbfounded by the experience. Their
response is more likely to be summed up as, "I knew that
bastard would do this to me if he ever got the chance."
They foresee outcomes, understand why something happens, accept consequences. They are seldom crushingly
surprised.

This difference in reaction is well known to management, and there is a growing body of outrageous literature
(not to mention "management awareness" seminars and
training programs) devoted to the unique problems of
supervising women or teaching male supervisors how to
"handle" the unfamiliar emotional reactions they can
expect when they try to correct, praise, or discuss certain
subjects with women subordinates.

For all the millions of dollars companies are spending
annually on their latest executive toy (the favorite brand
of which is "human resources development"), management is moving so far off base that it is hopelessly trapped
in a bog of behavioral psychology—a management
"science" being rapidly developed to hide the imminent
collapse of the vaunted male leadership capacity under

31

the onslaught of women in the workforce. It is for this reason—because male management is just as confounded as its newest female employee—that women who incorporate the essential x factor into their career calculations can outwit the entrenched hierarchy and make their jobs work for *them*, instead of vice versa.

Quite simply, the x factor might be labeled "perspective," or realization that working is a *game*. All organizations share a rigidly defined structure and mutual goals. The conduct of business is confined by specific rules which shape the nature of the game and ordain the resulting patterns, traditions, and operating procedures. Deprived of this crucial x component, most women have never thought about their jobs in realistic game terms.

Those who have noticed strange rites of passage tend to discount their observations as contrary to common sense. Still others reject any budding awareness in hopes the unsettling confusion will go away if they just ignore it. Even women who have reached the top echelons (for women) reveal their blissful ignorance of the x factor in publicized newspaper and magazine interviews. Young women college graduates who become bitterly disillusioned their first year out of school are totally unenlightened.

It's almost as if working women have stumbled, been driven, or deliberately plunged into a foreign territory that is completely encircled by ancient trees and impenetrable except through a few guarded gates. Only since the advent of Title VII of the Civil Rights Act (especially as amended in 1972 to cover the bulk of all occupations) have the number of gates increased to accommodate the entry of those who were previously denied access. But the interior geography of this foreign country (known as the Business World) has not changed since the Industrial Revolution first discovered and laid claim to it.

Most women are completely unaware that once they

pass through the gates, they have entered an alien land with customs, traditions, security forces, and mores of its own. What's more, the natives speak a strange, oblique tongue, and the signposts are in cryptic ciphers. Although the terrain is criss-crossed with well-trodden paths, there are few visible directions to guide the unfamiliar strangers. Most of the male inhabitants are outwardly cordial, but they are far too preoccupied, if not openly hostile, to do more than brush past the legions of female visitors who wander aimlessly in ever-widening circles, unable to help each other because one is more lost than the next.

This indeed is no-woman's land, even though some long-time visitors have set up housekeeping at a few choice crossroads near the outer perimeter. The settlers are of little help to the influx of new visitors because they have never penetrated far inland and have had too few conversations with inland natives to learn the language. None of them was ever offered a map of the territory, so most believe that the interior is an uncharted jungle.

They are wrong. Every inch of the Business World has been surveyed and plotted many years ago. It may be true that printed maps no longer exist, but that's because they aren't needed. Natives know the original layout and are seldom fooled by obliterated signs. They recognize that the meandering paths constitute a game board, that explicit rules govern one's progress from place to place, that penalties for unacceptable moves are swiftly enforced.

Although many women have heard it so described, very few are willing to believe that business is a game. Games, after all, are for children, and business is serious adult activity—the most serious of adult concerns because it is the most highly rewarded in prestige, status, and money. Furthermore, top business executives commingle and cohabit interchangeably in the upper levels of politics, government, and academia where the major policy decisions of the world are formulated. To reduce these important people to mere gameplayers is an affront to the idealism of many women.

On the other hand, there are plenty of women who eventually do perceive the game characteristics of business. Unfortunately, lacking a suitable tutor, they're apt to misjudge which game is being played. Consequently, many intelligent women can be found playing checkers while their opponents are playing chess. They have been able to identify a game board and certain playing pieces, but from there they extrapolate to simple games they know, failing to grasp the more complex moves allotted to certain pieces. They get checkmated early in the game.

Another typical misjudgment can be illustrated by cards, where businesswomen seem to be playing a sophisticated rummy although they have been promoted to a table playing poker. In both games there are no partnerships; all play only for themselves. But the object of play is fundamentally different: in rummy, the idea is to get rid of all your cards or to accumulate in your hand matched sets or sequences; in poker, the object is to *win the pot*, which consists of bets made by players who gamble that they have the best hand.

Clearly, "working" is a game women never learned to play. Not that it mattered much when they weren't allowed on the playing field anyway. But now things are different; women can no longer be arbitrarily excluded. That means that working women (all 40 million of us plus the millions of others still waiting in the wings) have a compelling reason to learn the rules of the game.

The Name of the Game is Corporate Politics

In any game, proficiency comes only with practice. Thus women at every level or point in a business career should start playing immediately, no matter how inept or awkward they feel. It's worth remembering that success is not determined solely by your own skill or experience; the quality of your opponent's play has at least as much influence on the final score. Many women will discover that they have a knack for the game; others will need more and longer practice sessions; some may decide they'll never be any good and drop out entirely. But even this last group will benefit from understanding the game because everyone who works for pay in American organizations is part of this national sport, if only a cheerleader or part of the clean-up force.

The game of business is played out in as many arenas as there are organizational facilities in the country. There are innumerable variations of the official game, some so intricate they challenge championship players, and some merely local options adopted by government, nonprofit, or academic groups. The basic rules given in the following chapters are sufficient to understand the theory of the game, recognize the official game board, the playing pieces, the scoring, the general rules, and the penalties for infringement or irregularities.

The game of business has acquired several euphemistic titles, but experienced male players refer to it by its generic name—corporate politics. It is the x factor, the missing component in the female "qualified" equation. The objective of the game is money and power. The rules are ridiculous (because essentially it's a little boys' game), but they are rigidly adhered to (because children, as every mother knows, are stubborn and irrational about silly, made-up rules).

Once you know the rules, it's easy to predict opponents' moves, at least easier than when you don't even know you're in a game where explicit rules govern the play. Women, at this point in time, stand to make wonderful

35

players of corporate politics and ultimately—when they get to be dealer—they can exercise their prerogative to change the rules to "dealer's choice."

CHAPTER
2
You're in
the Army *Now*

* Louisa owes her fortuitous product-buying position in an entertainment complex to the vice-president of her division, although he is not her immediate boss. Between them is a nervous male manager with whom Louisa frequently disagrees on business decisions. Her friend the vice-president encourages her to talk to him "about your problems" and once said, "Why didn't you come to the meeting and say that?" She explained that her boss, Bob, wouldn't let her attend meetings, but the vice-president said, "Come to the next one anyway." She did, and when her opinion was sought, it conflicted with Bob's. Ever since, her relations with Bob have deteriorated so markedly that he calls her dirty names. Her predicament is wrecking her self-confidence because she always heard that you have to do what the "big boss" says.

* Beatrice is the only woman in a department of male professionals. She feels contempt for her male colleagues and supervisor, all of whom she considers weak and timid for combing their hair, dusting off their shoes, buttoning on their jackets, and answering "Yes,

sir!" when summoned to the office of the assistant manager, their superior. She knows they despise the man and have no respect for his decisions so she thinks of them as "two-faced" and cowardly in not sticking up for what they privately agree are the "right" things to pursue.

* Mary is a young publicist who accepted a new job as publicity director of the branch office of a large institution. She is thrilled at the opportunity it offers because she will handle the publicity needs of four different departments and report directly to the managers of those operations. She was disgusted with her previous job because she reported to a single individual who she felt restricted her. She's heard that several older men turned down the position she now has, so she feels very lucky.

* Marguerite worked in the promotion department of a TV network in a department headed by a male supervisor younger and less experienced than she. When a corporate vice-president asked her help to produce an important rush project, she agreed instantly because his assignment was challenging, interesting, and exciting. He was extremely pleased at the accomplished way she took over the project, but soon her own boss complained that she was neglecting her regular work and loaded her with routine, trivial tasks. After six months of working day and night and weekends to satisfy "the demands of her job," she had a breakdown from sheer exhaustion.

If there's one place most women have never been, and never hope to be, it's in the army. Therefore it may come as a shattering revelation to find out that collecting a regular salary from a business enterprise means that you are part and parcel of a classic military organization. Not some slap-dash medieval legion where knights-errant occasionally jousted off to defend the honor of their lady fair, but a modern, mercenary, well-equipped, scientifically staffed military operation.

It is no secret to management that contemporary corporate structure is descended from the military. The only confusion concerns which original branch of the family spawned the present generation. Robert Townsend, the former president of Avis and author of *Up the Organization,* credited the mess that major organizations created for themselves to the fact that "for the last two hundred years we've been using the Catholic Church and Caesar's legions as our patterns for creating organizations." Early-twentieth-century business texts cited the *Maxims of Napoleon* as a guide for shaping industrial organizations. Naval enthusiasts have traced the prototype to captains of the East India Trading Company who came ashore in New England, backed up by riflemen, and founded the initial American business enterprises in their own image. Peter F. Drucker, often called the dean of business consultants and author of several standard management references, acknowledges the military debt but attributes it to large-scale industrial development which precluded efficient operation under the aegis of a single tycoon.

No matter, as of 1978 the military pattern has become so entrenched in the corporate way of doing things that it's doubtful it could be changed even if somebody tried. It might even be true that there is no other way to structure a large organization (whether a corporation, a government bureau, or a university) than the tested military hierarchy. Of course we can't know that yet because so far in history only half the population has been heard from on this subject: the ideas, brains, and creative instincts of women have had no part in fashioning our society's organizations; these are strictly male cloning productions.

Regardless of how or why the military mentality overtook the corporate structure, it is absolutely critical for aspiring women to understand that this is the primary layout of the business game board. Unless you grasp this fundamental fact, you will never master the simplest of moves, nor comprehend the theory of the game. Once you *do* catch on to this cardinal fact of working life, the whole scene in your office milieu will light up like a pinball machine as if you'd hit the jackpot.

Nothing clarifies the mysteries of male-female job relationships quite as much as the initial realization that you are in the army now, and have been for all your working life. (The only exception might be very small companies of a dozen employees or less where the owner-manager dominates the operation and runs it on an autocratic basis. In such a situation, success or failure rests entirely on a one-to-one personal relationship with the owner-boss who may or may not imitate the military matrix. In any case, there is little chance to play games because there is no place to move.)

Women, for the most part, start out at ground zero when it comes to functioning in a military unit. Practically none of the women in private industry has prior experience with army life. The few who may have been in the WACS or WAVES were confined to huge clerical pools and excluded (as they still are) from the relevant army experience which is combat duty. The rest were nurses and are still nurses. They may have noticed that it's a little different being a nurse in the army or a nurse in a big medical complex, but they wouldn't connect the similarity to the twin organizational structures because a narrow profession like nursing remains the same. A nurse cannot be promoted to doctor, in or out of the army, any more than an executive secretary can move into her boss's executive chair. Some women have had peripheral connections as the daughter or wife of a military man, but that experience is worse than nothing. Army wives are deliberately isolated from the real life of the men whose outer trappings include a covey of subservient females.

Not only do women have no useful military background, those who are career-minded and ambitious find

40

the thought anathema. Striving women are naturally inclined to be independent, rebellious, and assertive. They have already thrown over the pervasive cultural conditioning which pressures women into submissive, secondary roles, so the well-known army requirements of mindless obedience, mass living, and incessant order-taking are repellent to their psyches. On these grounds alone, they tend to reject interest in things military and exhibit little curiosity about the subject. They may also reflect women's general abhorrence of war and the machinery to fight wars. (In 1975 all nineteen women in Congress voted unanimously against U.S. involvement in the Angolan war and by substantial majority opposed military spending for the B-1 bomber.)

At this point someone is bound to observe that many men have mercifully eluded military service, and those reaching adulthood after the draft was canceled are as uninitiated as women in army protocol. True, and these young men have, and will have, difficulty adjusting to life in the corporate structure during their first year. But, unlike working women, they are clued in very early by male associates and management. Their receptivity to the system is light-years ahead of women's for a variety of reasons, all offshoots of their upbringing and social conditioning.

By and large, men without actual military experience have not escaped constant exposure to military orientation. Among their first playthings was a set of toy soldiers. They built forts in kindergarten and in vacant lots, owned successions of toy guns, and played cowboys-and-Indians or cops-and-robbers during childhood years. They saw movies, watched TV programs, read books about great wartime adventurers, and identified with these military heroes. Some had close pals who got drafted or enlisted, with whom they went through the experience vicariously. Fathers, uncles, grandfathers, or older brothers regaled them with stories of wartime feats and service exploits.

41

Few boys grow up in our society without becoming imbued with the grandeur and thrill of militarism and the respectful awe due the martial arts. It is part of their education "to become a man."

Unfortunately they learn more than national defense from this manly indoctrination. "War," says Susan Brownmiller in her monumental study of rape, *Against Our Will* (New York: Simon and Schuster, 1975), "provides men with the perfect psychologic backdrop to give vent to their contempt for women. The very maleness of the military—the brute power of weaponry exclusive to their hands, the spiritual bonding of men at arms, the manly discipline of orders given and orders obeyed, the simple logic of the hierarchical command—confirms for men what they long suspect, that women are peripheral, irrelevant to the world that counts, passive spectators to the action in the center ring."

Girls are raised to fulfill their expected role of peripheral and passive spectators. If they'd once wanted to join the boys in the fort, they were chased away. Sentimental movies and maudlin books taught them all they know. War and the military life are man's responsibility; to women it means writing letters, mailing cookies, raising fatherless children, volunteering for menial Red Cross chores, and—always—waiting patiently and tearily for the valiant men to come home. It's no wonder women bring an unreal and bewildered attitude with them into business. In the first place, they don't suspect that an office is structured like a standing army. Secondly, they don't know where or what the action arena is.

You're Invading an Alien Country

For a long time I didn't understand how profoundly this female ignorance of and indifference to military protocol interfered with the business judgment of in-

42

telligent, alert women. I am indebted to the viewpoint of two early childhood education specialists for helping me to resolve the issue. In an article titled "Sex-Role Culture and Educational Practice," Patrick C. Lee and Nancy B. Gropper suggested that the best way to fathom sex-role stereotyping is to examine the phenomenon on the basis that females in our society are being brought up as part of a separate culture—one distinctively different from the male's civilization.

When I began to view women's job problems through this anthropological lens, the disparities in men's and women's attitudes toward employment swam into focus. All around, I saw confirmation of this "alien culture" theory. It was abundantly evident that females in a business society operated on a different plane and judged the workplace from a perspective that stemmed from a different acculturation. Their communication patterns, physical gestures, group affiliations, dress customs, cultural artifacts, game skills, avocations, and competencies did indeed reflect dissimilar cultural values and norms from those around them. From these observations, I became convinced that women will be forever short-changed in business unless they perfect techniques and unorthodox modi operandi to compete in a world they never made.

When women enter business with serious intentions to succeed, they are almost immediate victims of traumatic culture shock, although they can't identify the pain. The classic symptom is frustrated, bewildered emotionalism. They rail in anger or confusion at the "craziness," "meanness," "stupidity," "male chauvinism," "unfairness," "dirtiness," or "senselessness" they seem to see all around them in the work milieu. If the shock is particularly severe, they begin to mistrust their judgment, their intelligence, their ability, even their self-confidence. In the end they either decide to make the best of a bad situation or flail at windmills in an attempt to maintain their integrity. They are suffering from a chronic case of sex-culture shock.

The antidote for a businesswoman of today is exercise, exercise playing a uniquely female brand of corporate politics. The central strategy in this game depends on analyzing the pertinent male cultural conditioning which exerts control over men's actions and involuntary reactions in the business environment. That information is essential to pre-plan your own moves accordingly. *The purpose is not to "join them" but to surpass them.* Key maneuvers are contingent on making accurate predictions of your opponents' moves, then outwitting them at their own game.

The first step in analyzing the "foreign" business culture is to appreciate the impact and extent of the military influence. Some women are overwhelmed at the immensity of such a task and ask if it's possible to acquire working knowledge without similar experience and with no reliable information sources. Some even wonder if it's worth the effort. Yes, it's worth the effort, and it's not hard for smart women to catch on. It has been said that the scheme of the armed services is a system designed by geniuses for execution by fools. That's as good a description of the corporate copy as you'll ever find. And since women will be relegated to the "execution" end for quite some time, the jobs and the companions they encounter will not be overwhelming.

All you really have to learn about the military are those specific elements which have been carried over to male-dominated business. Guns, thank goodness, are generally discouraged as office equipment, and physical slaughter is eschewed. What business has adopted lock-stock-and-barrel from the military is organizational structure and the concomitant rules to maintain mass discipline. Along with the structure have come remnants of the attendant warrior psychology, including a camouflaged form of the conquering-hero rape instinct (as we shall see later), and a popular slanguage replete with military pomposities to dramatize everyday banalities.

Fragments of the military-industrial edifice are usually visible to long-term women employees who are in the midst of it. Their difficulty lies in relating the various parts to each other and distinguishing genuine rules from obsolete "book" regulations that are tacitly ignored by all. Then there are unwritten, flexible canons that give rise to the invisible organization that rides in tandem with the formal structure in every company. To untangle these male business interrelationships—and eventually penetrate them—it is necessary to understand the primary characteristics of military structure which are duplicated in private enterprises.

Where Do You Stand in the Pyramid?

The word "hierarchy" originally referred to a governing body of ecclesiastics organized according to successive ranks or orders and ruled by a chief Hierarch. Unquestionably the principle of hierarchical organization is very old, but judging by the paralysis of contemporary bureaucratic versions, it has just about reached the point of no return. Nevertheless, we are universally stuck with it for the foreseeable future. This ancient device is your guide to psyching out your employer corporation and your job within the network. The grand design of hierarchy is replicated in every department, division, branch office, or other fractionated part of the overall corporate entity. Whatever your job, you are part of the grand hierarchy and also a functioning unit within one of the sub-hierarchies.

The symbolic shape of a hierarchy is a one-dimensional pyramid (see diagram next page). Its capstone is the top executive officer—the most powerful final arbiter, the ultimate decision-maker. Polishing rough edges of

THE CHAIN OF COMMAND

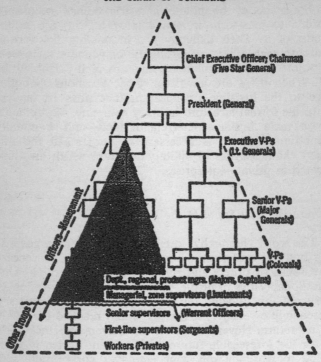

Notice how mini-pyramids (shaded area) pervade the superstructure. Jobs can be stratified further by inserting layers at any level in the pyramid. The chain-of-command is in the vertical fretwork of reporting lines.

the pyramidal hierarchy is a favorite pastime of the military and its business shadow, so that explicit titles may vary from time to time but I will use those army terms which are most easily recognized. The general, then, is the head of the army and buck privates are at the bottom of the heap. This minimal knowledge is enough to plot the three corners of the triangle: the general at the top and thousands of privates spread across the broad bottom base.

The inside of the pyramid is made up of layers, or levels. Not every general is head of the army; there are several subordinate levels of generals, just as there are several levels of corporate vice-presidents under the president and chairman of the board in private industry. The top man is a five-star general (chairman of the board); one level below is the four-star general (president); on the next level reside lieutenant generals (executive vice-presidents); below them the major generals (senior vice-president); and progressively down the levels through brigadiers, colonels, lieutenant colonels (assorted degrees of vice-presidents), down to majors, captains, first lieutenants (various regional and departmental managers) and finally second lieutenants (junior executives just "graduated" from management cadet training). These successive layers represent decreasingly important or less powerful officers. The layers fan out from the top down because the less powerful the level, the more positions located at that rank. From the middle of the pyramid down to the bottom base, the layers are composed of "other ranks" or enlisted troops which are sharply differentiated from commissioned officers—or management.

The power in a hierarchy flows from the top down because the functional logic is simple: when a task is too big for one person, divide it. The top executive general assigns portions of his work to subordinate generals who are directly responsible to him for performing those specific tasks. When their assigned tasks overwhelm the capacity of the subordinate generals, they in turn subdivide their work and assign specific functions to other subordinates who, of course, are directly responsible to them for performance. These subordinate officers delegate down the line to another level of subordinates, and so it goes, in geometric progression, until you hit bottom—that's the only level in the hierarchy which is purely subordinate because there's no one lower. All the other levels (with the exception of the capstone) are in a dual position: they themselves are subordinate to their immediate superior officer but are superiors of those to whom they've delegated work, those who report to them. In a hierarchy, no one is an island; each position is intertwined in the stratum.

The intent of hierarchical organization is to subdivide large and complex tasks into manageable components and then to reassemble or coordinate those elements to accomplish a proscribed purpose. There is an inner flexibility to the system that can accommodate to changing circumstances. If tasks become unmanageable due to geographic distances (global warfare or international operations), technological inventions (nuclear weapons or new industrial developments), or numbers of people required for the tasks (peak mobilization of World War II or peak employment of 1960s), new classes of subordinates can be created by adding lateral levels.

Such added hierarchical levels can be inserted at any layer in the pyramid without changing the internal structure because the relationships between the levels remain constant. This practice may produce higher pyramids, but the "distance" between successive levels remains the same. A new insertion inevitably pushes all lower levels further downward. This automatic downgrading occurs frequently in the corporate structure. Whenever a new job is inserted between you and your boss and you are told to report to the new individual (who now reports to your old boss), you have witnessed insertion of a new hierarchical level. And instantaneous demotion of your position.

With each descending level, the power, responsibility, authority, and status diminish in a prescribed ratio. So do the importance, difficulty, and prominence of the assigned tasks as they are consistently subdivided down the levels. The rationale behind subdivision is to insure that no task exceeds the ability of its performer. In practice, the principle turns into an idiot's nightmare as both military and business tasks are broken down into dehumanizing fragments. Management is greeting the influx of women workers (up 75 percent in twenty years) with open arms and plunging them into the low-paying, low-status jobs at the lower end of the skills spectrum—as usual. The proportion of women in higher skill positions on the pyramid ladder is dropping steadily although the numbers are increasing. To disguise the reality, office walls are painted pink and blue to satisfy "the feminine desire" for pretty surroundings and it's called "job enrichment."

"If It Moves, Salute It"

To avoid chaos in a hierarchy, the levels are clearly labeled with authority tags which identify occupants. This is the rank, or job title. The military set the mode with a profusion of pay grades and differentiated titles; government clearly numbers its job ranks as GS 1 through 18; corporations make an unholy mess with hodgepodge, undifferentiated titles and numbered job classifications intermingled. It takes an "inside" detective to unscramble the rank of, say, four hierarchical levels when all share the one title of vice-president. An M-6 supervisor in one department may have the rank and salary of an M-8 supervisor in another department of the same company.

Many subsidiary presidents report to corporate vice-presidents. *But the rank system is intact.*

In the armed services rank is formalized with an intricate set of insignia, badges, patches, and stripes which announce one's title, tenure, honors, and importance to all and sundry. The insignia tell soldiers and officers alike whom they must defer to, and this unquestioning respect for superior hierarchical rank is the first lesson drilled into raw recruits in boot camp or cadets in officer training schools.

What recruits learn is that the superior is entitled to respect and deference and obedience solely because of the *rank* he has attained, not for any personal qualities, good, bad, or despicable, and not for any performance or competence attributes. The hierarchical structure is abstract and impersonal. Only the task to be performed and the authority required to perform it are delineated; people are considered expendable inasmuch as war obliterates a lot of personnel, but the system never collapses. In other words, it's the uniform (or office) that matters. Not the person in it.

This impersonal quality indigenous to hierarchical structures is an early stumbling block for many women entering this foreign environment. They assume *they* are *important* and that they can make the task or job into something better or more important to the company. This is literally impossible in a hierarchy; expanding a defined job means moving into someone else's territory or, as women often end up, doing two jobs for the price of one. It's not uncommon to hear women explain their excessive devotion to duty by saying, "They need me," "The work had to get out," "I always have to correct or redo half the material I get." The sense of responsibility reflected here is admirable and necessary as long as you are doing your own job, at your own rank! Redoing someone else's work is not your job. Assuming responsibility outside the parameters of your function is not your

50

job. Taking on added duties out of goodwill or "helpfulness" and without commensurate compensation is being exploited, since someone else's failure to perform is not your problem. (Unless, of course, you are the supervisor in charge of exactly that, in which case it *is* your responsibility to get the work out.)

In a hierarchy, the person in the *rank* position gets credit for satisfactory performance of duties belonging to that rank. If you do somebody else's work, it may be a gracious gesture, but it has nothing to do with performance evaluation at your own level. When jobs are ranked, it doesn't matter who fulfills the duties as long as the obligatory tasks are performed. It's immaterial whether the incumbent is overqualified or minimally competent as long as the limited tasks assigned to that slot are completed satisfactorily. Medals of honor are sometimes awarded to military personnel in recognition of actions "beyond the call of duty" because a rank-structured hierarchy demands, and expects, nothing more than one's spelled-out duties. This fundamental impersonality also means that no hierarchical position "needs" a particular individual to fill it; anybody will do, heartless as that sounds. Women who desperately "need" a job can easily be misled by zealous supervisors into believing the job "needs" you and extra effort makes you indispensable. Not so in the rigid rank hierarchy. Its impersonal machinery goes into operation very fast when there's a staff cutback or elimination of plants or branch officers for efficiency reasons.

Who Gets into the Officers' Club?

In addition to the ranking system, the military structure endowed business organizations with its classic differentiation between officers and enlisted men. In the armed services these two classifications are sharply distinguished by pay, social standing, professional status, privileges, responsibility, and advancement. Officer candidates are the future commanders and leaders; enlisted men can progress through noncommissioned officer ranks until they hit the ceiling which is imposed just below the starting rank for future leaders.

Noncommissioned officers do not jump into commissioned officer ranks no matter how capable, long-serving, or ambitious. Some of the traditional differentiations between officers and noncoms are reportedly being eased somewhat, but the dual categories are ingrained in the hierarchical mentality. The purpose is to prevent "unqualified" people from reaching important leadership positions by preordaining the promotional track, depending on where one enters the system. Enlisted men enter as buck privates at the bottom of the pyramid and can progress rather easily to corporal and sergeant. After that comes a point in the lower-level hierarchy where additions or subtractions in layers can easily be made as the army needs more or less interim supervisors. Some familiar gradations are staff sergeant, sergeant first class, master sergeant, first sergeant, and sergeant major. Running parallel to sergeant grades are technical specialists 4 through 9, all equivalent in pay grade and rank. Next comes numbered gradations of warrant officer rank, the highest of which is the ceiling for servicemen who entered at the bottom and worked their way up.

This is the arbitrary breakover point in the military structure because the next pyramidal level is second lieutenant—the commission given to graduates of West Point or other colleges designated as reserve officer training schools. The promotional track of candidates who enter the system as junior-grade lieutenants runs upward via first lieutenant, captain, major, lieutenant colonel, and colonel to the various levels of generals.

The rank levels of sergeant and warrant officer have special relevance for working women because these are

52

comparable to first-line supervisory positions (sergeant) running up through increasingly responsible supervisory positions to the ceiling (warrant officer). At this level, there is a broad gray band across the corporate hierarchy which signifies the crossover from supervisor to management status. These two words are not synonyms although they are used interchangeably by many career counselors. It's true that management people are also supervisors, but the majority of supervisors are not management. It's hard to pinpoint the transfer line because corporations have messed up titles so thoroughly, freely duplicating titles at lower levels to make jobs "sound" more important, that the demarcation is blurred. Insiders usually know where the shift from supervisor to management supervisor occurs because the line always exists in individual companies.

Even the military prototype is slightly confused. Warrant officers enjoy officer status and privileges (they can go in the officers' club, for instance), but they do not have full officer responsibility. Their duties are more administrative or technical in nature. This level in the military model is such that a young, inexperienced college graduate with a second lieutenant's commission immediately outranks a warrant officer-4, who could be a superlative administrator with twenty-five years' service and several honor medals earned in action. Long-tenured women executives should have no trouble locating the corollary level in the corporate hierarchy. It is the point at which a just-graduated M.B.A. could be brought in and made the boss of a woman who has headed a department successfully for many years. In today's employment market the M.B.A. graduate is part of the management or leadership cadre. As in the military matrix, potential leaders in corporate hierarchies do not enter at the bottom of the pyramid. They are brought in at some midpoint, bypassing the lower ranks.

Anything as riddled with lateral layers as the hierarchical pyramid must also have strong vertical connections. How do the orders from above come down the steps and reports from successive levels go up? In military parlance these vertical connectors are called the chain-of-command and, amazingly, the linkage is simplicity itself: every person reports to one person. To repeat, every subordinate at every level is responsible to one superior and one only; everyone in a hierarchy has one boss— their immediate supervisor. All official information— orders, directives, reports, requests, and certainly decisions—funnel through these authorized channels, traveling meticulously from one level to the next, whether going up or down.

If you have ever got entangled with a government bureaucracy you learned more than you care to know about "going through channels" because civil service has achieved the *reductio ad absurdum* of this hierarchical principle. Large corporations are not far behind; inefficiency and delays are so rampant that managements have set hordes of systems analysts, organizational experts, and communications specialists to work on the problem— with little luck so far. In one respect, this is a good omen for up-and-coming women because crafty moves are possible in the game of corporate politics with adroit use of red tape. Utilizing red tape for one's own advantage is not unusual, but coming from women who have been so easily duped in the past it is almost sure to catch men players off guard.

Clearly you must master the red tape vertical fretwork of the hierarchical structure, beginning with the one-boss, chain-of-command tenet. In the military this doctrine is instilled through relentless training in discipline, in the habit of unquestioning obedience to assigned authority. That's tough to teach Americans because most of us, including male bosses, hate to be disciplined. Once trained in the principle, however, they love the authority designation which puts them in a position to discipline others, no matter how minuscule the area of responsibility. Often the lower the degree of authority, the more insistently it's invoked, human nature being what it is.

Human nature or no, *absolute deference to the authority invested in your immediate boss* is the undeviating Number One Rule of the game. If I were to estimate which business canon is least comprehensible to women, I'd probably pick this one. Most women have no clear realization that every job in every corporation is so encased in the hierarchical network that, structurally speaking, your boss has life-and-death power over you. Your one-and-only immediate supervisor constitutes your sole connecting tie to the hierarchy (whether that cord is a lifeline or a slowly tightening noose). There is no way you can leapfrog, bypass, overrule, ignore, challenge, disobey, or criticize your boss and not get penalized in the game. That is the inviolate rule of the game, so much so that this rule makes the game. Without it, there would be no game at all. The rule applies to everyone in the corporation except the one at the top—who won the game!

Since this unquestioned authority of each boss is the controlling law, all activity in the game stems from it. In essence, the major tricks and ploys needed to play the game successfully are designed to (1) manipulate your immediate boss to your advantage, or (2) get out from under the thumb of a particular immediate supervisor. Your immediate boss's power over you derives from the rank of the position, not the person. Obviously, a shrewd player selects her immediate boss very, very carefully! Never take a job until you have had a sufficient opportunity to interview a potential boss at enough length to surmise your personal empathy or rapport. Of course that selection process is not possible when new supervisors are assigned to take over an existing group, so all players enjoy a period of hectic gaming, as we shall see later. Any woman, incidentally, who is offered a job without being interviewed and approved by the person to whom she will report directly *can be positive* that the job is a nonactive, inconsequential position, or (as happened to me once) she is a pawn in someone else's vicious game.

So, your most important relationship in any job is the one with your immediate boss. It is critical that you develop as good a working relationship as possible with this person. If that becomes totally impossible, your only option is to get out. Staying in such a position is employment suicide. Women employees frequently observe or get caught in destructive boss-subordinate situations and are appalled because "nobody will do anything about it." Nobody *can* do anything about it *according to the business game rules!* If you take a boss complaint to the personnel department, they will simply return the problem to your immediate boss, possibly however, through your boss's superior. If you go over your immediate boss's head to the next level, that superior's hands are tied by the rules. The immediate boss has supreme power in a stipulated area, and every man knows better than to infringe on it; such a move is "not fair" in the male game, it's an outright foul. Naturally, a superior can remove or reprimand a subordinate who proves to be an inept supervisor, but the power inherent in the rank remains with the occupant until such time as that supervisor is physically removed. Given the intransigence of this rule, every single move in corporate politics is predicated on its existence. The game is a dance choreographed around this configuration.

Under the discipline tenets, to usurp any fraction of the authority that belongs to a superior is a punishable offense in the armed services. And nothing seems to bring out the militaristic origins of the business system more quickly than an attempt to infringe on a male superior's circle of authority. Men know that to bypass anyone in the line of command is to deny him his right to exert his authority and prove his importance. I am using the pronoun "him" with deliberation in this context because the authority principle is all too frequently violated when the legitimate chain-of-command has a female link. Women supervisors must always be alert to enforcing their right in the chain-of-command formality. Simplifying the system in the interests of getting the job okayed quicker or done more efficiently is not a smart move in the woman's game. Any moves that deteriorate your legal range of authority in the orderly chain weakens your position. That's why male superiors of women supervisors try it so often. It's known as "the helpful male" ploy: "You weren't here so I just took care of it for you; I didn't think you'd mind." You can let him know you do mind, of course, but the better tactic is to keep your eye open for an opportunity to pull the same thing on him and sweetly repeat the same words. Just be sure the retaliation move infringes on his authority circle and is not merely a piece of work that he'd be glad to palm off on you anyway.

Enforcement of this disciplinary rule is so strict in the military that no provocation save death is sufficient for a subordinate to resist or disobey a superior's order. The dramatic conflict inherent in the situation has been grist for the novelist's mill. Women can absorb much of the mentality of the hierarchical culture from reading such novels. One outstanding example is Herman Wouk's *The Caine Mutiny* in which navy Captain Queeg appears to have crossed the boundary from autocracy to insanity. The ship's entire personnel are convinced he has doomed them to certain death by his handling of the ship in a hurricane, and most of the action revolves around subordinate officers who are better qualified to take over command. The terrifying dimensions of the conflict between military discipline rules and self-preservation are starkly outlined, but the denouement with its court-martial trial is dazzling in illuminating the mind-set of the military mentality.

Navy ships make convenient vehicles for fictional works because the hierarchy is condensed into a manageable unit. The old movie *Mr. Roberts*, now a staple on TV late shows, illustrates another aspect of the chain-of-command. Mr. Roberts is second in command to a tyrannical captain and favors a management style directly opposed to dictatorial methods. The story dramatizes the relationships—and authority limitations—among men at different levels of the hierarchy, but the crux of the lesson to women lies in the futility of humane instincts and well-meant promises when the power to countermand lies higher up the ladder. The plight of the intermediate supervisor is clear. The point of this self-indoctrination is to comprehend the values, motivations, and responses that are governing men you must deal with in the business environment. Staying one jump ahead of your adversaries is only possible if you can predict their likely moves in advance. Mothers and teachers do this all the time when they anticipate children's possible actions and want to counteract them beforehand.

"Who Promoted Major Major?"

Modern literature is replete with subject matter on hierarchical themes, but by far the best prepared text for a course in playing corporate politics is Joseph Heller's famous World War II novel, *Catch-22*. In this case the movie version will not do; you must read the book (and reread it every few years as you move up a notch or two on the business ladder). This excruciatingly funny, savagely incisive novel about an isolated air squadron in the Mediterranean could be transplanted in its entirety (minus the bombing missions) to the everyday working week of the average businesswoman. You will meet almost all the male bosses you've ever had, and be primed to recognize those you've yet to encounter. ("Actually, Major Major had been promoted by an IBM machine with a sense of humor.") For all its side-splitting humor, *Catch-22* is a brilliant evocation of the hierarchy in operation and shows how different men respond to their rank positions and duties. For women, there are buried nuggets of priceless hints on outwitting the red-tape restrictions—and instructive glimpses into the placement of females in a typical hierarchical situation.

Should the relevance of *Catch-22* to the present business scene escape you, there is a sequel published twelve years later by the same author which is right on target. Joseph Heller's *Something Happened* is literally set in the business milieu. It is about life and working in the middle- to upper-middle management levels in a typical corporation. It is *Catch-22* shorn of its wartime exhilaration and transposed to its peacetime equivalent. To get the full impact of the hierarchical transference, the books should be read in sequence, first the military, then the private industry prototype. Both books are undiluted specimens of male-culture mentality, so women who want to see themselves in a full-length three-way mirror— the way they appear to male bosses and colleagues— should take careful note of female characters in the novels, and men's attitudes toward these women.

Understanding the military substructure of business organizations—the stratified pyramid, the rigid rank system, the chain-of-command network—reduces the initial confusion so often felt by working women. Knowledge provides an essential piece of equipment—a permanent spotlight—to illuminate shadowy corners of the office milieu. You'll need this essential tool to make intelligent judgments about your placement in the company's formal structure, and management's determination of the worth of your job. For instance, the extraneous nature of secre-

59

tarial and clerical jobs can be perceived in the glare of the hierarchical spotlight. At what level in the hierarchy do these jobs fall? What rank (including salary and title) is attached to such positions? Where is their connection in the vertical chain?

The unfortunate truth is that secretarial functions *do not belong anywhere.* These jobs are *outside* the pyramid, nowhere entwined in the network. They are not even bottom-level jobs because there's no vertical connection that joins them into the hierarchical ladder. Secretarial jobs can occur indiscriminately throughout the layers, from top to bottom, with no substantial difference in ranking. In fact, there is no formal rank attached to these jobs; they are anomalies. Because these disembodied positions float aimlessly throughout the pyramid, they are not subject to the rules which apply at real levels, especially the one-to-one boss stricture. Secretaries and other general clericals are often responsible to two or more ranked individuals, and uncertain as to the relationships. To which immediate superior is a clerical worker responsible? The two executives for whom she works? Which one? The clerical supervisor in personnel or office administration? The sales department manager? Or one of the sales representatives for whom she processes paperwork?

Working women's confusion in a hierarchical milieu stems largely from their historic exclusion from the "real world" inside business enterprises. The typical female introduction to business via clerical jobs leaves a trail of misconceptions which later haunt those women who get a step on the ladder. But even then, women continue to receive the treatment of outsiders not subject to the standard rules governing men at identical ranks. This widespread mistreatment of ranked women employees leads to tension, aggravation, and bewilderment on the part of ambitious climbers. They can be seen running around distractedly trying to satisfy demands of several

60

supervisors or unwittingly deferring to colleagues of equal rank.

Marguerite, the TV promotion executive who collapsed while trying to please two bosses, was mercilessly exploited by the executive v-p, who thoroughly understood the authority rules, but gambled—successfully—that a female subordinate would not. As the superior link in the chain-of-command, it was within his purview to detach her from her regular duties while she worked on his project. Instead he got invaluable assistance from another man's subordinate by playing on the woman's eagerness to do a job *that wasn't hers*. Naturally her real boss got furious—at the superior player's interference in his authority realm and the employee's connivance, as he would see it. The only maneuver open to him was penalizing his female subordinate with mounting demands on her time by assignment of needless or trivial chores. Marguerite didn't know the military rules. Had she been an accomplished player of corporate politics she would have parlayed her strong point (the need of the v-p for her services) to force him into making the mandatory move within his power—freeing her from the petty tyrant to whom she legally reported. The two male supervisors were playing against each other under the standard rules; she was squeezed in the middle, a victim of ignorance, although in a position to make a desirable improvement in her own situation.

Sometimes women employees unwittingly force bosses to "pull rank" when they fail to accord proper deference to superiors as enjoined by the military legacy. I once watched a bright, talented young woman destroy her chances at the very beginning of a promising professional career. She was well liked by her female co-workers, experienced veterans in the field, who gladly answered her eager questions and enjoyed the opportunity to teach the lively, fascinated newcomer. At first her male supervisor was very pleased with his new employee, but when her proficiency grew at an alarming pace, his ardor diminished perceptibly. He became super-critical of every task she completed perfectly and increasingly kept her under his thumb. She became distraught trying to satisfy her boss; the more women colleagues applauded her work, the more he tore it apart. One day his anger exploded when he overheard an older woman explaining a technical point to the neophyte. He peremptorily dismissed the older woman (who was not in his group) and railed at the younger woman, finally commanding: "When you want to know anything, you ask ME! I give out all the information you need around here!" She lived in terror (and disgust) thereafter and eventually quit, unable to fathom his antagonism.

He was an ex-navy officer who jealously guarded every prerogative of his business rank. The young woman had violated the military code and demeaned his authority by seeking advice from inferior-status people (her female colleagues) rather than him. The factual situation further confounded her because her boss literally did not have the professional know-how that she could obtain from peers. Had she known the implications of the business-military ranking system, she could have learned from her friends while concealing the truth from him. To play corporate politics (i.e., gain her own ends), she would have asked him first, then sought competent advice from knowledgeable colleagues. She could have deceived him into thinking he was the one training her although her real aim was to accumulate professional techniques from respected co-workers.

Lifelong failure to perceive the military grounding in office structure accounts for the prevalence of deluded "Aunt Toms" who think authority comes from longevity or assumed officiousness. Such women are usually minor functionaries, but they continually try to impress others with an assumed superiority which they mistakenly believe was accorded to them. For many years I had a professional acquaintanceship with such a woman who was duped for a quarter century and refused to believe it even when forced to retire "early." Outside of work she was friendly, sociable, widely traveled, interested in music, and a permanent volunteer in children's hospitals. In her office she was a veritable witch on a broomstick. After a couple of beginner's jobs, she had settled down in one corporation for twenty-five years. She was a devoted, conscientious worker staunchly loyal to her employer. Early on, she learned the deference rule and was blindly uncritical and almost obsequious to male superiors. Women colleagues who came into her orbit over the years regarded her as a prissy, old-fashioned, irritating pest— or a management fink. For a preponderance of her working years she doggedly interfered with other women's work, taking on a role as emissary of management due to her seniority. The department heads never discouraged her and, in fact, often they dispatched her as an unofficial courier to "straighten out" problem employees who would predictably quit after a period of her tutelage. During all her twenty-five years, she was assigned to a single, extremely limited task and was never promoted to so much as corporal. Yet she played at being a toy sergeant, interminably trying to whip other pfc's into line, blissfully unaware that she was never given the authoritative rank to do so. Her male superiors tolerated her amusedly (and exploited her irritability quotient when it suited their purposes) as long as she continued to perform her one narrow task satisfactorily. Mostly they laughed at her pretensions, secure in the knowledge that any one of them could puncture her balloon of self-importance whenever they felt like it.

Aside from making herself hated, her example was destructive to incoming women cohorts who never knew whether to comply with her unbidden dictates; she confused the authority picture for them. Especially when she was used, as long-seniority women frequently are, to

63

do personnel dirty-work for cowardly male managers.

Working women who hope to function effectively in a hierarchy must be fiercely protective of their rank rights, but at the same time they must be sure they know what their position actually is. On the other side of the coin, they must have a clear perception of the formal authority designations so they cannot be hoodwinked by individuals (male or female) who lay claim to authority they do not possess.

"Catch-22," Doc Daneeka answered patiently, when Hungry Joe had flown Yossarian back to Pianosa, "says you always got to do what your commanding officer tells you to."

"But Twenty-seventh Air Force says I can go home with forty missions."

"But they don't say you have to go home. And regulations do say you have to obey every order. That's the catch. Even if the colonel were disobeying a Twenty-seventh Air Force order by making you fly more missions, you'd still have to fly them, or you'd be guilty of disobeying an order of his. And then Twenty-seventh Air Force would really jump on you."

For over a hundred years, working women have been caught in the corporate Catch-22 which pitter-patters on the heels of its military model. The colonel said you were to get paid only half of what men got paid and could never go anyplace no matter how many missions you completed, and if you didn't accept his orders sweetly and uncomplainingly you'd be guilty of insubordination and be thrown in the discard pile and get no money at all. Well, the rule still stands that you have to do what your commanding officer tells you to, EXCEPT when he tells you that the rules don't apply to you because you're a woman! Rules are rules and they apply to *everyone*. If you learn the rules and play the game according to the accepted regulations, you've finally got a chance to win because neither your immediate boss nor the commanding general can pull a fast switch on the energetic female troops of today.

CHAPTER

3

You're in the Ball Game —Fight, Team, Fight!

* Clarice objected when she was frequently told to complete projects that had been assigned to an equal co-worker. Her male supervisor wheedled her with statements such as, "You know you're much better at that aspect, and we can't afford to turn in a performance that will make the team look bad."

* Jean was offered a seemingly substantial promotion to fill a management supervisory vacancy heretofore held only by men. She turned it down to her women friends' amazement, saying, "Who needs it? All that extra responsibility and headaches in addition to the activities I now supervise isn't worth the little extra money they offered."

* Arlene is a very competent senior employee who asked for an additional staff member to ease her consistently heavy workload. She made this request because her immediate superiors were always younger men who were so unfamiliar with the background and ongoing requirements of the distribution operation they headed for short periods before moving on to better jobs that much of her time was diverted to teaching

66

them the procedures. She was reprimanded for her "poor team attitude" since everybody around here "pitches in as necessary to get the work out."

The military influence on business is morphologic; it relates to the form and structure of organization, *considered apart from function*. The functions of private industry—the everyday operations—are governed by another formula which has its genesis in a more familiar though not unrelated activity—team sports. Working women have long noticed that sports talk is endemic among men in business plants and offices, but few women realize that working for pay in American corporations is comparable to playing an extended version of a favorite masculine ball game.

The combination of military structure with team sport operation is a natural one from management's viewpoint. Both industry and the armed services have mutual purposes insofar as integrating widely dispersed operations into an interlocking force and coordinating the performance of countless individuals into a cohesive unit. They also share identical methodologies by having an overriding goal (to win the war; to make a profit) to be achieved through a series of orderly steps which are carefully planned in advance, taking due account of both internal and external realities.

Where business and the military part company is in the handling of people, the deployment of human resources. Both entities depend on manpower to accomplish their objectives, but the relationship of employees to employers is radically different from that of soldiers to the armed forces. Even though residues of military dictatorship sometimes seep into corporate systems, the rigid, impersonal, enforced discipline demanded by military life is patently unsuitable for private institutions in an individualistic, democratic society. Voluntary employees have one potent option denied to active service personnel: they can quit at any time or place. Conversely they can always be fired. To control its volatile labor force, business needed a more compatible system than military discipline. Organized team sports fills the bill.

The advantages of the team sports matrix are many. First off, team membership is voluntary, as is employment, but must be requested or applied for. To secure a place on a choice team, the applicant has to offer a needed skill or the potential for usefulness. Once accepted, the rookie agrees to abide by the formal rules of the game and the team. A novice who does not measure up to expectations, or does not follow the coach's directions, can be dropped and replaced with a more amenable candidate. Promising athletes can be enticed by offering special attractions such as better accommodations, respected trainers, congenial surroundings, scholarships, excellent equipment, or more practice opportunities.

Secondly, the objectives of organized sports teams overlap those of military operations. Teams too have an overriding goal—to win the game. This is attempted by way of orderly moves, all of which require close coordination among players and most of which are subject to disruption by external forces, specifically the opposing team. What more ideal prototype could be found to forge the disparate individuals located in the various levels of the militaristic hierarchy into an efficient civilian corporate mechanism?

Important as the objective similarities are, there is an unparalleled psychological bonus attached to the sports replica. Men *love* sports. Almost en masse, without any encouragement, they follow favorite teams, watch games, admire players, bet on scores, discuss proficiency, mimic the professionals, evaluate the strategy, and are roused to heights of excitation by championship performance. Men understand sports, appreciate the intricacies, and enjoy the competitive atmosphere surrounding organized games. As employees in a sports-imitative milieu, they feel comfortable, part of the organization, one of the fellows. They have gone through preliminary training on the school teams and Pee Wee leagues years before; they sense what is expected of them; they are bonded in a familiar male camaraderie. They feel they have finally grown up "to be a man" and made it into the major leagues—the wage-earners' team.

This job terrain, like that of military service and organized sports, is an exclusive male domain. When men enter the gates of the Business World, the map of the territory is in their head; they have been playing with miniature models all their lives. Given the significance of this sports phenomenon in the male culture, it behooves us to take a closer look at its development.

Where You Missed the Ball

Kicking or throwing a ball around is an asexual instinct in its basic form. Games of this genre develop spontaneously among children of both sexes in all countries and through all ages of history. Child development specialists consider ball games to be natural outlets for young children's excess energy, tensions, aggressions, and emotions. Physically such games are immeasurably beneficial in aiding development of the large musculature and fostering coordination in fine muscle control. Physical therapists are well aware that disuse or misuse of muscles causes them to atrophy. Medical authorities agree that physical exercise is a critical component in achieving full development of the human organism, female as well as male.

Despite this knowledge, female bodily expression is gradually discouraged in our society as girls are diverted to less strenuous, restricted pursuits. If exercise is healthy and ball games are instinctive exercises for children, why are girls turned against their nature? The answer lies not

69

in the physical but in the social disciplines inculcated by youthful games and group play. During the first six years of life, children have little if any group spirit. Every mother of preschoolers knows their tots can't play together for five minutes without some kid whacking another with a shovel or grabbing at a clutched toy. The first job in civilizing the species is teaching children to play *with* each other. By school age they must be capable of relating peaceably to the larger class group. That is, recalcitrant boys must be taught this group interrelationship; little girls are already shunted off into the doll corner or, in more progressive kindergartens, to the sink where they individually slop water all over washing toy dishes.

Within these few years after birth the socializing discipline has taken two polarized directions, one for boys and another for girls. The natural ebullience of children is controlled in different ways. Boys are encouraged to rein their hyperactive spirits for a few hours of the class day, just until they return to the playing field where they can assert themselves and gain recognition from peers for their athletic prowess. Girls are rewarded for sustained quietude and meek subservience. Outside of class they have no comparable playing fields to release their pent-up energies and are beginning to be chased off the boys' territory. Those not easily daunted acquire the reputation of "tomboy," a temporary phase tolerated for a few years but subtly discouraged. Mothers add to the suppressive process when they dress small daughters in clothes inappropriate for rough-and-tumble play or protectively pull girl children away from important learning experiences: "I told you not to play with those rowdy kids, I knew you'd get hurt. Now go to your room and get out your dolls and nobody will hit you." With such seemingly innocuous sentences are girls prevented from growing up and understanding the business world!

"Mom, Billy Won't Let Me Play!"

Around age nine, boys consolidate their random swinging at balls and haphazard racing around bases into a primitive social structure, the team. Baseball becomes a religion of sorts and rules become a fetish. At this age, boys argue passionately over what's "fair" and "not fair." The notion of rules and what they signify is a drawn-out learning process. Six-year-olds don't understand rules nor the idea that they are the same for everyone. Seven-year-olds grasp the general idea and want to follow rules, but they are vague about how they operate. Charges of cheating often have to do with violation of some rule a child made up to apply to everyone else. Parental, teacher, and peer pressure keeps refining the concept of rules for boys and emphasizing their impersonal, all-inclusive nature. In boys' pre-teen years the group game rules, decisions by coaches or umpires, suspended fouls in competitive play become hotly debated issues. By the mid-teens rules have become second nature to boys, and their impulse is to test them just to see whether penalties ensue. Teenage boys take chances on the playing field and in everyday life, but knowingly, experimentally.

The bulk of this important learning about the "rules of the game" takes place during the formative years, and since so much of it is carried out in the guise of team sports, most girls simply don't learn the same material. You might think that jacks or hopscotch or jump-rope have rules, so girls also learn but with different activities. Indeed, girls do learn from their genteel pursuits, but *what* they learn turns out to be self-destructive when carried forward into adult life. Girls' games teach meaningless mumbo-jumbo —vague generalities or pre-game mutual agreements about "what we'll play"—while falsely implying that these blurry self-guides are typical of real-world rules.

71

As an example, popular girl "sports" include playing jacks or jumping rope. These endeavors do require some physical skills which can be practiced to produce increasing dexterity; picking up threesies or foursies obviously takes more finger control than picking up scattered onesies. But these aren't rules; they are skills on a par with hitting a ball with a bat. The only *rule* I remember from girls' games is "no touching." No touching the crack, another jack, the rope, the line—or each other. When two or more girls play such games together, they are not playing *with* each other or *against* each other; they are mutually engaged in isolating, solitary activity. Any girls' game can be played equally well alone, or by turns if others want to join. But a boy who devotes endless solitary hours to perfecting a skill does so in anticipation of using the skill to solidify his place on the team or to perform well in the actual game. Girls never know about the game—they think the skill is the end-all and be-all.

For traditional girls' games there are no umpires or officials, no opposing team of critical judges, no advantages to be gained from collaboration. There are no libraries full of books explaining the rules, extolling the fine points of the game. No enthusiastic adult trainers anxious to promote latent talents. No television play-offs to watch envied professionals who have carried the game to its exciting peak of performance. Girls' games are children's games which are outgrown early in childhood and never resumed because they have no intrinsic educational value; they teach nothing. Brought up under the delusion that these hobbies are comparable to boys' games, adult women continue to compete against themselves, judging their ability without realistic standards. The objective of girls' games is never to beat anybody or perform under competitive stress, but merely to improve an agility in a vacuum. The extension of this childish concept—relentless self-perfection in limited endeavors—can be seen in the self-isolating way many women undertake paid jobs. They have not been taught that it doesn't matter how good you are but how well you perform in the game, as part of the team, that counts.

Secrets of Success They Don't Want You to Know.

... Rules Are Friends. Boys' teams operate under very strict rules which have an impersonal application. Boys and men learn they must abide by these regulations, for, if they don't, they or their team will be penalized. A good player can't limit himself to learning only those rules that apply to his position; he must know all the rules, those that govern the overall game as well as those specific to each player's function. Eventually the more proficient players try to outwit the rules by perfecting techniques that so closely verge on the fair line that opponents are deceived or unable to retaliate. Much of the fun in playing comes from this constant challenge to outmaneuver a skilled opponent within the confines of the rules.

In effect, without rules there is no contest; the rules are part of the enjoyment of the game. Rules in the male sports culture are friends not enemies. They are toys to be played with and manipulated because they are inanimate and impersonal. Rules never change to accommodate less skillful players nor can they be altered at the behest of a team member, a coach, an opponent, or the audience. The team and the players conform to the rules, never vice versa.

... Players Have a Position. The traditional boys' games are far from pointless childish pursuits. They are training grounds for life, preparation for adult imperatives of working with others, practical education for the discipline of business. The most popular games of baseball, football, and basketball are all team sports, and a structured, organized team is a well-defined social unit. Each individual member occupies a special niche on the team; the

73

functions of each position are prescribed, as is the territory or region of play for that function; each player knows exactly what his duties are and how they dovetail into operations of the rest of the team; each player knows that he must practice his personal skills so that his performance is a credit to the team and a contribution to its success; and each player knows that he has to perform smoothly and cooperatively with the others if he wants to retain his place on the team. If there's a conflict between individual glory and the greater glory of the team, then personal virtuosity must be sacrificed. If not, the star may find himself ostracized by teammates or eliminated by the coach. The exigencies of team play mandate a higher god than the individual—the good of the team, the success of the common effort.

. . . **Male Camaraderie Is Fun.** Team sports also teach boys an awful lot about members of their own sex. They learn very early that all boys are not equally good at doing everything. Some can run faster, some hit amazingly well, some throw better, and some catch better. Some are klutzes at everything but insist on playing anyway. Some teammates are nice, some are mean, some are tough, some are loudmouths, some are smart, some are kind of dumb. Nevertheless they must get along together, adjust to each other's personalities and competencies because a team needs a full complement of players to go into a game. Fighting among teammates is intolerable, an exhibition of poor sportsmanship which justifies removal of the troublemaker even if he's the most valuable or skilled player. To retain his place on the team, a player must abide by both the written rules and the unwritten codes.

It is often maintained that team sports teach boys about human nature and human relationships. Such claims are arrant nonsense. All-boys or all-men teams cannot possibly teach anything but inter-male relationships, and by natural extension that girls and women don't have any part in

74

these games. Team sports confirm that exclusively male camaraderie means fun-filled, satisfying times.

... **Don't Talk Back to the Coach.** Organized team sports also teach boys indelible lessons about authority relationships in the all-male culture. It soon becomes clear that every team needs a leader, a decision-maker, an arbiter. Rugged individualism or uninhibited democracy is no more effective in team sports than it is in the military —or in civilian organizations. The coach or the captain is the ultimate authority and the motivator. The coach evaluates skills, assigns positions, decides who plays in the first lineup, who gets benched, who is substituted. His authority is unquestioned. His orders are followed by all team members who learn never to disagree with the coach on the field. He makes the final decision when it comes to planning strategy and dictating plays, although all players participate in the planning sessions. Coaches are viewed as harsh disciplinarians. Their job is to "build men," which is to say, fearless, aggressive, unflinching, courageous, unstoppable, unemotional, single-minded robots programmed to synchronize their efforts to win the game.

... **You Can't Win 'Em All.** Without question the objective of team sports is to win the game against a reasonably competent opposing team. There's no great glory attached to beating a weak opponent. Golfers get handicaps to even up unequal abilities; teams which consistently win without meeting any challenging competition are in the wrong league or are apt to lose their fans. Nobody truly admires an easy win, and a nonchallenging game is no fun for either the players or the spectators. (Little boys yell "No fair" if all the good players gravitate to one side; if there's no contest in abilities, the game is no fun.) Winning is the object of the game, but winning is worthless unless there's a reasonable test of skills involved.

So what team sports also teaches is that you can't win them all. By the same token, you can't lose them all and still hold up your head. The aim is to win as many as possible, but in an evenly matched contest you're lucky to win as many as you lose. To this end, players practice constantly to improve individual proficiency and to strengthen team coordination. Despite heroic efforts there is always the specter of defeat, the inexorable chance of being beaten. Thus *losing* becomes part of the wider game. If there were no possibility of losing, there would be no sense in trying to win and no motivation to improve.

. . . Take Defeat in Stride. For all that losing is a common experience in team play, failure is a disastrous experience on an emotional level. Considerable sportsmanship training is devoted to coping with this situation. Teams learn to take defeat in stride, to develop attitudes and mannerisms to display in public and to the rivals who vanquished them. Players also learn to control interpersonal rivalry with aplomb. Good sportsmanship in this context is obviously a learned attitude, and an invaluable lesson. To handle evidence of failure—disappointment, discouragement, embarrassment, misfortune, inefficiency, bungling, incompetency, mismanagement, criticism—with good grace is a crucial life skill.

Failure in the sports culture is not treated as a demoralizing agent but as a revitalizing force. Losing a game is the signal to practice more, to improvise better techniques, to improve team coordination, to do whatever is necessary to correct the past errors so as to go forward with a determination to win the next one. Any tendency to give up or feel intimidated is firmly squelched. To accept defeat and not fight back is to act like a "sissy"—a girl!

Mothers of Little League boys fondly reminisce about the days when a team defeat desolated their child as if the world had ended. By the end of high school or college that same son may laugh with his mother over the long-gone childhood days when he took things so seriously. In the ensuing years he will have learned how to lose graciously and matter-of-factly, and how to utilize these inevitable experiences for his future benefit. He will not comprehend that his mother has been denied a similar growth opportunity, that she is still at the Little League starting gate, personally feeling demolished, distraught, and disconcerted by any little imperfection, rebuff, blunder, or awkwardness.

. . . Nobody's Perfect. By its very nature team sports forces candid self-criticism. If a new player drops the ball repeatedly or strikes out constantly or incurs penalties over and over, it's pretty hard to deceive himself that he's an outstanding player. Team members are exposed to unrestrained assessment of their skill and performance by coaches, teammates, rival peers, and the audience. Adulation and praise come from the same sources, but it's a mixed bag, the hoots and catcalls intermingled with applause and encouragement. Realistic, dispassionate analysis of each player's weaknesses and strengths is part and parcel of team development. When peers and coaches criticize an individual's performance, it is understood that they do so to guide and direct or to correct poor habits. As a result, players are inspired to practice more and are motivated toward higher achievement. When necessary for the team's good, other teammates reinforce this need for self-discipline and self-improvement by supporting good guys and sabotaging lazy ones or show-offs.

Every team player also knows that the other side is mercilessly dissecting the team's performance on both individual and group bases in order to spot its weak points. Observers from next week's opponent team were probably in the stands sizing up their coming rival. Spectators also indicated their approval or disappointment in the game. Team performance is always a form of public display. A player's competence or bumbling cannot be hidden. The young male athlete learns to accept the pattern and not take it personally as a measure of his total worth because a steady diet of appraisal within a peer group leads to an inescapable certainty: nobody's perfect. Everybody makes mistakes; everyone has off days; the best-laid plans go awry; if you fall, you get up and go on. If you persist, you'll eventually win, but it's no stigma to lose while you're trying. These are the building blocks of confidence held together by the mortar of athletic competition during the male formative years. And this is the stage at which girls are excised from the learning process.

. . . **Competition Is the Prize.** From early days when they assemble together, boys tend to divide any chance group into "teams" even though the sides may consist of one member each. In many cases the extemporaneous teams are far short of the required players, but it doesn't matter; boys are picking up the habit of testing their strength or skill against another with matching competence. *They are competing.* In the child's world there is no viciousness or enmity attached to such playful rivalry, it is a necessary ingredient to having fun. The competitive impulse adds salt and pepper, the spices, to an otherwise bland and tasteless dish of aimless exercise. Without the motivation of showing his friends and rivals how much he's improved his physical skills, it's a rare boy who would willingly spend hours practicing how to throw or catch a ball. What drives him on to self-improvement is eager anticipation of the prize—the chance to demonstrate his prowess in a real game. He wants to test the results of his hard work, to compare his hard-won proficiency against the ability of others within the safety of the same rules. In the male culture, competition is the reward. Competition is the fun. Competition is what makes it all worthwhile. Without the prospect of competition, personal competence loses its meaning and zest because it lacks the quantifiable measure of success—the rules of the game.

Obviously, when boys grow up and enter the business world they are acclimated to the philosophy and spirit of the sporting environment. Without being told, they sense the similarities in the business world and fall into the rhythm. Grown-up girls thrown into the same environment are thrown for a loss. There's nothing familiar about the atmosphere. To a large number of women, the activity going on around them in business doesn't make any sense for a long time, if ever. Because of their naïveté they exhibit signs of mental retardation or arrested development in men's eyes, which serves to strengthen the male conviction that women as a class are temperamentally unsuited for business. That's nonsense. Once women understand that business functions as though it were one big ball game, the veil of obscurity is ripped away. That doesn't mean working women will immediately overcome deficiencies in their upbringing, but at least you now can see the game board and recognize what kind of game you're watching.

Most women have a tremendous reservoir of applicable experience to draw from when figuring out the patterns of the working-sports game. For all the sexist repression of girls' athletic participation in competitive games, an amazing number of women admit that they always felt like "tomboys." They enjoyed team sports and still do. Better yet, they have an understanding of team sports structure, however rudimentary or however long buried. For many, their lifelong interest never went underground, and they remain avid partisans of the national pastime, baseball. Those who are mothers of boys active in sports are intimately involved with the pains and pleasures of the developmental stages their sons are going through. Working women in my observation are less prone to constrain sports enthusiasm in their daughters and can learn through them. All this, plus the recent emergence of dynamic women champions in professional tennis, golf, Olympics, school basketball, softball, track and swimming, strongly suggests that women are better equipped than they suspect to function in the sporting milieu of business. Very few need to adapt or adjust their thinking to fit into a man's sport world; most need only unleash their native instincts that were shackled years ago to rejuvenate their dormant enjoyment of sports and active play.

Still, women must practice to develop proficiency in the lost art of cooperative teamwork, so where can they do it? Their natural practice team is other women. Athletes should by all means join (or instigate) company-sponsored softball leagues and nonathletes should join "business" teams composed of other women at their level in their own company or outside firms. Cooperative teamwork is a human relationship; it cannot be learned out of books but has to be practiced in action. Since businesswomen have no other teammates, they must practice their skills and develop their prowess with each other before they can survive a contest with corporate Joe Namaths or O. J. Simpsons.

Margaret Mead, the foremost student of contemporary culture, says, "American women, as housewives, are the least cooperative women in the world. They can't even bear to have anyone in their kitchens . . . girls don't learn to cooperate with anybody." In direct contrast, she says, "We have a belief in our society that boys learn to co-operate with their same-sex peers in games more than anything else." This American sex-culture gap seriously handicaps working women if they don't make up for their lack of teamwork experience, because cooperative ability is considered a prime requisite for management jobs. This deficiency (exhibited to management in their handling of *other women* especially) probably accounts for the majority of supervisory women being labeled unqualified for further advancement.

Who's on First?

Lack of familiarity with team procedures can lead women to wrong assumptions about their job status. One is the delusion that having a job means you are automatically in the game. For men, yes. For women, no. Women must apply and qualify for the team. Otherwise they are routed to a peripheral role: one of the team hangers-on who mop sweaty brows, massage tired legs, carry water and lemonade, launder uniforms, or cheer on the lucky male athletes. From time immemorial women did not belong on the team itself; they were allowed near the sidelines for whatever menial duties they could perform or to stimulate and satisfy players' sexual demands. In transposing the team to business, none of that changed. Women are always relegated to their outsider role and their sexual function. They can get on the team only when they act like accomplished players, insist on their right to qualify, and make sure the operating rules are applied to them equally. The first move for women in playing corporate politics is to make sure you are on the team!

According to the rules, a team member has a definite, assigned position to play. So the first thing to find out is what your position is and exactly what duties are implicit to that position. Casual comments such as "Nice to have you on the team" mean nothing unless you know what position you're assigned. From the sidelines women got the impression that the business "team" was an amorphous group all working together, each person doing whatever they could do best, or fulfilling any duty that needed doing at the moment. Translate that into the real situation—an organized baseball or football team—and see how fast it falls apart. Does the second baseman play

81

third base when the spirit moves him or because the third baseman let his mind wander? Does the shortstop move onto the pitcher's mound because he doesn't like the way the game is going and thinks he can pitch better? Does a team member step up to bat just because he feels he can hit a homer better than the next guy in the lineup? No—he plays his own position and lets others play theirs.

Women must analyze their job situation to make sure they have a team position. For instance, a woman hired (or promoted) to replace a man can feel relatively sure that she is on the team roster. Even if she encounters difficulties in being allowed in the male locker room (accepted as one of the group), she still has an official duty position. In situations of "made-up" jobs (i.e., a new title or position created specifically for a woman), the woman must watch out that she is not an assistant to someone, particularly a male. "Assistant to" jobs are unlikely to be team positions. Under certain circumstances they may be valuable spots for a woman who has carefully evaluated the learning potential inherent in the job and knows how she intends to capitalize on the education. At other times, an "assistant" job is mistitled; it really indicates a deputy manager or assistant supervisor or junior professional. To be properly classified as a team position, the job must entail some area of independent duties or responsibility and/or be in line with the promotional track to higher jobs as evidenced by the fact that current executives have progressed from that position level.

When you're assured you have a legitimate place on the team, the matter of performance—doing *your* job on that team—is paramount. Good team members are counted on to handle their specific responsibilities, and that's all. (Sound suspiciously like some military rules?) No ballplayer runs all over the field playing assorted positions; the rules are very strict about that. But every team member is expected to do whatever job is assigned and do it as well as possible. Young women players are most guilty of violating this latter injunction and wonder later why they can't get promoted to better jobs. The scene is repeated every day in almost any business office. A beginner gets a job which is (admittedly) dull, boring, and far below her capacities. She feels vaguely insulted and demeaned, so she does the job very sloppily or carelessly, paying little attention to errors and deadlines. She treats the job as if it exists in a meaningless void, indifferent to its relationship to others' jobs. She might, indeed, spend much time doing some other job which is more interesting, hoping she can move on to more challenging work. With that approach she has almost no chance to get out of her rut because she is signaling loud and clear that she doesn't want to be, or doesn't know how to be, a good team player. She is not covering her base, so to speak, and no one would trust her in another position. She is announcing that she doesn't know how the game is played, so whatever latent skills she has will never be tested.

All legitimate team members become experts on the rules, but women who are fighting to hold their place must be especially vigilant. They must keep watch every moment because their tenuous hold will be threatened from two directions: more proficient players will try to fool them, assuming they are amateurs on rules; and violations will be penalized more harshly for women than men. A woman team member cannot allow such oversights—she will be revealing her ignorance, her unpreparedness for team play. The rules are inviolate; they apply impersonally to all players and all sides. Women promoted to supervisory positions are often caught in this trap. Under the guise of "helping her" to insure that she does a good job heading her operation, her male manager will allow subordinates to come directly to him with problems, bypassing her. He is violating a basic rule, the unbroken chain-of-command, and if she unwittingly allows such fouls to go unnoticed, she will find herself off the team—an empty title-holder who lost control over her assigned responsibility.

Always remember that the game of business is played out on the sandlots, the playgrounds, or the ball parks of the men's early childhood. The behavior of men players is often childish, not necessarily vindictive or vicious. The strategy for women in playing corporate politics is to not let any rough boys kick you off the ball field again!

Knute Rockne Is Alive and Well in the Executive Suite

For all practical purposes, women can comprehend the sports syndrome in business by relating it to any structured team sport they know—baseball, softball, basketball, soccer, hockey. But upward-bound women must recognize that management patterns its functions after the most sophisticated of all team games—football. It is no accident that 80 percent of businessmen who comprise today's chief executive officers told *Fortune* magazine some years ago that football was their favorite spectator sport. Many top executives actually played the varsity game during college and never let an interview opportunity go by without bringing up their football star past. (Many U.S. Presidents felt the same way.) College textbooks often introduce business management subjects to inexperienced students by using the illustration of a football platoon. (The assumption is that Business Administration freshmen will immediately understand the structure of a football team!)

Devotees of football will see close analogies to management problem-solving and self-aggrandizement. More than any other sport, football is a power game, the power of brute physical strength wielded by huge, tough, resilient men. A high element of danger is present because miscalculations can result in serious physical harm to individual players, but without risk-taking there's little chance of scoring. The kinship of football to military maneuvers is closer than in other games; military academies routinely produce superior football teams and fanatic fans consider the Army-Navy game the ultimate engagement in football contests.

The teams are large, eleven men each, putting twenty-two men on the field at all times, and the play shifts constantly from offensive to defensive situations requiring entirely different tactics, just as business must respond to alternating conditions in the marketplace. Because coordination among team members is tighter and more crucial than in other games, the responsibility of individual players to maintain their skills at peak levels is great. Professional football teams pay enormous salaries to secure the best available players so the contests are as evenly matched as possible. Nevertheless football games, like business games at top levels, can be affected by a large range of external forces which must be counteracted with pre-planning or split-second decisions. The weather, the wind, the condition of the field, the known abilities of the opposing team, the immediate strengths and weaknesses of one's own players, the vagaries of chance, including accidents or physical incapacities, the tension and motivation of teammates, the decisions of coaches, referees, and umpires, simple human error, and innumerable other variables multiply the elements of chance to phenomenal levels. Top management in business feels an intense affinity to the head coach of a football team; their problems seem almost identical.

The stronger the personal identification of a top business executive to his football past, the more violent his antipathy to women managers is apt to be. He will be so convinced business (management-football) is the apogee of a man's game (great men against great men) that he will feel that women are positively unqualified to compete against the strongest, most powerful, best-trained men in the world. Such affectations are managerial daydreams, of course, because the game of business is not a literal physical clash between male brutes. It is a symbol, a computer model, a paper game, a psychological contest. Competitive large-scale business does resemble football contests, but the business game is a mental competition— it's played in the head not the stadium. Not a single technique needed for the game is inherited or inborn— the talents, mental agility, abilities, attitudes are learned. Men teach them to each other but adamantly refuse to teach them to women. Too bad about them; women are smart enough to teach themselves, and their practice field can be everyday situations confronted on every job.

The physical emphasis in football is very misleading because the modern American game, dominated by the forward pass, is nine-tenths mental to begin with. The rules have been exquisitely refined through the ages to eliminate mayhem and murder, once a common occurrence in football, and to emphasize speed, precision, timing, throwing, deception, and planning, especially planning. In the transposition to business, these planning characteristics of football could be taken over almost in toto. These are the only fundamentals aspiring women need to learn from football: perceiving the goal; figuring out how to reach it; motivating the team to do it, and being prepared to counteract attempts to prevent it. And what have you got? The management skills of leadership.

Keep Your Eye on the Ball!

The most important thing in football is the ball. The object of all the activity is to get possession of the ball, for without it a team cannot score. The ultimate aim is to ground the ball on or beyond the opponent's goal line (for a touchdown), but the vast size of the playing field makes that impossible without small interim gains to move the ball within striking distance of the goal. Meanwhile the defensive team is devoting all its efforts to blocking such progress by halting the offensive team in its tracks or, best of all, getting the ball away and heading for the opposite goal line.

This is also a description of the way management feels about the competitive business situation in a free enterprise system. The ultimate goal of every company is to get and keep possession of a share of the marketplace—the potential buyers of its products or services. Direct competitors are forever trying to prevent them from accomplishing that goal by getting hold of the ball and capturing a larger share of the available market for themselves. The ebb and flow of a football game, the shift from offensive to defensive, the dependence on many players to carry out the action, the sheer size of the playing field where so many unexpected things can happen to frustrate plans and actions *is* analogous to the game of business, the big, broad master game of making a profit.

"Keep your eye on the ball" is the cardinal order issued to team players. It is a coach's perennial warning to players engaged in the action. Under the rules the offensive team which has the ball must move it a stipulated distance on each try (scrimmage down) to retain possession; the defensive team must prevent this. The team gets four chances to cover ten yards, and if it succeeds in accomplishing that advance, it keeps the ball and has four more chances to proceed another ten yards. If it fails to meet this interim objective, the opposing team automatically gets the ball and the offensive has forfeited its opportunity for the moment. With so many men after one elusive little ball, the most effective tactic is the obvious one of trying to hide the ball from rival players. Elaborate stratagems are worked out by football teams to deceive opponents as to who is carrying the ball. If opponents can be fooled into chasing or tackling the wrong players, the real ball carrier may be able to run a considerable distance unimpeded, thereby surpassing all objectives in one dazzling play.

Good football players are ham actors who devise stunts and ruses to baffle the defense. They run hard, pretending their empty hands are coddling the ball; they seemingly slip the ball to a passing teammate but actually keep it, while both players act as if the exchange maneuver had been completed; they fade back, raise their arm as if to throw the ball, then don't; they run in one direction, then veer sharply to throw off a chasing tackler; they hunch shoulders, adopt deceptive stances, yell loudly, or make myriad subtle movements designed to mystify opponents. These diverting tactics of faking, feinting, and trickery, plus psychological efforts to distract attention from the ball, *are highly regarded* in football—and in business. They are calculated techniques, deliberately planned to disguise the true nature of the play in progress. When successful, they are testimony to the brilliance of strategic planners, evidence of supreme performance on the part of players.

Ambitious businesswomen must be especially mindful that *lawful deception is admirable* in the games of football and business and is therefore widely practiced. Women who cling to the romantic notion that "fair play" refers to those vague non-rules from the female culture can be set up as gullible victims of clever ruses; external business competitors as well as male opponents on the inside game have no hesitancy in using the most polished techniques of professional players. Fair play means playing according to the rules. Period. Therefore, women who look over the field with clear-headed realism and learn all the rules can counterattack with delicate refinements of the same techniques. Women are naturals at playing this artful dodger game because their powerless, subservient position in society has taught them to cultivate an unlimited repertoire of manipulative, two-faced, guileful tricks to survive economically. Women have these skills in spades and have practiced them all their lives. Pretending to be a dumb blonde, a satisfied sexual partner, an enthusiastic laundress, a rattle-brained driver, a subservient wife—when the opposite is true but not politic to admit—is no different in intent or technique than business "perceptivity." Edna, the management trainee, described in Chapter 1, who was sidetracked into the less lucrative branch of banking, was the unwary victim of this typical management ploy. She was never told there were two training programs (if indeed there were!), and when she found out the true situation too late, she was greeted with innocent management smiles and smug: "Oh, I'm sure we must have told you about the double programs, you must have forgotten." She didn't forget anything; she'd been duped because she "trusted" the word of respectable men who were simply playing the game according to their legitimate rules.

To be a successful player at corporate politics, it is essential to remember that business plays by the venerated football rules. Nobody on the team broadcasts secret signals or reveals strategy to awestruck kids hanging around the practice field.

Diagram Your Moves!

Within the framework of free enterprise (competing companies fighting to gain possession of the marketplace ball), dazzling plays to outwit opponents and score heavily are the dream of every top management group, just as they are to coaches of football teams. The only way to make such dreams come true is through ceaseless planning of your options and your moves. This includes: analyzing all the elements, forecasting the responses of rivals in reaction to your moves, calculating the distance to be covered, weighing the skills and weak points of each player on both sides, evaluating the time and effort required, balancing the risk and its rewards vs. the losses that accrue if the gamble fails, anticipating all external interferences or conditions that could deflect the plans. Both football teams and management teams juggle many elements, some permanent and measurable but most unpredictable, so planning becomes a complex, hydra-headed monster.

Planning expertise is a learned facility improved over the years with constant practice. This is the skill that management-training programs are supposed to develop by gradually adding more and more relevant elements to the trainee's mathematical and psychological formula as successive jobs become more responsible. Pre-planning is a prerequisite to business decision-making. The presumption is that the person in authority has access to all the necessary information and will therefore make logical, intelligent, successful decisions. If that assumption were true in real life, there would never be any company failures, any profitless years, any financial fumbles, any employee problems. Or, at the least, there would never be any change at all because all competitive businesses would be such perfect teams that the games would be a stand-off, with nobody able to win or lose. Obviously that is not the case in the real world or in the game world. So planning comes down to a gamble—calculating the odds, playing your hunches, and praying you win rather than lose.

Obey the Golden Rules for Rookies

Getting in tune with the pulsing football cadence of modern corporate life may be a large order for some women. The clash of the male/female cultures is especially evident here where the rules must be followed and the etiquette of play scrupulously observed to maintain your long-sought place on the team. Aspiring young football enthusiasts are advised at the start of what they must do to become valuable team players. Most of that advice is pertinent to women who have just joined a management team.

1. Perfect your skills with determined, conscientious practice to master those abilities which earned you a coveted spot on the team. (Know your job duties and perform them well.)

2. Never lose your head in practice or in the game. A thoughtless act may cause you to be banished because emotional outbursts may cost the team a victory. (Don't let anger or fear drive you to impulsive actions that you may regret.)

3. Never disagree with the coach on the field but express your well-developed opinions in pre-game or post-game strategy sessions. (Never criticize or challenge your boss at meetings where others are present.)

4. Do not be aggravated or angry when a substitute takes your place. That teammate needs the practice and experience as much as you do. (Don't try to do everything or be all things to all people.)

5. Do not become discouraged or depressed when a play fails to score. Find the weaknesses and strive to correct them. (Learn from mistakes and put-downs. Figure out better tactics for the next try.)

6. Take advantage of the "psychological moment." If you recover a fumble, complete a long pass, or make a long run into scoring position, press your advantage and capitalize on your opportunity to confound the opponents; try a trick play on the next down. (Don't disparage any success you achieve. Publicize and promote yourself at every opportunity.)

The principles of team play are among the most important unwritten rules in business. Men instinctively know them and follow them. The women in the three introductory anecdotes harbored vague and distinctly female notions about "the team" and "team play." Consequently they were easily fooled and intimidated when male superiors threw out spurious appeals to their "team spirit." When it comes to grasping team codes, many women understandably react at the level of seven-year-old children who still confuse "rules" with things adults tell them to do. The female acculturation halts subsequent development which leads to a sophisticated appreciation that "rules" are impersonal regulations which apply to all and must be obeyed by *everyone playing in the game.* Not knowing this (and their concomitant right to invoke the rules), women meekly accede to atrocious supervisory requests that exploit their ignorance. In effect, they become a handy ball, an object tossed around playfully by male team members whose prime interest is improving their own performance statistics.

Put yourself in the superior's position and figure out

the shrewd management gains that resulted from exploitation of the three women.

Take Jean's case. If you can get an expensive management supervisor (a) for a couple of extra thousand dollars added to her salary compared to the previous man's $35,000 salary; (b) promote a woman to fulfill affirmative action policies; (c) don't have to replace Jean's $18,000 position because she can be cajoled into combining the two jobs, worth a minimum of $53,000, for approximately $20,000—what an enormous budgetary coup you have achieved! Significantly, the woman rejected it not because she realized she was being asked to cover first and second base simultaneously, but because the salary increase wasn't "worth it." That particular department head fumbled his stunning play only because he was so greedy that he didn't offer enough money; otherwise, Jean would have been successfully conned.

Arlene didn't grasp the team premise that the supervisor is the coach, to whom she should have looked for direction. Misguided for years with phony "team" talk, she did "whatever had to be done," which in her case meant *everything*. All the young management trainees whizzing over her head came up smelling like roses because she actually managed the operation, no matter who had the title. Instead of asking for a subordinate (which proved she was the sucker that male superiors took her for), she should have asked for the managerial job which she was clearly performing. Failing that, she should have reduced her workload to fit her real team assignment which obliged her to follow orders from her supervisor, not take over the decision-making merely because she knew what had to be done. In team play, even star players do not tell a new coach how he should run the team. If she had acted out her subordinate role according to team rules, the distribution center would have fluctuated wildly in performance, depending on each management trainee's ability to catch on. The fact is, Arlene is unwittingly doing three jobs: her own production assignment, including supervision of her subordinates; her immediate supervisor's job in making operational decisions; plus his supervisor's job, which is to teach the management trainees. Her department head has a great deal going for him: a distribution center that runs efficiently, consistently, and cheaply; a reputation "upstairs" for giving trainees responsible positions which boost them well on their way up the ladder; a healthy rapport with these potential future executives because he avoids all troublefree nitty-gritty that might come up if he had to teach them the everyday procedures himself; a successful departmental record that he can cite to parlay his own advancement.

Clarice has a common problem in that many male supervisors fill in for weak favorites by getting more competitive female "team members" to do double duty. She was entitled to (and could have requested) a definitive explanation of her team assignment—the exact job she was getting paid to perform. She could have used the admission that she was "so much better" to negotiate significant raises for herself as a reward for doing another player's work. Or she could have pointed out that the co-worker's inability to perform up to standard or hold up in the clinches was not her responsibility to correct. The unwritten rules are quite specific that each player is required to fulfill those assigned duties which add up to overall team performance.

Male players do not get into comparable exploited situations because their male superiors know that other men will instantly recognize an irrational request or illegal play, and won't fall for it. Men immediately ask for a raise when they discover they are valuable players at several positions. They don't confuse the phrase "team play" with the generalized word "cooperation," which means something quite different. A team in the organized sports context is a group of individuals in the same rank, each with clear-cut duties and responsibilities, who act in a harmonious and reciprocal relationship to each other to further a mutual goal. Perhaps the key word for women to remember is "reciprocal."

CHAPTER
4

Jargon
of the
Business Game

In the evolution of separate cultures language undergoes distinctive changes even though the tongue had a common ancestor. English as spoken by the British, the Americans, and the Australians produces three distinct dialects, each distinguished by its own picturesque pronunciations, incongruent slang terms, borrowings from obscure languages of native aborigines or one-time conquerors, nontranslatable idioms and colloquialisms. The language of the separate male and female cultures in America has undergone a similar transformation. While proper literary English became the predominant speech of the isolated female tribes, the jargon of business is a cultural vernacular descended from the all-male military-sports tribes. Most of the words sound and spell alike, but the meanings can shift drastically depending on one's cultural associations.

The anomaly is dismissed by management as a generalized "failure in communications," but the fissure goes deeper than that. Male business terminology is almost foreign speech to women, replete as it is with secret codes, double meanings, and colloquial slang. Translation is essentially a matter of making the nonspecific specific because identical words or phrases can have a vague, abstract, philosophical meaning in the female culture but a concrete, explicit, practical meaning in the male culture.

The working world vocabulary falls into three general subject categories: military derivations; sports lingo; sexual allusions. Entering or established working women must learn to translate this jargon correctly or they will miss the deeper meaning and true significance of what's being said to them, about them, or around them. The male-culture business dialect is countrywide, so to speak; it is not to be confused with special terminology which grows up around localized trades or professions. The argots of computers, medicine, printers, insurance, accounting, law, and such are technical languages which everyone working in that field, male or female, must learn.

As fresh phalanxes of women pour into the workforce, management is becoming increasingly aware that male supervisors have difficulty conveying orders to female subordinates. The men are trading ideas and observations to help each other cope with this mysterious situation. Men are, in fact, trying to learn the female language in order to motivate and "handle" women employees. Naturally this puts them one step ahead because they could end up in the powerful position of being the translators to a bunch of illiterates who are put in the intolerable position of accepting the translation, however inaccurate or skewed, because they don't know any better. And that's just what's happening; male interpretations of female vernacular are bizarre distortions, and the resulting pidgin is gobbledygook. In some places the situation has so far deteriorated that male supervisors are advised to have a third person present when discussing certain areas with women. In fact, some companies require it, according to Ray Killian, author of *The Working Woman* (New York: American Management Assoc., 1971.) This preventive measure is necessary to guard against the supervisor being misquoted to his or the company's embarrassment. This could even involve lawsuits for improper language or mistreatment.

It would be better for women to learn the *men's* language and translate *to* them. Theoretically men shouldn't object; they keep saying that women aren't assertive or aggressive enough in business. Taking control of the communications system would be a very powerful move.

Understanding a foreign language is one thing, speaking it is something else. A Russian-born friend of mine likes to watch UN debates on television to see how the Soviet ambassador reacts when the simultaneous translator shifts into an innuendo slightly while transposing the Russian speech into English. He's sure that the non-English-speaking Russians understand English better than most Americans but they never reveal it publicly. The value of understanding a language but pretending you don't can be a shrewd political move. The natives are off guard, secure in the knowledge that you don't grasp a word. They talk freely, discuss things with each other that they'd never say to your face, even talk about you in your presence. Mischievous natives can be spotted immediately if they try to mislead you with translations, misguide you with wrong directions, make a fool of you to test your lack of comprehension. All of these ploys will be tried by male natives in the Business World because they hope to drive out the female invaders, no matter what company policy says. A prime weapon for successful infiltrators is learning the language fluently but secretly.

One amazing fact appears when a woman collects a garland of management prose: not a single phrase or idiom is witty or amusing. The language of business is deadly serious. Any halting linguist who dares laugh or poke fun at a business communiqué may expect to be told "to get down to business," that is, be serious. Management males, established or aspiring, are a singularly humorless bunch. They have spoken their private jargon so exclusively that most of them have lost command of the universal English language. As television talk show guests they have turned out to be bores and bombs. For public-speaking engagements they hire a covey of speechwriters to dream up dreadful little jokes to launch a dull speech. For everyday communication with the public they depend on platoons of public relations practitioners to mouth platitudes on their behalf. By now the corporate cliché has become so ossified that businessmen can only talk to each other. This is fortunate because a working woman can easily pick out the favorite lingo in her company or department by listening for jingoistic phrases. Here are some examples to get you started on your phrase book.

Military Metaphors

References to military rank titles and actions have a predominantly pompous tone. They relate closely to the hierarchical structure and identify business as a glorious wartime battle. The famous "case history" method devised by the Harvard Business School to teach professional management was described by an M.B.A. graduate in these terms:

"It (a case history) describes a real event (although the names may be disguised) that happened in the course of some real business campaign, at times giving a general's grand view, at times a corporal's blurred impression; it reports on conditions in the trenches and bunkers of the business front, on the progress of armies of salesmen marching against each other, of supply convoys steaming down the channels of distribution. It is a factual listing of men, money, and materials risked; of brilliant victory, of losses beyond imagination."

99

Admiral: Chief executive officer of a multi-unit company, especially pertinent to conglomerates or diversified corporations. Derived from admiral of the fleet, highest naval officer equivalent to general. Indicates a navy man has control of the company and other ex-navy personnel will probably be found in the upper reaches.

Ally or allies: Friend(s) who can be counted upon to support your argument or uphold your opinion; co-workers who are on your side, no matter what, in staff meetings, executive disagreements, or internal power plays.

Arch rivals: Long-time corporate competitors in the same market, as Coca-Cola vs. Pepsi-Cola.

At Easel: Superior's command to subordinate who is standing at attention. An order to relax, to talk things over man-to-man. Found useful by female players to de-fuse sexual aggressors.

Attack: Move aggressively to gain added sales. A company can attack the market (introduce a new product), or attack a competitor (counteract inroads on its brands or sales outlets), or a problem as in "Let's attack it from a different direction."

Battle: Head-on confrontation with a rival competitor, as in "the battle was waged on television . . . or in supermarkets." The battle for markets, or the battle of the marketplace. (*Never* refers to a personal conflict between employees.)

Bite the bullet: Face an extremely painful but unavoidable fact, such as take a loss in this quarter. Equivalent to "stop kidding yourself."

Blitzed or bombarded: Saturated a market region with a sudden explosion of advertising, promotion, and sales incentives. A concentrated, short-term activity, as when introducing a new or improved product or "attacking" a competitor's dominance in a market.

Brass: Refers to metal insignia worn on collars and shoulders by military officers, stars, eagles, oak leaves, which indicate high rank. Corporate brass are executives in line for the presidency or chief operating officers.

Flagship: Technically the ship commanded by the fleet admiral. The diversion, company, or regional office which is consistently most profitable and held up as a model. Often consolidated with the headquarters office. Executives are usually higher paid and have higher status than those of the same rank in less profitable or smaller divisions. In diversified corporations probably identifies original business of company before expansion.

General: The chief executive officer, the head of the company. Nowadays reserved for an old-fashioned autocrat (usually the founder of the company) who exerts dogmatic control and dictates policy without consulting subordinate officials.

Keep your head down: Stay out of the line of fire; avoid taking part in a disagreement between equal or superior colleagues; don't take sides or expose your position too early when a management or supervisory change occurs.

Officer: One of exclusive group of top executives whose names must appear on all legal documents; composed of chairman of the board, president, several executive vice-presidents in charge of major operations, the chief financial officer, the treasurer, the controller (or comptroller), and the general counsel (lawyer) who frequently doubles as corporate secretary. Some officers achieve the rank by virtue of the incorporation laws, not because they have strong influence in running the company. The qualification "top officer" usually indicates an operating power position.

Officer candidate school: Harvard Graduate School of Business Administration, and by extension other prestigious universities known for business administration disciplines. Can also refer to internal corporate training schools or executive development courses offered to selective managers.

Outflank or *outmaneuver:* Successful use of a clever stratagem to win a point without forcing a direct confrontation with another. A good tactical maneuver for women corporate politicians. In past tense, i.e., "we were outflanked," means the other side won something behind your back without your being aware of it. Has identical meaning in sports lingo.

Police the area: Clean up the office, coffee room, or employee public room. From military police actions; to enforce trivial standards of neatness or orderliness.

Pulling rank: Using your superior position to get something free or undeserved, as in tickets, takeover of corporate suite, or the season box if home team is in the World Series. Male superiors frequently use to exclude females from attending conventions, conferences, or industry meetings, or to usurp choice expense-account travel arrangements.

Shoot: Speak to the subject or set forth an idea or plan. Usually indicates prior preparation, as opposed to "Let's hear what you think," which presumes spontaneous remarks.

Strategy: A long-range plan. Stems from military science of plotting and directing large-scale operations which will have significant impact on winning the war. Conspicuous by its absence in corporate planning which seldom looks ahead further than beneficial life of chief executives. See Tactics.

Tactics: Short-range maneuvers directed to engagement in a single battle. Often used interchangeably with strategy, but strategy technically refers to the overall plan, while tactics are methods of achieving necessary steps to implement the strategy. Most common characteristic of corporate planning which rarely looks further than current quarterly profits. As result, "putting out fires," that is, coping with immediate emergency problems, is a prime business tactic.

Under fire: Under intense pressure to perform or vindicate self in violent clash of opinions. Usually in public as when superior says of one member of assembled group, "Well, he hasn't proven himself yet."

Under the gun: Under pressure from above to produce desirable performance results, whether a departmental profit center or an individual employee who has been given a "warning" or a "second chance." Usually a private communication.

Sports Vernacular

Sports metaphors abound in business talk, as might be expected. They are colorful, action-oriented, motivational words and usually have an incisive meaning. One neutral sports phrase can communicate a world of meaning (to receptive men) without forcing the speaker to long explanations or loaded words. If a male manager calmly and smilingly remarks to a male subordinate, "I like to think I'm the quarterback," he communicates volumes, depending on the context. He is saying any or all these things: "Watch out. You're stepping out of bounds. You're forgetting who's the boss. You've argued enough for your viewpoint, now drop it! I've heard you but I've made the decision. I know you might get hurt as a result of this action but do the best you can under the circumstances and you'll probably be okay."

The male subordinate could laugh good-naturedly, say, "It was worth a try," and leave the office, their relationship unimpaired because none of the explosive words were ever said. They understood each other; they spoke each other's language. The same complacent comment made to a woman subordinate might be greeted with a blank stare or a flippant, "So?" Not getting the message, she might keep right on arguing her point, insisting on detailed explanations for the turn-down, trying to over-rule it. The supervisor, unskilled and uncomfortable at expressing business decisions in everyday English, would get involved in a long discussion with her. She would be effectively challenging his authority, ignoring his decision and his right to make it, while bringing on a critical analysis of her own work or her uncooperative team attitude. All this because she didn't know what the word "quarterback" signified.

Unlike military expressions, which are almost exclusively symbolic or ego-building when used in business, sports idioms are specific and literal. Team argot is the functional everyday language of business operations, which enshrines it as the major communications medium. As such, it is charged with de-fusing the most volatile situations in contemporary corporations—the interpersonal relations among employees and especially between superiors and subordinates. Sports terminology can define, to a confused man, exactly what the duties of his job are without recourse to job evaluations or specifications. If told, "Your job right now is essentially to run interference," he knows where he's at. His job may be clerical in nature, as are many women's jobs, but he could interpret the limits and quickly perceive when someone was overstepping his boundaries by asking him to perform extraneous tasks. He would know that his job entailed clearing the path and easing the workload of the important player, the ball carrier. He would not expect nor try to get the ball and run with it himself; his present job is to anticipate work that might interfere with the efficiency of his main teammate and complete assignments that speed the ball carrier on his way. He might, over a period of time, perform the same job for different teammates—but not simultaneously. His observation or a signal from the quarterback (his boss) would tell him who the current ball carrier was. It is highly unlikely that he would ever be fooled into "running interference" for another blocking back like himself, no matter how much pressure was exerted.

Business sports language can cut across any team sport vocabulary and differ in separate sections of a company. One department could adopt baseball and another football. These minor variations reflect the athletic interests of the manager, or, possibly, those of the employee group, in which case the manager adapts his idioms to the office favorite sport. Regardless of the sport, the most literal words are nouns that describe positions on the team, duties, responsibilities, territorial limitations. The verbs are less explicit but are more rousing, intended to inspire interest and motivation.

Women usually know the words themselves (can anybody escape sports news in our society?), but they don't know exact definitions, primarily because they think this talk is male gregariousness rather than standard business talk. The easiest way to figure out the sports identification in your work surroundings is to listen to the men around you. Interspersed with the working expressions will be social chitchat about yesterday's game, but that's not important except to identify the most vocal linguists. Listen for sports references when your boss talks to you; pick out the sporting lingo used spontaneously at meetings or conferences; be alert to sports allusions in office gossip or casual group discussions. Once you've identified the most important sports in your group, watch some of those games on television and get the feel for them. Basketball, for instance, is hectic, inhumanly fast-paced, high-scoring. Baseball is elegant and leisurely by comparison. Ice hockey is vicious and chaotic, while football is deceiving, the mass rushes concealing exquisite pre-planning and the huddles signaling moves to carry out the plans. If you find yourself working with a bunch of football fanatics, you can be pretty sure you've encountered a tribe of management-bound hopefuls.

If you were completely turned off sports in adolescence, you may have to go back and fill the gaps in your education. Read sports pages and books to pick up the attitudes. Subscribe to Billie Jean King's excellent magazine *women-Sports* to better appreciate why, as a woman, you were athletically derailed at puberty. Try the library juvenile section (or raid your son's bookshelves) to find out what advice coaches give to young men just entering on team play.

Those of you who are avid fans (30 million women watch the Superbowl!), or active athletes, have current experience in cooperative teamwork and can quickly make the connection to work situations. You have no experience in the big leagues, however—the male working game—because no women have been allowed on those teams. Men still resent female invasion of their private sanctuary, and women who reveal their familiarity with the language are mistaken if they think they gain entrance by "speaking the same language." I've seen that tactic backfire on genuine women sports enthusiasts who join "the boys" in raving about teams, engaging in Monday-morning quarterbacking and contributing to the office pools. Although they might have an alternative to the weather for social chitchat, their sports enthusiasm further ostracizes them from the male working group who look upon them as weirdos or "unfeminine." Certainly not as candidates for the star quarterback role some day.

To start off your private dictionary of business-sports language, here are some of the more common buzz words and phrases. The list is endless and many other samples are deliberately (or unconsciously) scattered throughout this book.

Baseball associations

Ball-park figure: A rough estimate expressed in dollars and cents, indicates whether further negotiation is

106

feasible. Applicable to any budget or monetary item. A job applicant asking $20,000 minimum will know her request is reasonable if told "that's in the ball park." The same minimum for a job with a top scale of $15,000 would put her "out of the park." A ballpark figure is never the final amount or cost; that figure is given in precise terms once the specifications are known to both sides and the negotiating completed.

Batting average: A quantifiable performance measure usually figured over a long period, such as a baseball season. Expressed as percentage of successes (hits) in relation to attempts (times at bat). Compares players' performance under game conditions, not against an abstract norm. If women are told "your batting average is not too good," the proper response is "Compared to who?" One hit in three times at bat (i.e., nine swings) gives a .333 average, a championship batter! There's no such thing as a "perfect" average. When a businessman says, "I'm batting 1000 today," it is a light-hearted joke, meaning he got one item approved or got his way in one instance, but realizes this is not representative of the future or long run, when his "average" will drop to the most typical .200 range.

Clubhouse lawyer: A player given to argument on any and all points, especially matters dealing with the conduct and operation of the team by the manager.

College try: A player who tries to catch a ball hopelessly beyond reach. Eager, enthusiastic efforts, as in "giving it the old college try."

In the cellar: Last place in the league standings. The worst record; consistently unsuccessful. Similar to "at the bottom of the barrel"; can be caused by getting "on (somebody's) shit list." Connotes possibility of bettering record.

Out in left field: Out of it; don't know what's going on; don't know what you're talking about. Literally the player stationed farthest away from the batter and the bulk of activity which takes place in the infield radius. Excluded from "inside" information, as many women in predominantly male job situations.

Over the fence: A sure home run. A stunning performance or unquestionably profitable financial feat.

Pinch hitter: An especially qualified temporary substitute brought in to handle a special problem or take over in an emergency. Not a candidate for the position replaced as would be an "acting manager" or a "substitute replacement."

Seventh inning stretch: A fifteen-minute break in a long meeting where important decisions are still to be made. In baseball a time-honored custom when fans stand and "stretch" before their team comes to bat in the seventh inning; supposed to bring luck to a favorite team.

Team player: One who subordinates feats or glory for the good of the team; situations where the boss takes all the credit. (See Chapter 3.)

Football associations

Back-up team or *bench strength:* Full complement of trained, duplicate players who sit on the sideline bench prepared to enter the game at any moment to replace players who are hurt, tired, or otherwise removed. In management, the upper three levels of the hierarchy if they contain several strong executives who are fully trained to take over the top job at any time. By extension, a smart supervisor's move to train a subordinate for one's own job to pave the way for your own advancement to higher level. Considered a sign of a well-managed company or department.

Coach: The boss. The unquestioned decision-maker for the team. Not a player. One whose job is to motivate and help players perform well together. A current fad in management training as in "the best manager considers himself a coach."

Disqualified player: One who has been ousted from the game as a penalty for a personal foul. The severest penalty for prohibited acts traceable to loss of emotional control under stress as illegally tripping or hitting another player in anger. Significantly, women "disqualified" from management are usually described as "emotionally unsuited."

End run: Moving around the lightly defended ends of the line to avoid massed opposition in the center, as when women create new jobs for themselves rather than competing with men for an existing "man's" job. See: Outmaneuver or Outflank.

Huddle: Get together with selected co-workers before a meeting to devise ways to get one's point across against opposition; make a deal with collaborators who stand to benefit from cooperation. Literally, the team get-together before each play on the field when quarterback gives secret signals that tell each player where to position himself, what to do, to facilitate the play.

Jock: A male professional athlete; a thoroughgoing competitive team sportsman. The "jocko mentality" pervades highly competitive, nonregulated industries.

Monday morning quarterback: A pejorative term describing player or spectator who delights in explaining how something "should have been done," or "How I would have done it." An after-the-fact analyzer who points out the obvious—that something should have been done differently since the attempted move failed.

Punt: A quick kick of the ball in desperate circumstances when it's necessary to get out of an untenable position. A gamble against great odds.

Quarterback: A key player who calls the signals, i.e., tells other players what to do, and how. Absolute authority figure on the field as delegate of coach.

Tackle the job: Approach a task with single-minded concentration, as "Let's break the back on this." Overused cliché supposed to rev up team players. Often assumes setting priorities, as "Which task shall we tackle first?"

"Scoring" Is the Broad Connection

In the glossary of business jargon, one word is more important for women to recognize than all others. It serves as the conjunctive which joins the military mentality, organized sports, and big business. It is the connecting link which unites the prototypes and the offspring in an unbroken continuum in their attitudes toward women. The word is "scoring."

To score: To win a victory; to make a profitable deal; to accomplish a desirable act in the face of competition; to pile up points in your favor. To have sexual intercourse with a female peer one has aggressively pursued just for the purpose; to "lay" a desirable, reluctant woman; a man's tally of such consummations with different women at different times.

The same versatile word is used frequently in the female culture, but its associations are drastically different. It can mean anything from making superficial cuts in meat before cooking, to totting up points in bridge or Scrabble, to the orchestration for a musical composition, to an indefinitely large number, as in "scores of people attended."

The dominant theme in the male-culture language—and the business lexicon—is sexist pornography. Obscenity is the popular vernacular. Practically any male activity or objective can be—and is—reduced to similes with the female genitalia, erogenous zones, act of copulation, or ravishment. This is the lewd, lusty language of the military conqueror, the male locker room, the stag party, the sales meeting, the company convention, the board room, the executive think-tank. The presence of the disparaged

110

object, woman, inhibits men's freedom to "talk dirty" when together and thus becomes an insuperable barrier to their communications. It is one of the main reasons men can't tolerate the thought of women invading the region of management or other male-exclusive groups. Their facade of decency, gentility, and superiority will be irreparably destroyed once women see them in their true commonality: crude, illiterate, sexist, mentally deficient smut peddlers and voyeurs.

Relatively successful women frequently report an inexplicable, disquieting, and extremely irritating experience in business meetings. Every time the word "damn" or "hell" escapes a man's lips in a business setting, he immediately turns to apologize abjectly to any woman present. Since these mildly emphatic expletives can punctuate every other sentence when men get into heated discussions, the "pardon me" apologia to women becomes unbearably repetitive. One woman executive told me that a male colleague interrupted himself fourteen times in ten minutes and finally turned to her in anger and said, "Dammit, you'll just have to get used to this talk if you think you're going to be in business!" She hadn't said a word! Her question to me was, "Is it possible that any reasonably intelligent man in the mid-1970s *really* believes that a woman never heard the word 'damn' or 'hell' in her life?"

Of course it's not possible. Any man who was that far removed from the society around him would be locked up as a dangerous lunatic, not holding a responsible position in a business firm. What's happening is that these mild words (once daring "swear words" to the boy-child) are setting off a triggering mechanism in the men's heads. They are terrified that they might inadvertently slip into the male pornographic communications argot. Such an accident might suggest that she is "accepted" as an equal "with the boys" by being clued in to the secret codes. Or

111

it might let her know how deeply he despises women as a sex despite his outward claims of acceptance.

A few top executives, speaking on behalf of their lower and middle management men, have admitted that the presence of women is resented in those jobs because it would force the men "to clean up their language." Men literally *cannot talk* to each other in a business situation if they feel pressured to purge their language of all the phrases that are derogatory or place women as degraded sexual objects which are endlessly fascinating to men but must be "cut down to size." The greatest compliment men can give a woman who is successful in business and a worthy partner on the team is to say "she has balls." Women recipients of such high "compliment" report their inner reactions as "insane fury" or "murderous anger."

Another frequent experience reported by women executives is equally disconcerting to those who don't understand the sexual allusions aspect of the jargon. When a woman walks into a meeting room full of men engaged in casual conversation, she is often greeted by a sudden dead silence. "The first time it happened," said one, "I had a ludicrous reaction. I was wearing an elegant new pants suit and my first thought was 'My God, my fly must be open!'" Another woman found herself surreptitiously looking down at the front of her dress during the ensuing meeting to see if she had spilled something on herself during lunch. Another, who was being considered for a promotion at the time, thought, "They were talking about *me*, probably decided I shouldn't get the job."

These women properly sensed the "feeling" in the room, that something was being discussed which related to them—and it was something bad. What they didn't know was that the casual male conversation probably had nothing to do with them *personally*. They had simply interrupted a discussion being carried on in the everyday, familiar male business code, the sexual venacular.

This situation occurs with increasing frequency as women move into previously all-male jobs.

The woman corporate politician can capitalize on such situations because it offers her an opportunity to control the male group—and few chances occur in business. You are always in command of a situation where you control the communications system. You, after all, can speak English—and the men will be forced to talk *your* language, not theirs. Deprived of their titillating jargon, they will be talking in a stilted, unfamiliar dialect—nonsexist language. They aren't good at this, so the resourceful female will be the only one in the room who is not discomfited, not embarrassed, not stumbling around to express herself, not angry, and not guilt-wracked.

She will lose her advantageous position entirely if she —God forbid—should use the typical male expressions which derogate her own sex. Knowing a foreign tongue perfectly is one thing, as we said before, but control of the situation comes from never revealing that you know it, and never speaking it in front of the natives.

Locker Room Language: 80% Sex, 20% Excreta

Entwined in the sexological vocabulary of business is a subcategory which centers on excretory products. Some of these appellations are directly transmutable to women's bodily parts and some are double entendres, but all are considered unfit for the delicate ears of "the ladies" who are being referred to in these salty, colorful terms. Here is a superficial sampling of what successful men don't want you to hear (as if you didn't know!).

Ass: A free-swinging word usually preceded with definitive adjective such as "fat." Used as aggressive insult to denote a fool: "He's a horse's ass." To throw a person "out on their ass" means to fire them or ruthlessly banish them from the immediate vicinity. "Cover your ass" stems from military usage under low-fire conditions when the protective mechanism is to throw oneself face-down on the ground; means to protect your exposed side, as write a memo or otherwise "cover" yourself for a business decision or happening that can be used against you. Also describes a woman, as in, "She's just another piece of ass." Also the implied but unexpressed completion word for the obscenity, "Up yours!"

Bastard or *Son-of-a-bitch:* A hated or despicable person; one who plays unfairly or illegally. Many businessmen are "bastards" in the way they treat working women. The closest equivalent women can use is "MCP," or "male chauvinist pig."

Bitch: An aggressive, ambitious woman who speaks her mind; one who won't take any "shit" from anyone. In form "bitchy" is applied to a woman who stands up for her rights. Nowadays supplemented by explicit terms "Libber," or "Woman's Libber."

Broad: Any woman. Often used with prefix "dumb" or "damn." Physically attractive young woman called "chick," "dame," "pussy," "beaver," etc.

Caught with your pants down or *with your fly open:* Discovered in an embarrassing business position, as when a competitor beats you, due to some lapse in your own planning or lack of foresight. When a woman walks into an all-male group, members feel she has caught them in one of these positions, hence the sudden self-conscious silence.

Cocksman: As, "he's a great cocksman." A flattering appellation for management executives; implies they have not sublimated their sexual drive to business but can still "get it up" when attractive women are available. Not to be confused with "helmsman," which refers to one who steers a boat and is therefore another term for chief executive, as one who "took over the helm" of a company.

114

Crap: See Shit. But "crap" has additional connotation stemming from the gambling game played incessantly by soldiers, "shooting craps."

Fuck: Originally limited to heterosexual intercourse but now so common a swear word that it's seen on graffiti and overheard on school playgrounds as in, "Get off the fuckin' swing." "Fuck you" is a violent denunciatory expletive, but the word can be applied less strongly to inanimate or animate objects, as: "Those fucking call reports drive me crazy," or "What the fuck are you doing?" An aggressive sales campaign might be launched with: "Let's fuck the hell out of 'em (the competition)." Word still holds its original meaning when used by on-the-make businessmen who consider it a compliment to a female companion to exclaim, "I'd like to fuck you, baby," or more simply, "Let's fuck."

Girl: Popular demeaning term for mature working women. Used widely throughout business as in, "I'll have my girl call your girl to arrange it," or "The girls in accounting will take care of it," or "Who's the new girl?" referring to a lawyer, an M.B.A., an engineer, a vice-president, etc., if of the female sex.

Masturbation exercise or *Playing with yourself:* An exercise in frustration; fooling yourself; manipulating statistics or profit-and-loss figures. Attempted cover-up of unpleasant reality.

Piss, Pee: Refers to urination, specifically through the penis. "Take a pee" is go to the urinal. "Piss on them" presumes a directional stream.

Screw: Another diversified word similar to "fuck" in origination and used interchangeably. A businessman said to "screw around a lot," may be known for perpetual flirting, whoring, or sexual advances to female employees or prostitutes. Or the expression may mean he does not pay attention to work, wastes time on frivolous concerns, or twists facts to impress superiors or colleagues.

Shit: Waste material; hot air; lying. As in "He's full of shit," or "That's bullshit." To "cut out the horseshit" means to stop making passes at the wrong women, lying about something, or fooling around in an irritating manner.

CHAPTER
5

Women Players
Upset the Boys

It should be clear from our aerial survey of the business landscape that women who enter the working world with a continuous career in mind must be prepared to deal with the realities involved. Foremost among these are the rigidities of the military hierarchy; the team sports philosophy which management uses to coordinate work and interrelationships of employees; and the male-culture jargon which is the primary mode of communication as well as the expression of conscious and unconscious attitudes toward women.

This business trio defines the game board—the playing field of corporate politics—and explains the rules of permissive moves and conduct, including scoring, procedures of play, regulations, and violations. Willingness to abide by these principles and to play within the rules is almost a guarantee that a competent, ambitious young man will "get someplace" in his business career. Not so for women. The same knowledge, competence, and willingness to play is insufficient to assure significant advancement. Women who want to get in the ball game and stay on the team must overcome a uniquely female obstacle: transference from nonplayer to team member status.

It has become fashionable to say that women suffer from being excluded from male-dominated economic activities. This is not precisely accurate. Women's current employment problems stem more from the fact that females *always have been* included in business; it is *where* or *how* they have been incorporated into the male culture system that redounds to their disadvantage when they try to join the economic inner circle. Almost from its inception, industry has utilized women, sometimes on a scale so vast that females comprise the preponderance of employees, sometimes on a basis so small that the female contingent is statistically negligible. In either case, women have been included in the workforce—what they have been excluded from is the *game* of business: the pursuit of profit and power.

The historic dividing line between males and females in the workforce accounts for women's widespread obliviousness to the rules of the game since these apply only to active players. This sex segregation line is the universal barrier that purposeful working women must cross to gain a recognized position on the action team. Crossing the line can be problematic because the division is ofttimes vague and unspecified. Clerical workers as now designated are obviously on the wrong side; no one classified in the clerical ranks, regardless of job title, is a team member or active player. Women in those categories must jump the gap to get into the games. Sometimes the differentiation can be recognized by salary. For instance, classified ads that rave about a "great career opportunity" and then give the pay rate on a weekly basis are listing nonteam jobs; players' salaries are reckoned in annual figures. Low-paying hourly rated jobs such as telephone operators or retail clerks are usually nonactive, as is almost any job titled "assistant to" or "administrative assistant." However, the dollars-and-cents amount of the salary is not an infallible guide to spotting the partition. Many women take a serious reduction in salary to effect their crossover to a team status job inasmuch as rookie jobs on the active team often have a low salary affixed. The rationale is that astronomical increases are possible in active play, while statutory limits are imposed on nonteam jobs.

This classic split, which includes women in the workforce while excluding them from participation in the business culture, *still exists*. This is the established system and its contours haven't changed. Title VII does not alter the private enterprise system; the law simply decrees that women (and minority groups) cannot be forced into inactive categories against their will, that all people *who want to* must be allowed to try out for the team and, if successful, be allowed to play. That leaves the system and the rules intact. Women (and men) who so desire, or are unqualified for better jobs, will constantly supply the nonteam ranks which continue to exist (and are scheduled to expand).

What this means to newly enfranchised women is that their emergence as active-player candidates has changed the dynamics of the game. Women-as-a-class now appear in dual categories in the system: as traditionally inactive workforce members, and as prospective official players. No individual can belong to both categories concurrently. But women, like old-time Chinese waiters, all look alike to the male establishment, so the entrenched players are hopelessly confused, unable to distinguish between their new female cohorts and their traditional secretary or assistant. Behaviorists and game theorists acknowledge that a new player always changes the game dynamics, but when the old players can't distinguish the new participant from kibbitzers, waitresses, wives, sweethearts, mothers, typists, daughters, cleaning ladies, or "dates," they are dumbfounded and disadvantaged. Their actions go berserk, their moves become erratic, their thinking is muddled, and their game goes to pot.

119

Remember, the rules haven't changed (except that the newcomer can't be ejected arbitrarily), but the methods of play, the accustomed responses, the conduct and etiquette of the established players have deviated from their usual norm. The resulting disorder is not provoked by anything, right or wrong, done by the new woman player. The chaos is due entirely to the inability of male players to recognize, or their unwillingness to tolerate, an unorthodox participant. Since women's actions don't create the disruption, there is no move a woman can make to calm or settle the atmosphere. Should a woman newcomer unwisely try to soothe or ameliorate the mental upset of male players, she will only increase the consternation, at which point she will have propelled herself into the mess.

I recently saw a training film proposal sponsored by a giant company as a guide to help aspiring women employees. High priority was given to a recommendation that women recognize how much men are threatened and uncomfortable in this strange new situation; advancing women should "try to be nice to them" to help ease their discomfort. *Really?* What a convenient ploy for management! Throw an inexperienced female rookie into an all-star game stacked with professional players and then charge the nervous neophyte with full responsibility for maintaining team esprit! This sort of thing should be recognized for what it is: part of the backlash to halt women's invasion of the corporate home ground.

The fact is, this discombobulation of the experienced male forces is a temporary weakness in the defense line which women must turn to their own advantage. Remembering that women players upset the balance and disturb the game by their very *existence*, not by their action or performance, women must be prepared for this reaction. They will not be entering the game as another skilled, eager, sociable, accepted newcomer. It doesn't happen like that, as my friend Diane, an economist, found out the hard way. She is now settled in a company and job she likes, but it took her three job changes in as many years to figure out the dynamics.

Counter Their Sneak Plays

"In my first corporate job I joyfully jumped into the all-male group of economists, thinking we were all one big, happy family, everyone doing his or her best for the company. I'm a pleasant, easygoing type who never has trouble making friends or meeting strangers, so the last thing I anticipated was trouble in relating to my co-workers. All the men were civil to me, carried on a lot of joshing and chitchat, but little by little I got the impression they were laughing at me. Not to my face, but behind my back. Several times at staff meetings when I made suggestions that I considered quite pertinent to an economic profile we were doing, the others made a joke or laughed at my idea as if I were being facetious. They never took me seriously, including the manager, who played along with the boys and treated me very light-heartedly on a professional level. I was so upset some days, I used to go home and cry. Here I was, trying to be friendly and jovial and working very hard, as is my wont, and I simply couldn't make friends with the group. I noticed that some of the men went to lunch together, but they never invited me along. I became almost paranoid before I left that job, absolutely convinced for the first time in my life that there was a terrible defect in my personality.

"In my second job I was luckier—or so I thought. One of the men was especially pleasant and nice to me and

121

we had lunch frequently, discussing the job, the company, and the personalities of our co-workers and boss. I didn't worry much about the rest of the group because I had a 'friend,' just as they had theirs, and assumed I was a member of the crowd. Then one day my friend left 'by mutual agreement,' as they say when men are fired. I was shocked and devastated. As I tried to find a new friend in the group I picked up the office gossip and discovered that my nice companion had been heartily disliked by all the other men, including the supervisor. Nobody but me was surprised he got the ax. Apparently he had never fit in, for what reasons I don't know. I stayed in that job for nearly two years because I needed that particular professional background, but I never overcame my isolation nor the effects of my early association with the 'misfit.' I ended up an efficient, hard-working loner, extremely unhappy in my work life."

Diane is an intelligent, ambitious woman who did everything possible to prepare herself for a progressive career. She selected a field she enjoyed and one she knew offered many future opportunities for women. She was an honors graduate of the Wharton School of Finance and had roughly blocked out a career plan for herself. She is attractive, well spoken, and does indeed have a friendly, outgoing, unsuspicious nature. She had gained valuable professional experience in a small nonprofit economic firm before moving to the corporate environment, so she entered her jobs as an official team member. She did everything right and had everything going for her—but then her troubles started. She hadn't anticipated the change in dynamics that her *very presence* evoked. She was operating under the delusion that, having met the same qualifications as men, she would be accepted as an equal professionally and could easily soothe any ruffled feelings she noticed.

It took two "ghastly experiences" before she figured out what happened and decided to change her tactics. "I was such a jerk. I like men, so I naturally assumed they would like and respect me. Either I had to accept the horrible idea that I had turned into some kind of babbling idiot who can't get along with people, or else I had to admit that the working situation is different. I chose the latter alternative.

Recover Your Own Fumbles

As a matter of fact, Diane took two years to analyze her failures and devise personal techniques to counteract the problem. Although she didn't express it in game terms, she is an instinctive player of corporate politics who invented new moves for herself with a singular female focus after discovering that mimicry of male tactics didn't work for her. In general, she came to four conclusions:

1. Male hostility to women is impersonal and subtle in business associations.

2. How women are introduced to male co-workers sets the tone.

3. Women are unwanted intruders into a previously safe male enclave.

4. You have to take control by capitalizing on the male-group discomfort.

This is how she remembers her first successful maneuver in starting a job.

"First off, I admitted to myself that resentment and hostility toward competent women is a fact of business life. It has nothing to do with me as an individual or them as individuals. It is an undercurrent in the work situation where a lot of men are used to having the place to themselves. Like it or not, you are an interloper; they don't really want you there but are forced to accept you by powers on high. However, they have innumerable ways to subtly and covertly discourage you. Like ignoring your presence at lunch, never asking you to join the quasi-social cocktail crowd, humorously disparaging your work and ideas, 'forgetting' to tell you about informal meetings or decisions—a whole accumulation of little things.

"Then there's the boss. Most of them don't welcome a woman either, so they tend to fall in with their male subordinates and tacitly allow the elusive teasing. It seemed to me that all they care about is whether you might upset the little sinecures that exist, break up the old street-corner gang as the song says. The way I'd approached them—in open-armed friendliness, hugging everybody to my bosom—made me fair game for all the vultures and an easily evaded target for those who wanted to avoid me. I decided my natural friendliness was my best weapon—but I must use it to control *them* instead of being so trustingly naïve.

"The introduction was very important. As usual, the schedule called for me to report to Personnel on my first day to fill out forms for two hours and then report to my new department just before lunch, whereupon the manager and a few henchmen, or maybe my closest new working companions, would take me out to an expense account lunch. Then the boss's secretary would escort me to my new office for the rest of that day. That standard procedure may work for new men, but I'd been zapped by it twice. So I didn't follow the schedule. Instead I appeared unannounced in my new manager's office at 9:00 A.M. and finagled the guy into *personally* taking me around to every co-worker's office to introduce me and identify me. He was uncomfortable at the break in routine, but what could he do? Faced with an eager, friendly person like me? Then I went down to Personnel and fulfilled the requirements. But when I returned for the pro forma lunch, I acted like an old friend who knew everybody. In fact, one man who had missed me on my morning rounds felt kind of left out. None of the men were quite sure where I stood with the boss, so they became very wary of me—and that's exactly what I wanted. I felt so exhilarated that the lunch was actually pleasant.

"Later that afternoon, and every day thereafter for a week or two, I made it a campaign to drop into the office of every single man in my department on some business pretext or other. I checked off a private list to make sure I didn't miss anyone or play any favorites. At other times, I was all over the place, 'getting acclimated.' I wandered the halls, chatted with anyone standing at the elevators, introduced myself to all the secretaries and clerical people, interrupted for a passing comment whenever I saw one or two co-workers casually gathered in someone's office or at the water cooler. I hardly ever stayed in my office because I was scrutinizing everyone, trying to separate the fair-haired boys from the outlanders, the cliques and friendships, the sources of the grapevine.

"In my sweet, friendly way I kept them all off balance; they didn't know what I'd do next. When I'd stop a threesome and say, 'You people going to lunch? Where are you going?' they were trapped into inviting me along. The first time some smart aleck 'forgot' to pass along a piece of information, I waited till the next staff meeting when the manager was present and innocently said, 'Last week Joe accidentally forgot to tell me about such-and-such. Is there anything additional I should know about today's subject that might not have reached me?' That forced the manager to review the points under discussion 'to make sure everybody understands.' And obviously it served notice on Joe—and any others—not to make a fool out of me again.

"Gradually I gravitated toward one coterie which I pegged as the smartest and best placed of the lot. I had accomplished my purpose in establishing a basis for a professional working relationship with everybody although I knew who was who this time. I like this job, I'm doing very well, and I get along with all the people that count.

But I tell you, I never let down my guard. I sense that the minute they feel too sure of me, not afraid, they'll walk all over me just like the others did, and try to exclude me."

Play to Their Weak Side

Women are, as we've seen, absolute amateurs at the game of corporate politics. The disadvantage would be hard to overcome if it weren't for the change in dynamics of play. That one shift opens up the whole field to clever women just as surely as the forward pass revolutionized the game of football. Men do not believe that women— a lightweight, inexperienced, powerless team—can present a formidable competition in the exhibition game between the sexes. They think they have that game locked up because of their long experience playing together plus superior training, equipment, and know-how. Their self-confidence will be justified if the new female players try to copy the customary playing techniques, but their complacency will be shattered if women adopt creative, unexpected moves which opponents can't envision and which will knock them off balance.

An old football maxim goes: "There's a weakness in every defense; find it." One of the weak points in the male business assemblage is the inability to admit that women are as smart as men. No matter what statistics or IQ tests say, men cannot concede in their innermost being that a woman can outdo them at anything. This blind spot allows women to function quite openly in learning the aspects of business that are unfamiliar to them because men won't catch on to what they're doing for a long time—hopefully when it's too late. One rapidly moving woman executive confessed that she got herself into a managerial position which required extensive financial controls before she'd ever heard of a P-and-L

126

statement. She immediately struck up an acquaintance with the company controller, and pumped him relentlessly about his "fascinating job." He didn't suspect he was feeding her the pertinent information she needed to prepare a statement he had to approve. "He'd never have done it for a man," she said, "but he was so flattered by my attention—and assumed I didn't know what he was talking about half the time—that he burbled on endlessly."

Another pervasive weakness in the men's team is the ingrained cultural conditioning which trains them to think of women in stereotypes. Most of them have had no experience in dealing with women as people, as human individuals with a diverse range of talents, abilities, and reactions. A woman, they have been taught, is a "mother," a "sister," a "wife," a "daughter," a "girl friend," a "prostitute," a "nurturer" of some kind—nurse, waitress, cook, secretary, teacher. When a woman doesn't fall into one of these common stereotypes, he is unable to judge her. So he squashes the real person into a categorical image and never sees the human being staring him in the face. Men love to insist that they are logical, rational, cold-blooded realists. Objective scrutiny of their reactions to women shows that they are exactly the opposite of their fantasy: irrational, illogical, unrealistic, uncomprehending. They function automatically on an emotional plane that prevents them from seeing women as people. Many of them freely admit they "don't understand women," or "don't know what she wants." Good. They will not suspect that women in business are playing according to the male-defined rules by adroitly maneuvering to concentrate female offensive action toward their weak side.

Capitalize on Sex Stereotypes

Women players, of course, must be careful to avoid any

situation which puts them into an actual stereotyped position, if they can possibly avoid it. For instance, a male executive might well, during a crisis, roll up his sleeves, return to his old engineering department, and personally take part in solving a technical problem. He would be greeted with awe and acclaimed with respectful comments such as "The old boy still has his magic touch," or "You can take a brilliant engineer out of engineering but you can never·take the engineer out of a manager." A comparable woman executive who dared volunteer to type a top-secret management memo would suffer a different fate. Her unwise offer would instantly reclassify her in all minds as the secretarial stereotype she has fought to evade: "She's so good on the IBM, that's where she really belongs"—as some executive's private secretary, natch. At the present time, women cannot live down or intellectually combat the stereotyped classifications in which they are mired in men's minds. What they can do is use the stereotype when it suits their purpose, but only so far as to confound the opponents.

Take the situation of an older boss who treats a young woman subordinate as a daughter. He can be jollied along indefinitely by the ambitious female player who is seeking usable factual information about *his* job, the work specialty, or the management evaluations of other department members—her direct competitors. She would *become* the stereotype if she depended on him to "push her ahead" or fell into the role of the helpless adolescent. A "mother" image can be exploited by a female supervisor to control any younger males who treat her as such —just until "mother" has to crack the whip or lay down the law. She would revert to stereotype if she became overly friendly, helpful, and solicitous—"motherly"— toward a male subordinate. The stereotype image she manipulates cannot be chosen arbitrarily by a woman player. She must have clear evidence to identify the male player's stereotype blind spot (as applied personally to

128

her) before she plays to his unconscious weakness. Not all male sex-stereotypes of women are equally subject to manipulation. The "girl friend" sex-partner symbol is a whole different kettle of fish, as we shall see in Chapter 9.

To utilize men's traditional stereotype attitudes as part of an offensive tactic, businesswomen must become very knowledgeable about female stereotypes and the way these absurd ideas obscure men's vision of the playing field. Female stereotyping is almost ineradicable from the minds of contemporary American men. Even those who make strenuous intellectual efforts to overcome their formative training succumb emotionally to their old habits and instincts when under stress or faced with an unexpected situation. It's very clear in the game of business that men at all levels—from top to bottom—don't know what they're doing when it comes to treating female employees, subordinates or peers, as human individuals. They are trying to update their employee manuals to treat women "better" than in the past, but they are relying on other men's stereotyped thinking to figure out how to deal with female employees. "Psychologists say that women's nesting instinct is the basis for their desire to dress up work areas with plants, attractive furniture, and colorful typewriters," one male manager tells another with smug complacency. Ask yourself whose "nesting instinct" allocated the executive office space and furnished the top men's suites with priceless paintings and sculptures, designer furniture, hand-woven rugs, luxurious sofas, and a forest of trees imported from the Amazon jungle? It would never occur to even the most enlightened business executive that a woman who bought a desk plant with her own money might be driven by consuming ambition and the thriving vine is to remind her that "Some day I'll be in a position to order the *company* to build a greenhouse in my office if I want it."

This hereditary eye-disease afflicts all players on the male team; they have incurable cataracts when it comes to female players, so their reconnaissance of the field is blurred. Women with 20-20 eyesight and good peripheral vision are well equipped to fool them. Playing corporate politics is a healthy action game, not a parlor TV sport. The well-trained professional player intercepting a pass doesn't turn around and hand the cherished ball to his opponent, saying, "Gee, pal, I'm sorry about your poor eyesight; here, this is supposed to be your catch." Nor can working women "feel sorry" for an incompetent or weak boss by doing part of his work or retrieving his fumbles. Such tactics will get her frequent turnover in new bosses as each is promoted because she made them "look good," but all it does for her is dig a six-foot plot. A self-effacing woman allows herself to become the stereotype of the loyal, grateful, supportive, helpful female. Those myths (so widely circulated in business circles) that women don't work for the same reasons men do, or don't want the same monetary and status recognition as men, can be exploited as easily as any stereotype.

Vivian was a public relations writer whose male boss thought women were "happy" if they felt their work was important and they were lavishly praised and thanked. In line with that belief, he asked her for monthly typed reports summarizing the results of all projects and regularly submitted them as *his* reports to an important client by retyping the front page and changing the names. For several months Vivian played out the stereotype myth. She prepared conscientious, thorough reports angled for the client, just long enough for her supervisor to feel sure he could depend on her work. When she was reasonably confident that he no longer read the reports but routinely passed them along in his name, she gradually changed the approach. She began writing for the supervisor's information, not the client's. Whenever possible, she unobtrusively buried comments in the body of the summary: "I don't know the final results on such-and-such because you took the project away in its printing stages and I have never seen it since," or "This was assigned to someone else, I'm not sure whom, so I can't report on its current status." Subsequently her supervisor began having trouble with the client, who eventually requested his removal from that account. A week later the client invited Vivian to lunch and said, "I've been getting your messages. I suspected for a long time that you were doing the bulk of the good work on my account. Now we'll do something about changing your status."

Vivian's game strategy could have paid off in a different direction, too. If her supervisor had been less simple-minded he would, at the very least, have read the reports before attaching his own name. In that case Vivian would have accomplished a different purpose—put an end to her boss's reliance on her to do his reporting work, which benefited her in no way but "helped" him enormously in looking competent. Neither player, incidentally, had violated any of the standard business rules. It is perfectly legal, ethical, and extremely common for male superiors to pass off work of competent female subordinates as their own; Vivian did her assignment (writing a memo to her boss) to the best of her ability. The next move was the supervisor's and he fumbled fatally because he expected all women subordinates to conform to his stereotype of working women.

Trust Your Intuition

Another pervasive weakness in the management defensive line may be used to your advantage. This is the universal male reliance on the power of "logical thinking." According to their own myth, men are geniuses at a tortuous form of slow, steady, step-by-step plodding toward obvious conclusions and bizarre deductions. They like to call this thought process "logic" and insist that the "cold,

131

hard facts of business" must be analyzed in logical sequence.

Women, it is concluded, think differently from men; they function with some silly, flighty mental quirk called intuition. For a change, nobody disputes the fact that women are especially gifted in this area of mind functioning—indeed, the mental process is called "feminine intuition." Because it is a female possession it has acquired the reputation of being inferior to rational, logical thought —but is it? What if it were far superior? What if it could be harnessed to overrun the obsolete Maginot Line of male reasoning?

The illogic of "logic" was brought home to me when I was in college. "Logic" was a required course and the star professors taught it. I got one of the few "A's" in my class and afterward the professor called me into his office and asked, "How did you do it? Your answers were almost perfect in oral and written exams but you never paid any attention, you did homework for another course, half the year you fell sound asleep in class, and I doubt if you ever read the text." All of which was true; I was bored to sleep in the course because I disagreed with almost every word and example the professor used. But since the marks had already been recorded, I told him how I passed: "I discovered in the early classes that your viewpoint and mine are diametrically opposed. I didn't have to study. The first thought that popped into my head as the valid conclusion or correct inference from the premises of the questions was bound to be different from yours. So I gave the nearest opposite as the answer and apparently it was always 'right' by your standards of reasoning." So much for the theory of irrefutable logic.

In business I discovered that statistics—so often the foundation of rational business decisions—are even more unstable than logic. It is possible to justify almost any conclusion statistically by picking a number, assigning a meaning of your own choice to it, and calling it statistical

132

proof. Another person can take the same numerical data, interpret it differently, and arrive at a contradictory result. Ben J. Wattenberg, one of the country's statistics popularizers, wrote a fascinating book, *The Real America* (New York: Doubleday, 1974) based entirely on numerical data and Census Bureau facts, in which he takes issue with most of the conclusions reached by experts who rely on the same data. With statistics, you pays your money and you takes your choice.

We have plenty of evidence that men's logical reasoning soars off into stratospheric flights of phobia when it comes to dealing with women as equal humans, but they don't do much better dealing objectively with their own kind. More male executives are attending company-paid psychology workshops than at any time in history. They are being introduced to role-playing, transactional analysis, behavioral science, counseling, sensitivity training, and group therapy—all designed to improve their management skills! One common feature of these therapeutic simulations is an attempt to *suspend rational thinking* in favor of instinctive feelings and perceptions. On the other hand, management disparages women's native gifts in this area as unsuitable to business needs, then it turns around and invests heavily in trying to teach its male executives how important they are!

Evidently a new weakness has developed in the male defense. If objective, quantifiable reasoning—an allegedly superior male faculty—needs shoring up with "inferior" female mental faculties, the fortification must be extremely brittle and ready for an assault. Under the complex demands of modern society and business, intangible factors have more impact on intelligent decision-making than phantom "facts" which are subject to personal interpretations or common rationalizations. Women frequently mistrust their intuitive feelings in business settings because they've been told to, or laughed at when they expressed them. Or, because women's intuition is sometimes fright-

133

ening in its speed when compared to the finger-counting pace of men's mental processes. Intuition functions with the lightning flash of an electronic calculator, announcing the answer in flashing red lights before the pen-and-pencil pushers of logical deduction have added the first set of numbers.

This is an attribute which has many uses for women in business. The trick is to camouflage it in terms men can understand. Their word for any thought they can't immediately justify is "hunch." "Hunch," obviously, is a fetal form of intuition and it's used extensively by businessmen, especially when they base promotional decisions on "impressions" of a person. They also understand vague intangibles like "common sense," or "sound judgment," both of which are useful to dress up intuition. Best of all, perhaps, is "rationale." Any good intuitive idea can instantly be embellished with other intuitive ideas. As long as succeeding ideas are presented as rationale for the first, the process will appear as logical thinking, which often is no more than unrelated ideas proposed in sequence.

A home economist who is asked to "sit in" on brand managers' meetings is not supplied with relevant sales data, so she *has* to use her intuition. "I'll hear something that sounds crazy from what I know about supermarket buying habits, so I make a definite statement such as 'I don't think we've zeroed in on the basic cause of the slippage in Cincinnati.' Mind you, I have no factual information, so I'm flying off the top of my head, operating on pure intuition, but I never qualify it with wishy-washy comments like 'I wonder . . . ?' or 'Maybe there's another possibility?' I make it sound very positive. When they question me, I say, 'Oh, would you like to hear my rationale on that?' Then I number every thought that comes into my head. Just saying, 'Number One, this . . . Number Two, that . . .' seems to qualify as logical presentation, even though the numbered items don't have

134

any connection. When it comes right down to it, the men don't have rationale, concrete ideas. They're just guessing too, but I found out I'm much better at that game than they'll ever be. The secret is using their favorite glory words; in our place the big rage is 'Can you give me your rationale on that?' Would you believe, they're beginning to show me some of the sales figures?"

Another woman, also in a consumer product industry, tried the opposite tack when her well-reasoned, carefully documented ideas were consistently ignored. As the only woman on a new product planning team, she originally buttressed her opinions with marketing studies, buying habits, competitors' sales estimates, and similar data. Despite her sensible presentations, the male product managers always voted in favor of their own preconceived ideas. Seeing that they refused to take her seriously anyway, she began to couch all her comments as vague "intuition." She made sure it got on the record when she'd say, "I'd like to vote in favor of further exploration on this item, but I have a *feeling* it would be a waste of time," or "My *intuition* tells me this is a good idea, it just *seems* to have potential." She presented her own ideas as if they came out of the wild blue yonder, unsubstantiated by anything but her female intuition. As further developments substantiated her judgment, she promptly reminded her cohorts, "Remember, I had a feeling this wouldn't live up to expectations," or "I told you I had an intuition about such-and-such." When her seemingly baseless "intuitions" compiled a track record for amazing accuracy, the men were forced to notice, particularly because she kept reminding them. When the group leader approached her one day and hesitantly said, "Uh . . . Mary . . . uh . . . you know we're getting close to the wire with the XL proposal . . . and we really need the benefit of your intuition before making the final decision," she knew her tactic had worked. "It's crazy," she says, "they never paid any attention to me when I followed the system they use to

135

propose new product ideas. Now I have this big reputation in the company for having a miraculous 'intuition' about new products."

The value of intuition extends far beyond manipulating stereotypes. It can be a most useful inner divining rod. Women often exhibit uncanny sensitivity to what's going on in their immediate surroundings. They often can just "tell" when something's wrong or an organizational change is imminent. They "sense" subtle differences in behavior or responses, even though men's surface attitudes remain the same. I think there is no question that these intuitive communications are valid and trustworthy —especially since men in business intentionally send out many deceptive messages to women. The woman's intuition is picking up the covert message, the real intent. As a female operating principle it is probably wise to never ignore your intuitive signals. At some later date, the justification or rationale for your "feeling" will come to light.

One woman executive told me she was offered a transfer to another department by a manager who had previously dismissed her interest in shifting jobs. On the surface it sounded like he was presenting the very situation she sought, but "I had a funny feeling that something wasn't right." Trusting her instinct, she turned down the transfer, but not without considerable agony and doubt that she was doing the wise thing after pestering for just such an opening. A month later she found out from a woman friend in the financial office that the department had been going steadily downhill in profitability for several months and was on the verge of being closed down. Had she accepted the "great opportunity," she would have been in the "fall-guy" position in that operation when it collapsed. "I am amazed at my intuition," she says. "I knew nothing about that department except what I'd been told, that it was a booming new section. Its real financial state was a deep dark secret. There must have

136

been something phony in the over-enthusiastic way the job was presented that tipped off my inner instinct."

Another woman has a boss who seems to ride a job-security roller coaster. "I can sense when he's in trouble upstairs. I don't know how, maybe something in his actions or attitude or tone of voice. Anyway, when I get the feeling that he's in trouble, I ask him for a raise or something else I've been denied, like a more liberal expense account. And I usually get it because at those low points he's scared to death he'll lose me or anger me."

When it comes to taking a new job, women frequently report unverifiable "feelings" that worry them because they "can't put their finger on" a definite reason, but a nagging warning bell keeps ringing. When the feeling is inexplicable but has a persistent gut quality, it pays to act on it because intuition has a much sounder base than surface intellectualizing. An office manager was offered a job by a new firm at a considerable salary increase and assurance that she would have complete authority over the administration of office services. "It sounds so good and it would be a big step up for me. They were especially complimentary about my 'diplomatic personality' because I'll be dealing with requests from their important executives. I'm torn because everyone's advising me to take it, but I have this awful feeling that I shouldn't." In the end, she didn't take the job and has been grateful to her intuition ever since. "I later heard the place was notorious for destroying office managers. It had several men executives who competed viciously trying to outdo each other and their favorite battleground was the administrative service area—you know, demanding dictaphone transcripts yesterday and wanting huge statistical reports typed up within an hour, storming down to the typing pool to see if their enemy's work was getting priority over theirs. I never saw any of those men during my interviews but some indefinable thing in the atmo-

137

sphere or the morale must have triggered my inner qualms."

Grab the Ball and Run!

Playing corporate politics is a game that goes on at many levels. There is one master contest of the war-between-the-sexes variety. But there are innumerable battlefields where individual women must find ways to outwit the systems that are deeply entrenched. There is no way to slip in quietly and unnoticed because the entrance of women players sets a turbulence in motion. This works to women's disadvantage because men players cope with the upset by rejecting women allies, by ignoring them, disparaging them, patronizing them, and forever trying to put them "back in their place" as mothers, wives, and secretaries. This is no place to help them put you down by meekly following their lead.

When new players enter and change the dynamics, it becomes an entirely new ball game. If the inexperienced new women players stand around and watch the old players to imitate their moves, the weaker ones will be mopped up in the first new innings. The rules of the game are so clear-cut that a beginner has plenty of room within the rules to practice individual methods of play. She must take advantage of the agitation on the field to discomfit experienced pros and keep them off balance so they can't mobilize against her. Women have an arsenal of tricks at their command, but many hesitate to use them, thinking it isn't fair to take advantage of another's weakness.

Come on, come on! You're not "playing house." You're in a ball game. If an opposing player drops the ball, you pick it up and run. If you can distract a rival so he isn't watching his base, you steal a base. If the infield moves closer, expecting you to hit a pop fly, pretend you will but then aim a fast low grounder through the unprotected hole. *That's* what "playing fair" is all about—playing within the rules but so cleverly and astutely that you give the other team a run for its money. And that's when you gain respect from male associates for your proficiency and talent.

PART
2

The Players,
the Penalties,
the Objectives

CHAPTER
6
The Goal
Is the Top of
the Pyramid

* Katharine is the first female Director of Personnel for a famous advertising agency. She is determined to recruit women for the managerial ranks, now running 93 percent male. This spring she placed an ad in the student newspaper of a large northeastern school she knew as a women's college although it had opened its doors to men a few years back. Under the headline "Management Trainee Position," she listed prerequisites which applied to a high proportion of female graduates: liberal arts or humanities degree; interest in writing, communications; enjoy working with people; diversified, progressive responsibility. She got six answers—all from men. "I reached the entire male complement in the graduating class and *not one of the women*," she says. "I can't blame the ad because the men responded swiftly and clearly indicated their recognition that this was a promising job opportunity. Apparently none of the hundreds of qualified women knew what management trainee meant."
* The career counseling workshop included nine unemployed women, all of whom had been laid off in the

recession of 1974 and were having great difficulty finding a job a year later. All were college graduates (some with advanced degrees) of the booming late 1960s and their nonsecretarial work experience averaged between five and eight years with only one employer. Without exception, they launched their career by taking the best of many jobs offered them on graduation, the "best" defined as the one that paid the highest starting salary and had an impressive-sounding title.

* Sally got her Ph.D. in chemistry about five years ago and took what seemed an auspicious job in a famous corporate lab. After three promotions, she quit. She took a new job as a management intern in a diversified industrial company. She is playing corporate politics to win.

During the past few years there has been an outpouring of solicitous concern for women who aspire to better jobs. Advice is coming fast and thick from feminist consultants helping other women, male agencies spreading their authority mantle, employee seminars complying with government mandates, vocational guidance testers fleecing insecure job-hunters, books, portfolios, and conferences teaching how to be an executive.

I see hundreds of capable women assessing their "executive ability," "leadership skills," "management potential," and other nebulous qualities. Many patiently list everything successful they did in life to find indicators for charting a career path. Ambitious women are urged to examine their personal attitudes, identify their interests, take stock of their aptitudes, remedy their deficiencies, strengthen their weaknesses—and reorder this weird accumulation into a marketable commodity.

There is nothing wrong with all this if its avowed purpose is to raise the consciousness of women who are looking at the world through rose-colored glasses and need to be jolted from their reverie. Nor is there anything intrinsically wrong with healthy introspection and realistic self-appraisal; indeed both are important tools for coping with contemporary life in general. But exactly how this emphasis on self-analysis will guide an eager woman to establish rational business goals is a mystery to me.

Use High-Power Binoculars, Not a Microscope

One major fallacy in popular career counseling is the presumption that women are sufficiently knowledgeable about business to make informed decisions before or after they've dissected their personalities. How could they be? Who honestly tells them about the vast range of jobs built into the private enterprise system? Who sets forth genuine career paths for women? What company is sincerely steering female employees into the pipeline to upper-level jobs? It seems patently clear that women are in no position to chart intelligent self-directions as long as the roads to advancement remain largely unmarked, unpaved, and untraveled. Worse yet, this understandable inability to discern shapes in a black void is twisted around to disparage them. Women are accused of limiting their own ambitions by getting locked into minimal aspirations, of making short-term judgments although the only landmarks visible to them are meaningless titles and immediate salary. Their difficulty is only compounded when advisors tell them to gaze through a microscope turned onto themselves. What they—and you—should be doing is training a telescope on the galaxies of opportunity!

At the very least you need high-power binoculars to survey the entire playing field. The microscopic focus perpetuates a dangerous misconception already held by most women—that "management" is a definable craft which one must be skilled in before getting a job, just as typing is a prerequisite for a secretary. Nothing could be further from the truth. Management skill is whatever a particular company or top executive says it is. There is no such thing as *a* management skill. There are as many ways of managing a company as there are chief executives, which is why corporations develop recognizably different personalities. Nobody who reflects on the matter even superficially could believe that a management job in the Howard Hughes empire is identical to one in the Metropolitan Life Insurance Company. Men, and certainly top executives, know that management skill is not a "thing." It is a developmental process and its components must be learned on the job.

Under the circumstances, self-scoring without knowing the score is a waste of time. It makes no fundamental difference whether a woman *thinks* she has management potential, she has to demonstrate it on the playing field. Companies which routinely favor men with ambitious drive pay no heed to that inner quality in women. Quite the reverse. A woman's stubborn insistence that she has executive ability often appears on the evaluation report as "manifests dissatisfaction with the job; thinks she should be a supervisor." The corporate woods are full of women with great management potential who have been consistently throttled *because* of their avowed competence. Very little of this covert systematic prejudice has been alleviated by EEO laws, so redirecting women down the same blind alley of self-improvement is counterproductive. The external realities are challenge enough, but they dictate quite a different game plan.

Those of you who absorbed the lessons of the military-sports chapters will readily see that modern corporations are looking initially for disciplined followers, not self-endowed leaders. Female corporate athletes need considerable active experience in the game to take part in the

146

gradual evolution from follower to team leader. When a novice takes up any unfamiliar game—bridge, bowling, baseball, or football—the first pertinent questions are: "What's the point of this game? What's the objective? How is it scored?" A beginner must have a rudimentary knowledge of what's at stake, a concept of the overall game, to make the most elementary moves. Does it matter if you hit a perfect grounder down center field if you don't know enough to start running around the bases? What difference if you are a master at bidding if you don't know it obligates you to take certain tricks? The game of corporate politics starts off the same way: appraising the ultimate objective, sighting your working goal.

Focus on the Chief Executive Officer

The clear-headed gamester can bypass the thicket of job abstractions which masquerade as worthy goals. For seriously ambitious women there is only one logical objective: to become the chief executive officer of the corporation. Which is to say, the president, the chairman of the board, or whatever title may blossom in coming decades to identify the controlling position at the top of the pyramid. To aim for anything less is to short-change yourself at the outset and to cut off your potential before you have any way of knowing what it is. Inasmuch as women as a class have no criteria to evaluate their business futures, and male management has no divining rod to unearth female potentialities, there is no way to predict the outcome of the game until women join the corporate teams with the express intention of becoming the captain. Prior to this second half of the seventh decade of the twentieth century such a suggestion would have been foolish and frivolous; from now on, any lesser ambition is female folly.

147

Considering the dearth of encouragement, it's probable that none of you reading this have dared let your imagination soar to the top of the pyramid. Mighty few women have plotted their first infant step up the hierarchical ladder because they haven't been pointed in the right direction. In a way, they've been playing pin-the-tail-on-the-donkey, that stupid game where a child is blindfolded and spun around several times to lose all sense of direction, then jovially headed for an unseen target armed with a minuscule arrow. The results are analogous when similar disorientation tricks are played on women in business. If they tear off the constricting blindfold, shake off the dizzying effects of ill-spun advice, and turn their field glasses resolutely at the panorama before them, their chances of hitting even a small target are multiplied beyond calculation.

If you're in a state of shock at the idea of setting your sights on the top job (considering that you are presently little more than a glorified clerk in your opinion), let's examine the rationale behind the game plan you're about to construct. In football, the goal is the area across the goal line, where players strive to put the ball by kicking, passing, or running. In business, the goal is the point toward which your lifelong effort is directed, the terminus you are striving to reach. By definition, a goal must be within the realm of possibility and worth achieving because its pursuit is a challenge. There is excitement and exhilaration in the striving, which implies a sense of steady and constant forward movement. The moving ahead is not the goal; the goal is the endpoint toward which you are moving. Interim steps ("My goal is to become a supervisor" or vague generalities ("My goal is management") or daydreams ("I want meaningful work") are not goals. To be properly classified as a business goal, the position sought should be viable over a long term—the extent of the game—because the goal is your terminus, beyond which you have no ambition.

The symbolic function of a goal is that of a beacon shining far ahead to guide you when other directionals misfunction. Women gamesters must identify the fixed goal to orient their course and the focus in the hierarchical structure is the point of the apex, CEO, the chief executive job. In the middle of the pyramid, as we have seen, positions can and do shift with the exigencies of the moment. Levels are expanded or contracted; job ranks are moved about; the entire core may be shuffled as happens in a reorganization or in a takeover by another company; whole sections of the interior are excised as economic conditions sour. Thus the vast central space of the pyramid resembles a movable mass forever shifting in minor or major ways. There is no immutable marker which women can depend on as they navigate through the shoal. Let's say you settle for a less grandiose goal than CEO and would be deliriously happy to attain the position of manager of the Widget Product Division. Good enough, but if technology wipes out widgets ten years from now and there is no such division just when you've become product expert and devoted twenty years of your valuable time to achieve your goal, what happens then? There is no such danger if you keep your eye on the CEO goalpost. Regardless of what happens, somebody has to run the place, if only to negotiate the merger or preside over the bankruptcy.

Scramble Your Signals to Protect Your Plans

One word of warning is in order here. Do not go around telling people that you're aiming for the CEO goal! To do so is tantamount to tipping off the opposing team to your strategy. Also, you set up formidable obstacles before you've even started playing. There are valid reasons for this caution, some obvious and some subtle. For starters, it "just isn't done" in the gentleman's

149

club. Even the son or son-in-law of an autocratic chairman is properly humble should he be forced to start near the bottom. Everybody in the company and the business community will know the younger relative is slated to take over the top spot, but nobody mentions it. There seems to be an aura of superstition that surrounds corporate power games, as if mentioning a legitimate ambition or expectation might scuttle its chances. Promotions to chief executive jobs always come as unexpected surprises to the victorious winners, at least that's how they tell the story to press interviewers. Men who fail to observe proper humility, who make no secret of their intentions to fight their way to the top, are not highly respected (though they can be mightily feared) by business peers who privately refer to them as ruthless or unprincipled.

What we've come upon is one of the unwritten codes of etiquette in the game. This admonition reads: Don't verbalize *high* personal ambitions. Men have little need to violate this injunction because an ambitious man's superiors instinctively know that he expects to move steadily forward, and act accordingly. A woman player, however, elicits no such response. It will be asumed that she *doesn't want* to progress, so blind adherence to the male etiquette code will destroy all her chances. A woman must convince superiors that she expects to advance as steadily as ambitious male cohorts. She must openly express interest in jobs one level above, discuss prerequisites, and drop hints about timetables. The rules require that you look only one rung ahead on the pyramidal ladder, so any mention of your guiding goal to become president is definitely out. The unwritten code aside, any such mention is bound to terrify all the men in your vicinity—and you can be sure the news would travel through the male grapevine like a brushfire. A couple of years ago there was a shaggy-dog joke making the cocktail bar circuit. It recounted the presumptuousness of a woman professional who was being interviewed for a job by an officer of a large corporation which was being forced to hire one female who could properly be classed as management. Everything had gone well in her preliminary interviews and her reputation was impeccable, so final approval was expected. Uneasy in his novel role of assessing a female subordinate, the management executive engaged in nervous banter and small talk, ending with the standardized clincher: "Why does an attractive girl like you want a job that means bothering your pretty head with complicated details of government contracts and regulatory guidelines?" And you know what she said? the shocked storyteller would ask. She said, "Because I intend to be president of the company and I consider this background essential." Listeners knew without being told that she didn't get the job. The reason the story was so in vogue in the executive club set was twofold. It contained the requisite ridiculous component (imagine any woman . . . ?) and it hit a super-sensitive male nerve —the emerging fear that these crazy women *might* try to invade the last bastion of male exclusivity, the executive suite.

Set Your Sights on the Top

It's a foregone conclusion that corporate chief executive officers, like presidential candidates, are not plucked at random from disinterested bystanders. You can't win a lottery if you don't buy a ticket, and no woman will get to the top of the corporate pyramid who doesn't set her sights on the job. Consider that you are going to work somewhere at some job or other, for some forty years of your life. Why not aim for a job where you can retire early if you want and be guaranteed an extravagant pension to sustain your later activities? The undisputed fact is that corporate CEOs make more money than anybody because they set their own salaries. They don't work any harder than many a conscientious supersecretary or millions of middle-management supervisors. They just do different work which they learned via subsidized on-the-job training. And if they get fired for incompetence (which happens more often than you think but not as often as warranted), the blow is softened with a $100,-000 annual consolation salary for many years or the rest of their lives. Getting fired at top hierarchical levels may be a psychological blow to inflated egos, but it certainly is not a financial disaster. That alone should be a compelling reason to aim for the position.

A British business editor, Robert Heller, chided Americans for their "simple refusal to believe that anybody who has made millions, floated to the top of a large corporation, or both, can be an idiot." He could have been talking to American women, who are surely the most gullible swallowers of management myths. Unable to penetrate the citadel of corporate Wizards of Oz, women stand in inordinate awe of top executive jobs, even though it's likely that many intelligent, experienced women now working in under-utilized positions couldn't do worse than a number of current CEOs at running a large company. Those of us who frequent annual stockholder meetings agree wholeheartedly with the *New York Times*'s brilliant reporter, Marylin Bender, who notes in her book, *At the Top* (Doubleday and Co., Garden City, N.Y., 1975.): "A striking impression emerges from these rituals—how unexceptional the noblemen of corporate America are. One objective of the feminist movement is to secure for women the same triumph of mediocrity." In short, the prime personality characteristic required of women who want the highest-paid jobs in industry is perseverance—and being headed in the right direction.

Due to obvious circumstances beyond their control, women have plowed through the business world looking at their feet, hoping to find a lost penny or tossed crumb. We are geologic experts on the muddy base of the pyramid, whereas "management" looks down from the crest of the mountain. The view from the top is management perspective, and the only practical way for women to acquire it is by preparing themselves to assume the regal position. This matter of perspective is crucial to ambitious women; without it your approach to job situations is narrow and warped. You lack the sense of proportion that turns ordinary drudge jobs into meaningful endeavors in pursuit of a goal.

Perspective is often illustrated with a picture of a long, flat Kansas highway lined with telephone poles. The pole nearest you in the front is tallest and most imposing of all; as your eye travels down the line of sight, the poles progressively shrink in size until they converge at the vanishing point on the horizon. The objects nearest you always appear largest, but the spatial relationships and the relative size of poles, ahead and behind, change dramatically when you shift your physical position. These are deceptions of depth and distance—visual illusions—because the poles are actually identical in size; only your perspective distorts them.

Similarly in business situations, your perception of the relative importance of various jobs is influenced by your physical nearness. Many women stick at the same job pole all their working lives, neatly polishing the knot holes and planting flowers around the base because they think theirs is the most important pole in the lineup—which it is, but only from their own perspective. Looked at from even a short distance away, its relative importance in the vista comes into different proportion. Viewed from top management's perspective, its significance dwindles rapidly. Will anyone at management distance, for example, be able to *see* the neatly polished knot holes or care about the pretty flowers? Nice touches at eye level but how important from a distance? Not long ago a department store advertising copy chief bemoaned the excessive time and energy she devotes to her job. She loves her work even though it necessitates many hours of overtime late at night, Saturdays, and even Sundays during holiday sales seasons. She enjoys a fabulous reputation because each newspaper ad that comes out of her department is a polished gem of perfect English, quixotic humor, and clever artwork. By all the usual standards she is a top professional in her field, yet she is deeply disturbed because she has never been promoted to advertising manager. At first she rejected the notion that her perspective was nonmangerial and she might be polishing knot holes, but then she saw the difference. "For twenty years I thought my job was to turn out the best advertising copy I could possibly conceive for the store! It never occurred to me that my sole task was to attract enough customers to move the advertised merchandise and to make sure that decisions of buyers and managers were justified and profitable. With my talent I could have done that, without untold overtime and without driving my writers and artists up the wall in my demand for needless perfection. Instead, I treated every ad for 89¢ panties as if we were writing 'Ode to a Nightingale.' "

Seeing your job in proper perspective is not easy when you're deeply involved in the everyday pressures. Women like this copy chief tend to misjudge their job priorities and fall into the trap known as "gold-plating" the task, or over-emphasizing secondary considerations. Personnel executives recognize the existence of this normal human

154

proclivity to puff up one's job because companies that experimented in letting employees write their own descriptions for a job-evaluation program found most jobs magnified beyond recognition. Undoubtedly women share with men the human desire to increase their prestige and self-esteem by imagining their job as more complex and difficult than it is. But untangling fact from fiction is more difficult for women because they have been so inappropriately placed in the traditional job structure that many female jobs *do* utilize higher levels of skills and responsibility than are reflected in the job classification. This is apt to be true in industries where women predominate at lower levels, such as retailing, communications, or publishing. In other industries there are often a few low-level jobs customarily reserved for women because they produce more efficiently than men at the task. What that means is that women, not knowing any better, were willing to assume more duties than men to satisfy bosses' demands rather than job requirements.

There is no pat solution to the problem of seeing your specific job for what it is, except to cultivate the habit of looking down at your job from a management overview. If you always keep your secret CEO goal in mind, your assessments will be more accurate than opinions of your immediate superiors since your perspective will put *them* in perspective also. It takes a little practice, but it becomes a fun part of the game. In a way it's play-acting, and you throw yourself into the role by thinking: "If I were president right now, how would I measure the contribution coming from the specific job I now hold? Which of the miscellaneous responsibilities entailed are really important to the organization's goals—and which are inflated puffery added by some supervisor up the line or my predecessor? What can I learn from this spot in the hierarchy which will be useful to me as president?" Questions like these are invaluable to teach yourself how to concentrate on

155

the essentials of your work and how to minimize, eliminate, or quickly slop over the trivial stuff.

Watch Your Timing!

So far we haven't mentioned one subject which has a powerful influence on how you lay out your strategic game plan—timing. Time is the limiting factor which shapes the game and creates most of the pressure and stress associated with business success. Timing in this sense will be a wholly unfamiliar concept to women because it does not exist in the free-floating female culture. Nor is there a model to follow because no woman has yet had a chance to incorporate timed moves into her plan. The women who have attained a measure of corporate success today have crawled, stumbled, inherited, or been pushed into their positions; they had no occasion to think in long-range terms because they were handed a lifetime pass to stand still under the old practices. Timing becomes important only to those who envision steady forward movement toward a definite goal. The unambitious have no reason to concern themselves with time. Consequently an exhibited awareness of the business time element subtly reveals your serious intentions to management. Often the difference in attitude between aspiring men and working women is the unconscious revelation that time is a driving force in the expectations of men, while women do not feel its inexorable pressure. A demonstrated appreciation of time-measurement is part of the X factor which disqualifies many women for upper management consideration.

The game time clock has two faces: one is personal and individual; the other reflects the exigencies of business operation. At the personal level, timing is an extension of life. There are just so many years we all have to accomplish whatever we do in our time on earth. Once you assimilate outside employment into your life plan you find that it fills a definite niche of approximately forty years. The goal-plan spectrum covers approximately a thirty-year period figured from the age you graduate from college and enter the workforce until you reach your desired job objective. When you aim for top management, that objective must be reached—or be close—no later than your early fifties, so age twenty-two to fifty-two comprises a typical game plan span, give or take a few years at either end. By adopting a CEO goal you establish time-planning guides. First off, count the number of levels in the hierarchy through which you must progress to reach your goal in the allotted time. These may vary, as companies differ according to size and industry, but most corporations limit their levels to somewhere between ten and twenty. Taking the lower limits (ten promotional steps within thirty years) means that each upward move must be accomplished every three years. This time factor shortens appreciably if you must make fifteen moves in the same thirty years; you now have two years for each planned step.

Experienced corporate gamesters become very attuned to their personal time clock. They know when failure to move means automatic forfeiture of the ball. This is not necessarily automatic at every time period because early moves progress at a faster pace than later moves. Some of the moves can be completed in six months, while another may not be feasible in less than five years. Flexibility is possible as long as the average mobility rate is sufficient to cover the required distance in the apportioned time. Keeping your attention centered on a stable goal reachable by realistic time and distance calculations provides a new player with warning bells to signal when a career is getting sidetracked or immobilized. For example, if you've been working for six years and had one minor promotion, your time clock is backed up. You must advance two levels in the next year to get back on schedule.

On the business side of the clock, timing serves a different function. It indoctrinates you with the basic philosophy of free enterprise. You may not guess it if you've been floating idly in a repetitive job, but corporations are oriented solely to the future, never the past. The price of the stock last year is ancient statistical history; what counts is the increase in earnings this current quarter. A sensational product of yesterday is today's failure if a competitor has come up with a better idea. Time plays a major part in management decisions because industry hopes to keep pace with the changing marketplace and ahead of its competitors. Future projection—planning—is integral to corporate decisions because no company operates in a vacuum. Competitors, economic conditions, government regulations, money supply, labor resources, raw materials, relevant technology, consumer psychology —to name a few—are forces which have impact on policy decisions. All fluctuate in a momentary time-frame projected to the future. Last year, yesterday, this morning are gone, and what happened then has no significance except for any lingering impact of what happens tomorrow, next week, or next year. The infamous "pressures" of management are not indigenous to business, they are dictated by time. Mediocre executives can always be spotted by observing their anxiety levels as related to time. The frantic, last-minute, incessant emergency types are bummers to be avoided because they don't understand time-planning and will make your life miserable.

Artificial time pressures created by inefficient supervisors must be distinguished from realistic time strictures which operate continually in business. Real time limitations lead to inevitable compromise decisions and these perturb women who grew up in the timelessness of the female culture. When time is obliterated as a controlling element, any task appears in different equation. Routine household chores taken on an entirely different complexion if one has all day to work on a closet cleaning or ten minutes on the twenty-fifth of each month to complete the same task. The ten-minute time stricture will lead unavoidably to a compromise on thoroughness, compared to the careful attention to each detail which would be possible with no time limitations.

Full-time office jobs are *always* structured into time frames, the standard being eight hours a day, forty hours a week. This immediately sets up a compromise equation which eludes the comprehension of many women. They frequently resent the time factor and even revolt against it, feeling overwhelmed by unreasonable assignments and put upon by male superiors "who don't understand how much is involved" in producing a requested project. Chances are that those superiors are balancing the time element against work standards and assume the women subordinates are equally cognizant of the trade-off. Unfortunate as it may be, excellent job performance is more often measured by compliance with timing exigencies than superior quality of a finished product. The typical male supervisor's snappishness, "I don't care how you do it, just get it to me tomorrow," is a reflection of this conflict. So are management criticisms about hard-working women that they are "argumentative," "nitpicking," or "too fussy." A CEO goal orientation helps women overcome the destructive hangovers of female conditioning by focusing on the official time clock which controls the game and all its moves.

Line Jobs Are the Action Arena

Any woman aiming for a career in management must

be quite sure where those jobs are and how to find them. There's no doubt that president or chairman of the firm is a management job. To find the rest of the management track, work backward from the top. Find out how they got there and you will know which jobs or which divisions of the corporation are important to your future. There are many ways to get this information because the background of top officers is widely publicized. Dun & Bradstreet's *Reference Book of Corporate Management* gives business biographies of officers and directors of all companies reported in Moody's *Handbook of Common Stocks*. So do *Who's Who in Finance and Industry* and dozens of specialized directories for various industry groups. *Business Week, Fortune,* and other national business publications run stories about top executives, as do business-financial sections of Sunday newspapers and leading trade publications. If you are an employee, your search is aided by internal memos, promotion announcements, and company publications which proudly trace the job history of present executives. The grapevine is also helpful in dispensing personal information about executives.

Almost invariably you'll discover that the top executives of the firm came up through the operating departments—either that branch of the company which is concerned with "producing" whatever goods or services the company deals in; or that branch charged with selling or marketing the goods or services. These are the business operations directly responsible for making money, the only function of a commercial enterprise. Nowadays money itself (the prime rate, international exchange, investment capital, taxes) as opposed to "making it" through simple profit on sales, has become a major consideration in the affairs of complex business organizations, so a few top executives are beginning to emerge from financial operations.

To interpret your diagram of officers' promotional tracks, you have to refer back to the military origin of organizational structure. The departments your goal models come from are called *line* functions or departments, and the rest of the organization consists of *staff* operations or departments. The prototype of classic line-and-staff structure is, as always, the military, and today's corporate officers, most of whom served in World War II, are highly respectful of the organizing genius which coordinated a massive global effort on many fronts with armies from several nations. In military parlance the fighting arm—combat troops and their officers—is the line and all other units which recruit, support, feed, supply, or advise fighting units are staff.

Translated to business terminology it means that the front-line fighting forces are the money-making units: sales and production. The separation is readily identified in industrial corporations which manufacture a product and then sell it to another company, the government, or consumers. Nonindustrials (financial or service companies) have the same two divisions, but the names are different. In retailing, for instance, the "production" branch is buying; buyers and merchandise managers literally "produce" the goods the stores sell. In banking the profit-making product is money; one sector produces it by collecting it from depositors, the other loans it at higher interest rates. Whatever kind of business you're in, there is an equivalent dual operation wherein something is "produced" at one price and "sold" at a higher price; the difference, after deducting salaries and expenses, is the profit before taxes. This is highly simplistic, of course, because huge modern corporations have immeasurable room to manipulate income, expenses, pricing, and profits, but the fundamental activity is making money.

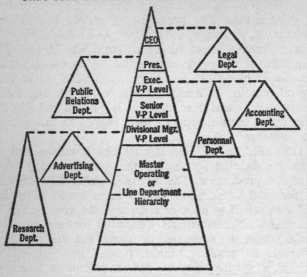

Staff departments are pyramidal ornaments to the master "Line Department" pyramid. Staff departments report to line executives at various levels of the hierarchy. Staff departments vary in size, depending on the needs of the corporation. Staff department internal structure duplicates authority levels and chain-of-command connection of operating pyramid except that the top job is head of department instead of corporate chief executive.

Staff Jobs Support the Fighting Forces

Staff departments make up a separate part of the company. They are not profit centers, they are expenses. (See diagram on preceding page.) However vital their services, they cost the company money to operate, and in an economic recession staff jobs are the first ones cut. These are departments composed of the specialists in assorted fields and their function is to assist the line executives. Staff departments serve as technical advisors or supplements to line departments. Thus, staff jobs are not in the line and therefore are not training grounds for future policy-making officers of the corporation. Both line and staff departments are set up according to military authority patterns —each person reporting to one immediate superior—but there is a significant variation in the area of authority. Staff vice-presidents have authority *only* over the people in their department; they report to a line vice-president who is their superior. Staff executives make recommendations to their line superior who then makes the *decision* (which can accept or ignore the staff suggestions). A staff executive is never empowered to make *policy* decisions; those are the prerogative of line executives.

Typical staff departments include personnel, purchasing, accounting, data processing, advertising, public relations, research, traffic, billing, industrial relations, medical, home economics, legal and, depending on the type of industry, technical specialties such as engineering, sciences, and architecture. Need I point out the obvious? That this is a list of the only departments women have been allowed to enter until the last couple of years? The sex-discrimination barrier is still almost impenetrable in line jobs, which is precisely why top managements can sit back and complacently announce that women are "unqualified" for upper management jobs. Of course they are; management has arbitrarily unqualified them by excluding them from the pipeline. The disqualification has nothing to do with women's innate or demonstrated capabilities or business acumen. It is a flat-out evasion of the equal opportunity laws, and it is pursued successfully because employees of government enforcement agencies are as untutored as women when it comes to understanding the organizational power structure and policy practices of business firms.

You won't be fooled if you keep your eye riveted on your CEO goal because the road to advancement today starts in management trainee programs (the business firm's officer candidate school) or in sales (now euphemistically titled marketing). Highly motivated women must start in—or cross over to—these primary line training positions if they intend to move deep into the business structure. Ambitious men have long read these road signs and made job decisions accordingly. Years ago Fletcher Byrom, chief executive of Koppers Co., turned down many job offers when he graduated from college with a degree in metallurgy. He chose to become a sales trainee at American Steel & Wire because it "might offer better chances for advancement." He was right, as his phenomenal career attests. Women must make the same decision today.

Sound Strategy Zigzags over the Field

Unfamiliar as they are with hierarchical structure, women often believe that any promotion is a step in the right direction, up. This is not surprising in view of the blanket refusal to grant them the most deserved upgrading in salary or status through the years, but a new danger now lurks. As a palliative to the past, managements are now offering insignificant supervisory positions to women (many of whom have been doing the work anyway) and touting them as big promotions. It's important that you not be tricked by this ploy. What's happening is that the grade platform of female ghetto departments and a few other staff operations is being raised slightly. Instead of keeping all women in the lowest "operative" jobs (assignment writers, junior editors, computer programmers, bookkeepers, personnel clerks, tellers, research assistants, and the like), many companies are upping long-term women a notch to first-line supervision. Industrywide we will soon have a generation of female super-clerks still vastly underpaid and exploited but with marginally higher salaries than their subordinates and impressive titles—impressive if you don't know any better. Despite the title, which could actually be "manager" of something, first-line supervision is definitely not management.

Margaret Hennig and Anne Jardin, co-directors of the Graduate Program in Management at Simmons College, have done a remarkable analysis of women's jobs which documents the horrifying development. Extrapolating pertinent job data from census figures and from major industries in which women are a majority of those employed (AT&T, insurance, banking, education, health, retailing, etc.), they calculated that 60 percent of people in supervisory positions today are women! Their study (summarized for me in a personal letter) was based on figures from 1972 since available statistical data is always years behind the times. At that time, the trend to promote women to these supervisory jobs had scarcely gotten underway, so I'd guess a current figure could reach nearly 75 percent. The age of the female super-clerk has descended with a vengeance! Hennig and Jardim, along with other perceptive feminist consultants, agree that most of these supervisory women have explicitly or implicitly been labeled as lacking in management potential.

165

They are effectively dead-ended after one tiny step offered by management. If nothing else, this evidence of management generosity should remind women gamesters of the pungent warning in the ancient maxim: Beware of strangers bearing gifts.

The difference between first-line supervision and a managerial function has nothing to do with the nature of the supervisor's work and the hierarchical level of the people supervised, not necessarily the number of subordinates. A first-line supervisor might have one assistant and part-time use of a secretary; a chairman and chief executive officer of a corporation might have only one person reporting directly to him, the president. Most first-line supervisors have many subordinates—all the billing clerks or telephone operators or copywriters or personnel interviewers or retail clerks or nurses. The first-line supervisory job was better described when it was called "chief" or "head," and the title still lingers, as in chief bookkeeper, chief operator, copy chief, or head nurse. The function of such a supervisor is to coordinate the work of her group, all of whom do the same job. Her authority and responsibility are limited to that task, and she was probably promoted from the ranks of the group she supervises. Subordinates of first-line supervisors are in the lowest professional levels or (significantly for women) in a specific clerical category.

A managerial supervisor has a broader territory of operation; her job entails more aspects of the larger function. This can mean that two or more first-line supervisors in separate functions report to her and she is responsible for scheduling and dovetailing the tasks of different work sections. In another instance, the editor of an employee magazine who supervises reporters, artists, and photographers would be equivalent to first-line supervisor, but the company publications editor who was responsible for the employee magazine, a daily newsletter, and bill inserts would be at a low managerial level. A retail clerk supervisor who was named assistant store manager might have no additional subordinates but the work responsibility would enlarge to include consideration of inventory replacement, delivery schedules, and customer complaints as well as sales results. At the managerial level, a supervisor is no longer a specialist. She does not *do* the work her subordinates do and she needn't know *how* to do it. Her job is to judge results and insure performance by others. Managerial supervisors get into planning, coordinating, personnel problems, motivation of people, and money, whether budgets or profit figures.

To avoid this low-level supervisory booby-trap in the alien land of business, women must maintain constant surveillance of the entire game board. It may be much better to transfer to another sector than accept a limited supervisor post. In addition to the line and staff cleavage, corporate jobs are traditionally divided into classifications. Job-evaluation and salary-administration programs, for instance, are generally handled under four distinct groupings: production workers, technical workers, supervisory, and clerical personnel. Executive, or management, jobs are peculiar unto themselves. Because no two managerial jobs are exactly alike, none of the standardization techniques used at lower levels is deemed suitable. So raises and promotions of executives are still decided by subjective means, opinions of superiors, and personal salary negotiation. If they call you "executive" or "management," don't let them apply standards which belong to lesser groups. Remember, the game of corporate politics is based on outwitting the opponent, especially when he tries clever deceptions to trick you. Gratuitous promotions or raises may come at the lowest levels, but the higher you go, the more certain the rules that *they must be requested*. If you are confused about your job classification, always play according to rules for the higher category where formulas give way to personal negotiation.

In practice, this categorization of employees produces five distinct promotional ladders, each with its own ceiling. This fact is hotly denied by companies accused of just such discriminatory systems, but when they are forced to produce their records in court, it's amazing how closely statistics correlate with practices which observant employees note every day. You might have to adapt the following list to fit special conditions in your company, but in general terms the separate promotional ladders evolve in this pattern:

1. Manual workers: often unionized; promotions by seniority to cleaner jobs or more complex equipment.

2. Skilled trades: start as unskilled craft workers or helpers, can move up to semiskilled or skilled classification; skills limited to a single trade, includes apprenticeship programs.

3. Clerical workers: includes secretaries and white-collar workers in "paper factories." Move to better desk locations.

4. Professional ladders: includes staff specialists and technical experts college-trained in law, accounting, journalism, personnel, sciences, engineering. Job experience all in same specialized function; can move to top position in that specialty. Certain staff executives can become members of management team where, as advisors to president or senior officers, they can exert influence on decisions.

5. Management ladders: start as trainees or assistant supervisors in sales or production departments; may

move in departmental track until these converge at upper levels. Otherwise many promotions and lateral shifts between marketing, manufacturing, finance, branch offices, subsidiaries, and some staff departments to encompass diverse exposure to entire operation. Can move to any high-level post in top management.

Study these promotional ladders to help you structure a game plan and evaluate promotions. To end up in policy-making positions, you must get on the management ladder in a line department even if it means starting over again as a low-paid trainee. (Certain unionized manual workers, the skilled crafts, and top-flight executive secretaries get paid more than management or professional beginners, but they have no place to go.) Major professional or specialty staff departments also have a managerial level toward the top which is treated as a mini-management ladder. So, notice especially the pattern of promotions and job changes included in management development. Broad, diversified experience in all the important operations of a company is becoming the primary qualification for upper-level jobs. Similarly, in the professions, every field has many facets and a potential management executive must have gained on-the-job experience in all the essential ones. Your long-range strategy must incorporate lateral moves to get the experience which paves the way upward. For all women who have been locked into a narrow corner of their field, the smartest way to promote yourself and your career is to move sideways. For a woman player, the shortest path to the top is not straight up, it is a zigzag field run.

Keep an Eye on Other Players All the Time

The contenders you'll face in playing corporate politics change constantly, depending on the situation. This game is played on several levels as well as on different fields. At one level the opposing teams are Women vs. Men; that's the primary team allegiance for all women in business. Then there's the game of an individual woman vs. a particular company's system (if things get tough she may need to call for reinforcements from the rest of the women's team). Then there's the game which pits a woman against her immediate supervisor. And last but by no means least is the game of teammates vying for the coach's approbation (and subsequent promotion), which eventually pits a woman player against men and women in her own age group who will be competing for increasingly fewer job openings as the pyramid narrows.

Most of this latter group will continue to be men because women are still merely dribbling into positions which lead upward. If you are lucky enough to have female peers, you must consolidate immediately to strengthen your weak position because the massive attacks occur in the all-star game of Women vs. Men. Should you run into a woman who refuses to join forces, let her go on her solitary way into the other frays. She will be out of the running soon enough since this is not a game for anyone who can't understand the rudimentary principle that success is contingent on moving from the strongest position possible. A female amateur who doesn't understand the rules of the game—and disdains her natural allies—will not be much of a threat when today's rookies turn into experienced rivals in future seasons' games.

By and large, the neophyte woman player must keep her eye on male peers who are practicing their techniques and perfecting their strategy at the same level she is. The number of players can be enormous and you can't keep track of everybody, so you narrow the field to those who are aiming for the same ultimate goal that you are. These are the age-group contenders you'll eventually face head-on.

Some peer men can be eliminated on the same basis as uncooperative women, that they aren't smart enough. Others may be clearly content to remain approximately where they are; not everybody is ambitious. As a rule, you can assume that those in a management trainee program have serious intentions to advance, but it's comforting to know that half of them will drop out within five years. Remember that figure. In case you get hassled with derogatory remarks about women "giving up" when you decide to change jobs, throw it back. The typical experience with culled male college graduates recruited into management trainee programs is that 50 percent of them quit the company by their fifth year. Incidentally, watch those who quit. If the smart ones are abandoning that ship, find out if they know something you don't; it might be your cue to join the exodus.

In nontrainee situations, you just have to keep your eyes and ears open. Observation and vigilance are perpetual traits of the corporate gamester, and it is essential to watch what men do to give off signals that they expect to advance. You can also make some tentative moves in your own game at this time. Remembering that men react to you as a stereotype, play up to the male tendency to tell women their troubles or dreams. Deft inquisitions by shrewd women fall into the class of "comforting" or "building up men's egos," so you might find out much valuable information. At the same time, you may calm incipient fears that *you* might be an equal contender—that is a silly idea, isn't it?

It doesn't take a psychiatrist to recognize that some-one with a definite goal, who calmly and deliberately sets about implementing it, radiates a sense of purpose and stability. Self-confidence is shaped by knowledge and prep-aration, which become a hallmark of the upwardly striving woman who is learning, learning, learning. With every increase in knowledge, with every successful play in the game, with every failure which is calmly analyzed to figure out what went wrong, the aura of self-confidence is strengthened. A woman player who has correctly sighted the ultimate goalpost in the game steers a steady course, no matter how many storms may batter her ship in the course of participating in a long-distance crossing.

The only realistic goal is the goal in the game, a touch-down. Not every player can expect to make a touchdown —and the challenge wouldn't be worth much if everybody made it—but the excitement and fun come from the striv-ing. Too many women are wracked with doubts, panic, consternation, confusion, anxiety, and depression because they can't pick a satisfying job out of the 40,000 listings in the U.S. Department of Labor's *Dictionary of Occu-pational Titles*. Its sister publication, the *Occupational Outlook Handbook*, describes over 800 occupations, and that's equally impossible to use as a guide.

As many women sense when they keep looking for that pie-in-the-sky, a "meaningful job," picking an occupa-tion, as opposed to planning a career, is a boring way to plan your life. A career, after all, is a complete course or progress extending through life, that can abound in remarkable actions or incidents. Let's face it, there's only one reason to work—to make money. If you ap-proach working realistically—that is, as a gambling game that everybody plays—you might find what you're looking for. A job can mean money, a challenge, a chance to use skills and talents you didn't know you had, a marvelous theater of the absurd to watch and participate in, an opportunity to grow up, to meet all kinds of people, to function in society, to have an impact on that society. And if you play skillfully, it should only take about forty or fifty hours a week, leaving you plenty of free time to develop an active, meaningful, satisfying private life.

CHAPTER

7

Can I Get There from Here?

Established working women might think that a CEO goal is crazy as far as they are concerned, that it should be reserved for women college graduates just entering the labor market. Not a bit of it. For one thing, the ultimate objective gives you the critical perspective needed to play the game. But more to the point, we are at one of those congruent moments in history when all auspicious elements are running in parallel formation. At this juncture, long-term working women have as many opportunities as beginners to push themselves ahead. Not quite to the top of the heap perhaps, but a substantial distance. One advantage of experience comes from years of being bounced around the hierarchical court, which presages a slight acquaintanceship with the rules. But there are far more pragmatic reasons to be optimistic. Those of you born during the Depression, now in your late thirties and forties, are standing next to a gaping hole in the corporate pipeline—and somebody has to plug it. This approaching hiatus has worried employers for many years because it was evident that the abnormally low birthrate of the 1930s would result in a serious shortage of trained men for management positions—just about now! Management's solution is to shove younger and younger men up the ladder even though they are not ready for the responsibility. That leaves vacancies further back in the pipeline, and these, too, are being filled with younger, less experienced men. In effect, second- and third-stringers are filling out the denuded management team.

Not only are most of these premature executives unseasoned by industry's own standards for management readiness, they aren't the cream of the crop to begin with. They can't possibly be, since they were extracted from a minute fraction of the population, thanks to the male-WASP self-perpetuation process. At the time these men were nominated as managerial candidates—twenty or more years ago—they were the residue left from a screening sieve which was universally in use:

Female sex—totally out

No college degree—eliminated nine out of ten males

Non-WASP (white Anglo-Saxon Protestants)—knocked out all blacks and other dark-skinned men; eliminated in wholesale lots most Jews and Italian or Slavic Catholics

This categorical exclusion on the basis of sex, education, religion, race, and ethnic origin narrowed the field of managerial candidates to 3 percent of the labor force, as reported by Vance Packard in *The Pyramid Climbers* (New York: Fawcett World Library, 1964) I myself had once calculated that management's beloved 100 percent quota of male WASPs reduced its pool to 20 percent—but I forgot to include the educational factor.

Such crude, dictatorial, unreasonable discrimination against the overwhelming majority of American workers is precisely what Title VII outlawed. (Educational requirements, per se, are not discriminatory as long as they are applied to everyone and it can be proved that they have some relevance to the job duties.) Title VII is the trump card that all women hold. The aim in playing corporate politics is to build a powerful hand behind it so the trump need not be played until it carries maximum value. The opposing players know you hold that trump, but they play as if *you* don't know it. The gamble pays off more often than not because an incredible number of women haven't the vaguest notion of what employment discrimination is. The law prohibiting 100 percent male-WASP quotas at all levels of business has been in effect since 1965. Look around your company, your office, or your department, and judge whether management has been scrupulously obeying a law which has been in effect for more than twelve years.

At the top, and for several hierarchical levels below, the male incumbents in large, established corporations are all handpicked under the once-legal system which airily dismissed 97 percent of the brains and talent in the workforce. Recognizing the razor thinness of this cross-section, you begin to understand why institutions like the Harvard Business School and the American Management Associations have been doing a booming business in the past ten years running company-paid executive training seminars and management refresher courses for executives. Some corporations have actually gone into the university business themselves, operating huge campuses to desperately train the motley male crew they chose for executives. These makeshift efforts to plug the corporate pipeline will work in makeshift fashion—unevenly. It is a *very* good time for experienced businesswomen to start playing corporate politics with a vengeance, and press their advantage.

Diagram Your Present Location

To figure if you can get there from here, you need a road map—a play diagram. You have to plot where you are in the corporate structure, and where you want to go, keeping in mind the personal time factor (how many working years you have left) and the game time clock (how many moves you must make in that period). If you've been working for fifteen or more years, you're in the third down; the time clock will show that a touchdown is unlikely because you can't zoom through that many levels or cover that much territory. (If you're close enough to make it to president of a major corporation, you are a rarity.) But you can make a field goal or two —senior vice-president of your staff department or your operating division. Don't piddle around aiming for trivial promotions; to play corporate politics you have to open up the entire panorama to establish your management perspective. Gazing down from your imaginary eminence, draw your personal map, a formal organization chart (see diagram next page). Lay out each level in your department pyramid from the top down, inserting name boxes to indicate each person located at successive levels. If an official chart already exists, you're that far ahead. If not, figure it out by watching who reports to whom in the military chain-of-command.

Women plotters who have less than five years' experience are still viable candidates for the ultimate CEO position. You should enlarge your diagram to include a rough chart of the entire company, locating your department in its proper relationship to other branches of the whole. Your game plan has a larger dimension than more senior women's. Chances are, if you've been in your first job for five years, it is past time for you to move out unless there are extremely promising extenuating circumstances. Very rarely does anyone move to the top of the first company they work for, unless they move out for several years and are later invited back.

Women in the middle, those of you averaging ten years' experience—anywhere from five to fifteen years—have options either way. On the upper side (twelve years' experience), you're tagging along at the tail end of the

177

PERSONAL ADVANCEMENT CHART

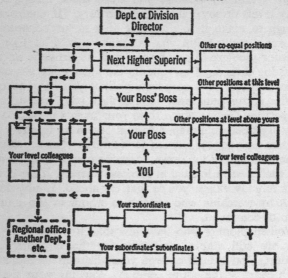

1. Start with You. Go downwards and block in subordinate levels to figure out how many levels from bottom of pyramid you currently are.
2. Plot straight up in direct line of progression: your boss, boss's boss, etc.
3. Fill in other positions at each lateral level, including your co-equal colleagues.
4. Track progression path of top executive(s) through all jobs they once held (dotted line) to calculate your own advancement possibilities or options.

low-birthrate era, which indicates spotty shortages of male managers in your age group. Approximately seven to ten years' experience places you in the early stages of the postwar baby boom that began nourishing the corporate pipeline in the late 1960s. Your male competition will be keener (and increasingly vicious), but nowhere near the head-on confrontation facing the current generation of college students when they move into the workforce, as equally trained young women and men competing for the same job. (College students should refer to Chapter 8 for specific advice on how to get on the right track.)

These are broad generalizations of course, but a long-range game plan takes some preliminary scouting. It makes a difference in your tactical planning if you know whether you are moving into pebbly, grassy, wet, or dry territory. Personal planning, like business planning, must take all variables into account, especially the allocation of human resources—the labor force. When you methodically plot your private options, you are concurrently learning the methods and practicing the techniques of management planning.

Psych Out Your Present Company

Once you have a fix on your own position, you need an aerial view of your employer hierarchy. What kind of an industry are you in? Where does your company rank in its industry? How well managed is it? Is it a good place to work? Is it worthwhile for you to play corporate politics here or should you change playing fields? Women frequently accept meaningless trappings of a company as indicative of its stature. "It's big; it has nice offices; the people are nice; everyone's heard of it." Not long ago the same could be said of W. T. Grant's stores, Penn-Central Railroad, and several major banks and brokerage houses—but they are now bankrupt, or dissolved.

In addition to the industry, psych out your company. Does it have an economic future and a personality to suit your own? Although corporations are structured alike organizationally, they all have distinctive personalities. The type of industry exerts a pervasive influence over the basic environment. Heavily regulated industries, such as utilities, banking, and insurance, tend to be slow-moving, conventional, placid, strictly run according to the book. Consumer-oriented industries which must react to public demand, such as retailing, food, cosmetics, advertising, automobiles, and television stations, are more hectic, high-pressure, and innovative. Companies in highly competitive fields (detergents, drugs and toiletries, motion pictures) are more dynamic than those where a few giants dominate (mining, oil). This business climate or personality is not always evident from outside nor from a myopic job at the bottom. You discover it through research, reading, and talking to other business people. Most women got into their industry by accident rather than forethought, in part because so few jobs were open to women but primarily because they entered as secretaries, and clerical level jobs are the same all over. That's not true of executive jobs, so women striving upward should seek out industries which fit their personal pace and life-style. After several years, one gets "locked into" an industry, forever associated with it, and switching to a new field becomes difficult.

All is not lost if you stumbled into an incompatible industry, because individual companies within that group can vary considerably. The company's personality is a direct reflection of the personal style of the man at the top—the chief executive officer. It pays to investigate him thoroughly. If what you see, read, and hear about him is distasteful or displeasing to you, you will not enjoy the game of moving ahead in his company. Conversely, if the man at the top sounds like the kind of man you admire, you will be a better judge of an interim superior

180

who doesn't fit the mold and could pervert your view of the future. The CEO's priorities can greatly affect your opportunities. If you're in a department the president considers unnecessary or antiquated, your chances of moving very far are nonexistent. The opposite is equally true —an ignored operation can come to life if the CEO says so. Of vital concern is his attitude toward women. If he's old-fashioned and obdurate, you are guaranteed the company will maintain minimal compliance with EEO laws, just the barest necessity, no matter how many signs Personnel hangs in the ladies' room. Don't waste your time there; your game plan starts with a new job at a better company.

Accumulating this information is not the least bit difficult. It comes easily and naturally as you read the business news daily. If you're not into that habit yet, you'll need a few concentrated hours for a crash research course. Many large companies have a library on the premises, and practically every reference book and periodical will relate to your company, its top personnel, and its business. A few hours there will suffice. Otherwise, the public library should be your lunchtime hangout for a few days. Ask the reference librarian for help if you can't find what you need. You're looking for current information, not history. The various directories published by Standard & Poor's or Moody's Investment Service will start you off. Then check the *Business Periodicals Index* for recent magazine articles—and hope the library has the issue you need. The U.S. Government churns out an endless stream of vital business facts and information including the *Survey of Current Business* and the *Federal Reserve Bulletin*, but these won't give you intimate facts about your own company. Above all, talk to friends and business people in other firms to get their impressions of your company and your chief executive.

With pencil in hand and your departmental chart before you, you are ready to plot your course. This is no idle exercise. The assessment you're about to make already exists; it's in the hands of the department manager or in the personnel department files. Somebody higher up has plotted your future (or lack of future), and as long as you leave it all up to them you remain the unwitting football in the game. To become an active player you must arm yourself. You might be thinking this diagraming ritual is superfluous because you can figure it out in your head, you know what's going on in your department. That's possible, but it isn't businesslike. Businessmen love charts, graphs, diagrams, and other sequential visuals which demonstrate "logical thinking." Plotting your own advancement chart gives you practice in a routine skill that may prove invaluable. Football players, in case you don't know, spend more time poring over their sketches and diagrams than playing on the field. The game of corporate politics is also played largely in the mind; the overt moves are a small part of the whole.

Study your diagram carefully. Is everyone in the department accounted for and located in the proper level? Examine the level directly above yours; which of those positions could you move into? Draw a dotted line to each possibility. Then look at the next higher level; which positions here are potential promotions from each of the immediately lower slots? Connect them with dotted lines. Continue this analysis and connecting lines until you reach the top job. Next, take a red pencil and start at the top. Draw a line from the department head down to each job he previously held. Do the same for the assistant department head. You now have two successful tracks connected in red—how close do they dovetail with options you sketched for yourself? If the variance is acute, you're in some kind of trouble. Either you miscalculated the relative importance of various positions or you forgot part of your department—regional offices or subsidiary operations, for example. If so, jot these down on the side.

Assuming you passed Step One satisfactorily, appraise each of the individuals ensconced in the successive positions you tracked as possibilities for yourself. Are they older or younger than you? How long has each held the job? Have you heard that any might be quitting or retiring soon? Are there any rumors about work changes or upper level promotions that might create new job openings? Finally, assess other people at your present level. How many of them might be seeking the same upward track as you? Do they have qualifications you don't have? (If so, list them on the side.) If your chart presents an optimistic picture, try a rough calculation on timing. How soon might you reasonably expect to make the first step; what is the average length of tenure in that spot before moving onward? And the next step? And the next? If you're one of the rarities whose chart confirms a viable advancement potential from your current position, you can jump to the next chapter. You are suited up with requisite equipment to play on the field.

Most women's advancement charts come out a mess, or almost blank. What this exercise does, on your first try, is illuminate a host of problems or reveal serious obstacles to promotion. That's the purpose, because you can't correct a problem until you know what's wrong. Not surprisingly the advancement difficulties women face are remarkably similar, regardless of industry, company, or type of work. That's because the overwhelming majority of nonclerical women employees are in staff departments that are severely limited in advancement potential. Being self-contained units with no spill-over into other facets of the company operation, the top people have no place to go and stay there until they retire. Often the only true

183

management level job is the department head although very large specialty departments may have a secondary level of managerial personnel. Sex discrimination is clearly visible in staff departments. If the higher jobs are held by men, and women are clustered at the bottom, there's no other explanation because all employees entered the specialty job with identical professional qualifications.

There's no question that professional staff jobs offer interesting occupations in the corporate structure. Women and men who have permanent interest in the physical sciences, mathematics, writing, statistics, psychology, and other college-bred specialties find lifelong satisfaction in pursuing their interest. Management-bound women, on the other hand, must recognize the practical limitations inherent in the line-and-staff system. Early in their career they must make hard decisions about their future and escape from staff departments to get into line jobs.

Face-offs at the Line of Scrimmage

More than likely your personal diagram will reveal that you have to extricate yourself from one of the following job traps.

Bogged Down. Line or staff, management rewards diverse experience more highly than super-specialization. This means that lateral transfers (with or without promotion) to various facets of the department's work are more valuable in the long run than straightforward promotions in a single operation. The internal breakdowns in activity will vary from company to company and department to department, but here are two typical examples. A personnel department subdivision will cover: interviewing and hiring clerical personnel, processing executive personnel, wage and salary administration, benefits and insurance, union negotiation, EEO and affirmative action, college recruiting, and so forth. A public relations department might include categories in: advertising, employee publications, external booklets, films, financial news, community relations, press representation, and consumer complaints.

An inexperienced woman might think that promotions in one function, say clerical hiring or press relations, indicate advancement because she reaches a supervisory level on a par with managers of all the other functions. Her personal advancement chart, however, will show that she's now bogged down. She cannot make another upward move because the next level requires experience in several other aspects of the departmental work. By moving upward in a constricted straight line she missed out on across-the-board training in other phases of personnel or public relations work. To get out of the cul-de-sac, she must devise ways to make lateral jumps, to acquire the missing experience. Her game plan will concentrate on sideways mobility.

Blocked. The intrinsic restrictions on upper jobs in staff departments leave many capable, broadly experienced women stopped dead in their tracks. You can locate this type of structural blockage on your diagram by studying the incumbents above you. If any of these are people your age or younger who seem settled into the job slot for the remainder of their career, you can't get past them. Or if a second-level job such as assistant vice-president is held by a sidetracked executive who was deposited there until he retires, you can estimate the precise number of years that opening will be closed off. The blockage backs up the promotional flow for those years, discounting unpredictable events such as death or unexpected overhaul of the department. A woman so blocked can be an extraordinary performer and get noplace, simply because there's no place to go. Her game plan must focus on a new job, getting hired at the next successive level in another company.

Wrongly Classified. Covert prejudice is hard to eradicate because it is frequently invisible to all but those women who hold certain jobs. The historic tendency to classify jobs held by females as "service" or "support" positions, regardless of the actual duties, leads to widespread misclassification of women's jobs. Many *line* jobs are shoved into a staff department merely because a woman customarily holds the job. If your diagram suggests that your job is an odd-ball or anachronism in your department structure, it's a signal to analyze your functions very critically. Why doesn't the job fit into the standard divisions? Who is really your boss? Which executive benefits from your contribution? What makes your responsibility "special"? Is your work really public relations—or is it sales? Are you a routine statistician—or is your type of research part of marketing? Do your mathematical projections belong in the fiscal office—or in financial planning? Is your title production assistant—whereas you actually manage an operation?

The chief designer (now marketing vice-president) of a famous textile company told me she was relegated to the publicity-promotion department for many years, presumably because she met with the editors of *Vogue* and *Harpers Bazaar* along with major retailers, leading manufacturers, and top buying offices to make her fashion forecasts and create seasonal textile designs. When she finally analyzed her corporate placement, she realized that the all-male sales force and the all-male production division didn't budge until *she* decided what fabrics would make money the next season. In fact, she was directly responsible for millions of dollars in sales and profits while technically classified as a minor functionary in fashion publicity—at a pittance salary. It took a long time, and adroit maneuvering, to convince the president that she belonged in the company's marketing operations because no woman in the history of that industry had previously held such a position or received the proper title and salary.

Comparable devaluations of "women's work" are common in the corporate structure. If there's anything about your job which "doesn't fit" according to the military matrix, or if you consult with line executives more consistently than your staff department head, become suspicious of your title or location. Expand your investigation to encompass functions in relevant line departments. A wholly different game plan may be called for, one which seeks a title change or job reclassification—with commensurate salary. This project takes perseverance and persuasion, plus your documentation. Work on the highest superior in the department where you want to *go* (no superior will help *reduce* his personnel!). A woman in this position is quite valuable to the company, so don't get discouraged. Stick to your guns.

Dead-Ended. This fate befalls many female executives whose numbers escalate yearly as companies comply with Title VII by appointing women to token positions. Such women get trapped in a small but essential staff specialty and are granted the title as head of that department while still comparatively young. They've hit the structural ceiling and can progress no further. If you are dead-ended at the top of your specialty, your only tactic is to expand the job responsibility, or search for another company with a larger, more prestigious department in that field.

Another dead-end is reached after excessive tenure in a single job. Management automatically labels anyone who stays in the same job for many years as unpromotable. The thinking is characteristically stupid because it ignores human diversity, but here it is, straight from a classic personnel manual: "Increased length of service on a given job actually reduces an employee's ability to change jobs, producing in him what is referred to as 'a trained incapacity to learn.' He becomes so imbued with problems and procedures of his present job he is unable to adjust to new circumstances and situations. The expert becomes too expert." Recognize a uniquely female Catch-22?

Here you are, stuck in a job you mastered ten years ago but forced to remain because of the company's rule that no female is allowed beyond this limit. Now that the law prohibits such sex-based limitations, you fall heir to another standard operating procedure which arbitrarily charges you with a "trained incapacity to learn." (Your expertise is well utilized by the company, however, largely to train a procession of male grasshoppers who are jumped over your head to progressively lucrative positions.)

Your game plan to defeat systemic dead-ending is fortified by Title VII. Women caught in this snare are well-advised to become authorities on equal promotion mandates to build their self-confidence while pressuring for long-delayed upgrading. Don't be deceived into saying you "love the job" and enjoyed it all these years because it's what "you really want to do." The strategic defense is constant complaint and insistence that you were ready for promotion years before but the stalemate is the company's responsibility and must be rectified for women, despite what the manual says about men.

Blatant Discrimination. If there have been (or are) advantageous openings which you sought and were refused in favor of a less qualified man, you are one of the millions who are daily victims of continued sex-discrimination. Some women don't recognize their plight because they erroneously believe that a prerequisite for promotion is prior demonstration that they know the work beforehand: "I agree he was better qualified because I've never done budgeting which is required at that level." Such comments are sheer lunacy or reveal deep misconceptions about business practices. Mobility and promotions in the male hierarchy are on-the-job training experiences. They are designed to teach promising employees more complex aspects of the business than were required at the lower job level. Management development, erratic as it is, is outlined to provide repeated *opportunities* for ambitious employees to face unfamiliar challenges to show how fast they learn, to demonstrate how well they cope in a new relationship, to manifest their mastery of broadened responsibilities. If you don't learn something new, it's not a legitimate promotion.

Women's mobility has been so circumscribed in the past that women who are now offered long-delayed promotions frequently know (and even perform) the functions and duties of jobs far above their level. An honest-to-god affirmative action program (which is day-dreaming of the highest order) would have to leapfrog many female employees several supervisory levels before they reached an equal plane with men wherein the next promotion is a learning experience. To judge your own qualifications for promotion or transfer, look at the *job you have*. If your performance has been consistently rated excellent or superior, you have mastered the work and are fully qualified for the next promotional *opportunity*.

If you don't get it, find out why. Request detailed explanations of how the decision was made, what qualities you lacked. If the explanation is reasonable, your game plan will be directed toward acquiring the necessary background so the next opportunity can't be denied you. If the explanation doesn't hold water, you have a potential legal complaint. You might have to flash your trump card—if you know you hold all the other tricks. This is a poker game, not an emotional wrangle, so make doubly sure you are following the chain-of-command rules as you pursue your case internally. Be prepared to defend your allegation with cold-blooded calm. Most important, offer an alternative solution or grounds for a negotiated compromise to management—either a better promotion than the one they illegally refused you, or a merit raise immediately with a promise of preference for the next available opening. Meanwhile, start a surreptitious campaign to round up all other women in similar circumstances. You won't be the only one, because companies

189

which blatantly discriminate in this day and age do it across the board. Organized teams of employee "women's groups" are working with management at many companies to focus attention on discriminatory policies. The more women in the group, the more successful the action. It's easy to fire one or two "agitators," but it's another story when there are twenty, thirty, or fifty women pressuring simultaneously as a coordinated team.

Blasting Out of the Secretarial Sand Trap

If you're one of the millions of female secretaries in industry and have followed the previous descriptions of the pyramidal hierarchy in Chapter 2, you know that your job *classification* puts you completely outside the structural system in organizations. A secretarial classification does not fit into any standard level in the hierarchy, which explains why the job has no future. Secretaries, in fact, seem to provide an endless supply of practice balls which team members at any and every level toss back and forth to improve their own game proficiency. A secretarial job classification is the supreme dead-end; there is no career mobility whatsoever attached to the job. A private executive secretary with an office on the top floor of the pyramid is in the same job as secretaries on any other level. There may be a difference in salary, but the pay increases represent merit and seniority raises, not promotional upgrading. Structurally, secretaries are out of it.

Functionally—that is, in the local operating team format—secretarial jobs are by definition inactive or non-strategic. A secretary is never a member of the team. A male boss who keeps playing on your sympathies with a lot of guff about "We want you to feel you're a vital part of this team," is generally trying to get you to work overtime without paying the time-and-a-half to which you are entitled. As a rule of thumb, active team members do not get paid overtime; they are "exempt" employees. They are paid annually (including bonuses in many cases) based on the team's seasonal performance results. Straight clerical workers are paid for the hours they are required to be on hand for supportive tasks, even if they just sit and wait.

Obviously, a woman with ambitions must blast out of this job classification before she can become a team candidate. The word "blasting" may overstate the real-life change since the job tasks are often very similar, but the chasm between secretarial classification and low-level hierarchical jobs is enormous. Golfers will understand the simile of the sand trap. As a secretary you are off the fairway, buried in an out-of-bounds sand trap strategically located to snare the duffers and the pros. When Jack Nicklaus or Arnold Palmer get into such fixes (and they do), they certainly don't stand there bewailing their fate; they calculate the best approaches to blast themselves out of the hole and back on the course.

In today's business climate secretaries have more chances than in previous times to finagle a transfer. Affirmative action guidelines stress the need for "posting" job openings (on bulletin boards or in ladies' rooms) to give all interested internal candidates a chance to apply. Find out if your company has a bulletin board or publication which lists job openings, and watch it carefully. (If not, call Personnel and ask them about job "posting"; that is quite a loaded word because most of the recent settlement decrees on sex discrimination have stipulated that the companies adopt a continual policy of job "posting.") Start applying for jobs in any department, even if you don't think you're qualified. What can they do but explain *why* you are not suitable? In that case, ask for a job which will give you the necessary experience. Or, if possible, emphasize those facets of your prior jobs which included the relevant experience. As a game tactic, this

191

persistent application for a different job will inform all the powers-that-be that you mean it when you say you want a shift from secretarial oblivion. (Be sure to read the rest of this book carefully so you can evaluate the job openings intelligently; you don't want to plop into a new dead-end.)

The truth is that secretarial jobs are rarely moronic. Many experienced secretaries end up gratuitously doing the work of high-level bosses. Certainly an alert, ambitious woman can learn a lot about a business or trade by observing and working closely with an upwardly mobile boss. Practically every woman who has achieved a measure of success today started out as somebody's secretary, inasmuch as no other beginning jobs were open to women prior to Title VII. But today, any woman who takes a secretarial job must (a) want to be a secretary for the rest of her life; (b) be bankrupt and in need of an immediate, temporary job to survive (note the qualification "temporary"; it's smarter to job-hunt on some company's time than on your own); (c) be a victim of P. T. Barnum shills who peddle "miraculous" job nostrums. (Industry desperately needs good secretaries, so deceptive tricks to induce young women into these jobs are practiced on every street corner, not to mention employment agencies which survive on secretaries.)

Since secretarial jobs are outside the hierarchical system, there are no detailed job descriptions which spell out the duties. A secretarial job title is a catch-all for a large number of legitimate jobs in a corporation, but as long as the vague, meaningless title "secretary" is appended, the job is open-ended, subject to the whim and caprice of each boss—and beyond the pale of the wage and salary schedules. It is a man-made job, tailored to fit female workers into a vast employment stereotype which bears no relation to the work performed or the salary paid. Furthermore, no two secretarial jobs are alike.

I have written dozens of résumés for women who were

technically cast in this job-mold by asking them to detail what they actually *did* on the job. I've uncovered office managers, production coordinators, talent search specialists, marketing researchers, ghost writers, editors, distribution supervisors, bookkeepers, consumer complaint representatives, real estate saleswomen, insurance adjustors, purchasing agents, and lord knows what else—all blanketed under the illicit title "secretary." One thread connected these jobs; the occupant of the title *also* (in addition to the job duties she performed daily) typed her boss's correspondence and ran innumerable errands, many of which were job-connected but just as many that were personal for the boss. An astute secretary who is practicing the game should not be duped into doing someone else's personal errands on company time.

One game plan to escape the secretarial trap requires a careful analysis, over a period of a month, of your actual everyday tasks. Write down every single thing you do, no matter how minor, casual, or automatic, including phone calls. If you discover a legitimate team job—that is, prescribed duties performed regularly, demanding some independent decision, judgment, and follow-up, within a clear-cut area of responsibility, however meager—buried under a secretarial title, you have a case for pursuing a job title change. Start your campaign with your immediate boss. If the job duties you perform are part of his task and add a definite contribution to his performance, see if you can get him to "promote" you to a nonsecretarial title. Don't go for "assistant" because that doesn't help you much. Try for a "junior" something or other which presumes that with more experience you can work up to senior or full-fledged whatever-it-is. Unfortunately, such "promotions" can put you in a lower salary bracket than secretary. It's worth taking the decrease if the change-over puts you into a hierarchical promotion track.

If your immediate boss is not amenable to helping your cause, jump him. As a secretary you can do that because the rules don't apply to your position. Try his boss, the department head, or the clerical personnel representative. Before moving into this fray, arm yourself with your accurate written description of the job you really do, and have a job title in mind for yourself. This potential new job need not be restricted to the same department or section in which you presently work; better if you could start anew in an entirely new sector. Don't get discouraged too easily if your first attempt fails but you like the company or have a vested interest in staying there. Many corporations are secretly revamping their goofed-up women's job classifications for fear they'll get nailed by the equal employment agencies for illegal job titling.

However, if your internal efforts at reclassification fail, revamp your written job description into a one-page résumé and begin looking for a new job one step above the function you identified. Assign a salary of approximately double what you're making and you'll be pretty safe in having hit the market price for that type of work when it is correctly labeled and not called "secretary." While you're looking through classified ads for possibilities, watch out for the new breed of code words which are trying to disguise secretarial jobs. Here are some standards to avoid like the plague. "Skills." The only time that word appears in a help-wanted ad is when they are trying to hide a secretarial classification; it refers solely and completely to typing and shorthand or its equivalent, even when it appears in an ad for an M.B.A./Financial Analyst! Here are some more: support services; assist. (president, director, busy exec); rt. arm; high class; sophisticate; brite; brite achiever; hardworking; plush surroundings. (Yech!)

These aren't your only options by any means, but you have to utilize the same methods as other ambitious women to find creative solutions. The other day I ran into a friend I hadn't seen for almost a year. She had been a top executive secretary for nearly twenty years, the last ten of which were as private secretary to the president of a successful but medium-sized corporation. Her company got involved in a takeover and was bought by a conglomerate. As the new owners moved in, her boss, the president and chief executive, was quietly moved out. The conglomerate manager brought along his own private secretary, so my friend was out of a job (as the top secretary in the original corporation, her salary—and probably inside knowledge—didn't "fit" the new owners' staff). When I met her on the street a year later, she was a changed person—lively, dynamic, animated, and full of self-confidence, compared to the poised, quiet, meek, and rather retiring person I remembered. She had gotten out of secretarial work at last and was doing extremely well at her new job. She was selling a line of office supplies and equipment for one of the large companies in that field, and loved it. "One of the reasons I'm doing so well is that secretaries in the companies I call on help me. They have never seen a woman sales representative before and they're so happy to see me they get me appointments with their boss and never let him turn me away as happens with men salesmen. But the important thing is: I know my business better than any man—can you *imagine* that all the equipment used by secretaries is bought and sold by men who've never used it in their lives and wouldn't know one tape or ribbon from another! Secretaries don't know that the real money in their field is all in the buying and selling of the equipment they use—and all men are in that end of the secretarial business."

Clerical jobs are in another can of corporate worms. Strange as it may sound, many purely clerical jobs are not nearly as dead-ended as secretarial jobs (which of course are broadly lumped in the "clerical" genus). It all depends on *where* the clerical jobs are located: if they are in *line* departments (that famous sales-production duo), they may fall into a category we might charitably term sub-trainee positions. If not actually *in* the pipeline, their proximity to its mouth is so close that aspiring women can adroitly get themselves sucked in. For instance, a clerical job in a branch sales office of a big corporation is so close to the beating heart of the organization that a woman who wants to work her way onto the sales team has an opportunity to learn the significant bits of information. She can fashion that kind of knowledge into an effective case to demand a transfer to the sales force itself (sales forces *never* have enough women to comply even minimally with Title VII; most have none). The entire computer software or EDP field is in an evolving state, so clerical women may find room to maneuver; job functions and responsibilities are often fluid and flexible because these corporate departments are relatively new and any unstable, not-yet-rigidly structured department offers potential for clerical women to move into promotional track jobs. Obviously, you have to apply for a transfer or upgrading to a job title that is not classified low-level clerical. The work may be identical, but the title, the classification, is what gets you into the hierarchical ranks.

Top executive men used to boast that they "worked their way up from messenger," surely the lowest of the clerical category jobs. But you can be mighty sure they selected the messenger job with a sharp eye on its proximity to the mouth of the pipeline. Then, when they were sufficiently armed with inside information and access to helpful male friends plus knowledge they picked up about the corporate operations, they made aggressive moves to get out of the messenger category and into a long-range career send-off position. Women are finally in the position to use similar tactics to get onto the fairway. As a matter of fact, a few large corporations have been making voluntary efforts to upgrade clerical women of long tenure; it's cheaper than filling clerical-style jobs with newly hired women. No matter, the movement can be parlayed by clerical women who want jobs with a future.

Selling Yourself on the Job Exchange

Changing jobs, you may have noticed, is an integral component of any game plan, if not the only recourse to structure one. To be realistic, there is no way to play corporate politics without keeping this component uppermost in your mind and foremost in your planning. I know many successful men whose first self-imposed task when they get a new job is to update their résumé and have it printed immediately. They intuitively realize that the time to start looking for a job is the day you start one; they are always prepared. Women, in contrast, don't start looking for a job until they are unemployed—which is the worst time in the world. Never quit a job, no matter how aggravating, until you have utilized the company's time and convenient facilities to conduct and finalize your search for a new position. The only "notice" you are obligated to give is the same length of time they are pledged to give you. The rules of the game are the same for all players, and the rules on termination are usually quite explicit. If you could be fired on one day's notice, that's the rule for you to follow when quitting. If the standard is two weeks' notice, you abide by that when leaving. If you've never thought of quitting and aren't prepared constantly to switch companies, better check the rules in your game; do you have a written guarantee that you can't be fired or laid off in return?

Unless you are extraordinarily lucky in your choice of employer, the odds are that you will have to change employers several times in the near future to get out of a rut. For upwardly mobile women, job-hunting is a two-edged sword. On the one hand, there *are* opportunities for women because corporations *must* get some executive or managerial level women on their staffs. On the other hand, employment agencies and executive search agencies serve as the screening agent to eliminate women for companies which cannot be caught doing it themselves. This goes on in a very underhanded, covert way, so ambitious women have to play a most sophisticated form of corporate politics when dealing with placement firms. It's a good practice field, of course, because you've got nothing to lose and everything to gain, and lots to learn. Women gamesters must be alert to the "games" that are being played against them in this area so they can devise personal tactics to circumvent the problems.

"Head-hunters" is the popular name for executive search consultants and management consultants who also help clients find managerial candidates. Until a few years ago, women were excluded from this job availability source because all of them limit their "search" to specific salary brackets, i.e., some over $60,000 a year, others over $30,000. A few years back, the break-over salary for women was $20,000 a year, and cracking that universal salary ceiling was a major (and almost impossible) achievement. Inflation has upped that amount somewhat, but only by a couple of thousand dollars, nowhere near the inflationary increase and still not on a par with men. Still, with the publicity drive on for "qualified" women, most head-hunters now say they are looking for women candidates. (If a company or search agency can prove it interviewed a couple of women, that gets them off the sex-discrimination hook—they don't have to hire them, they just have to say they "considered" them equally with men but, as usual, none of the women was qualified.)

Women must keep their names on the head-hunters' lists. *All* head-hunters are paid very handsomely by the companies for each executive they find for the organization, so the first guide for job-seekers is *never pay anybody* to find you a job. If you, as the job-seeker, are asked to pay, you have run into a commercial rip-off. The same

198

thing applies to employment agencies; the companies also pay them for all reasonably decent jobs (and for many indecent ones). Many employment agencies have a very poor reputation with women and justifiably so because they cheat on salaries ("I know a terrific gal and you can get her for $10,000 less than you'd have to pay a man; interested?"); they send women on wild-goose chases for jobs that are manifestly below their talents; or they ignore women when the company has secretly tipped them off that they want a man—or a young, attractive woman. Or —don't ever forget this qualification—they want "military officer background" or "varsity football experience," preferably team captain, thereby evading unlawful requests for "man only."

Nevertheless, these are the two primary sources for jobs, and women have to play against these odds as cannily as possible. Some employment agencies do get executive listings from companies they handle exclusively, especially in certain specialty fields, so ambitious women shouldn't ignore them entirely. Indeed some are highly reputable and specialize in legal jobs, the medical field, publishing, advertising, accounting, engineering, and so forth. The best way to weed them out is word-of-mouth; ask all your friends in your line of business if they've had any experience with them, and what it was. Or go interview them yourself. Notice, *you* interview them and don't give them any information about yourself that you don't want them to know.

Head-hunters haughtily dissociate themselves from the more lowly employment agencies, but for all intents and purposes they operate much the same, with the exception that they never send a woman on an interview unless she definitely satisfies the corporate client's prerequisites. This does not eliminate wild-goose chases for women, however; one of the "prerequisites" today is "Send us a couple of females who are *almost* but not quite suitable so we can cover our ass on this damn affirmative action thing—

as you know, we've got a lot of government contracts." You can't be sure, but *expect* to be conned with this ploy in any job-hunting campaign. Be especially careful in dealing with head-hunters that you never say anything uncomplimentary about your current employer; it's entirely possible the head-hunter *works* for your company, and anything you say will be bounced back immediately, not to mention news of the fact that you are job-hunting. Women gamesters use this knowledge for their own purposes when they *want* the rumor to get back to their boss or company that they are job-hunting at a much higher salary demand—and higher level, it goes without saying. The gamble is that your current employer will come to you with a counteroffer.

If you *don't* want news to get back to your employer, you must stay with personal contacts or *feminist-owned and run* executive search firms. The personal contact route, in addition to close personal friends who have connections with prospective new employers, includes officials of trade associations, professional societies, alumni groups or similar organizations. You don't say you're looking for a job; you merely let the word out very casually and offhandedly that you "might be approachable," or "I never refuse to talk to anyone." If you ever get any calls from management consultants or executive search consultants, they will usually approach you by saying they are checking up on someone else and have been referred to you for a recommendation. Or they may ask your help in recommending women who are especially qualified in this-or-that field, whatever yours is. Chances are, they are really sounding you out to find out (by your answers) what kind of a "team player" you are, whether you are knowledgeable about your field (if so, you'd know all the other outstanding women in it). This is one place where women help themselves by helping each other, that is, by recommending other executive women you know. Male head-hunters know nothing about qualified women, but they make their decisions on the basis of how many times they hear a certain woman's name. "Whoever I talk to, the name Mary Jones comes up in the conversation; she's probably our number one choice" (to lure away from her current employer), or, "Let's keep Susan Glutz at XYZ in mind, she's right on the ball, she knows everybody, she's a very skilled promoter of executives she knows."

For management-oriented women their *first choice in head-hunters* should be the new *feminist-owned executive placement* firms that are springing up in major cities. These agencies specialize in women's advancement and can be trusted to push the *woman's* interest. They are well informed about the special problems that women face because the woman-search firms are equally subject to sly discriminatory tactics by male management. For example, they will get orders for the lesser or lower-paying jobs while the real plums still go to male consultant firms (the system of payment is a percentage of the first year's salary, so 25 percent of $100,000 is a lot more than 25 percent of $23,000).

When dealing with any kind of placement or search firm, women's tactics must incorporate the awareness of common pitfalls. At all costs, evade the deliberate traps. Here are some no-no's:

Never put your birthdate, age, marital status, number of children, weight, hair color, or other such nonsense on your résumé or application form. (Once you have a job, it's time enough to give the relevant insurance, social security, and income tax information.)

Never reveal what salary you are making Put down the salary range you *want*. If the agency recruiter or prospective employer *insists* that you give this information, lie. (This is the Arab bazaar or Tijuana Tactic.) Put down the salary that men in equivalent jobs make if you know it; otherwise, add approximately $10,000 to what you got paid and you'll be closer to what the market rate for the job is. At high levels, the salary discrepancy can easily run $30,000 less for an equivalent woman. Unless the other company or recruiter has access to your employer's salary records (and believe me, it's even hard for the government to *subpoena* those), there is no way to know more than what you tell them about your salary. As a rule of thumb, women job-changers should aim to double their current salary on the next job.

Never say anything uncomplimentary about your current or previous employers. They were all the most wonderful companies and the "greatest bunch of people" in the country. The reason you left is always because of another "offer you just couldn't refuse" or because the company has such a marvelous back-up team of top-flight executives that it would take too long before there would be openings at your level of expertise and experience.

Never accept a job (or even a serious interview) without psyching out the company. Dash to all the financial and biographical reference books and call up everyone you know who has had any recent dealings with the company to find out what they have to say. Ask plenty of questions of your own at the interview. It's much more important to your game plan to know what you think of them, not what they think of you.

Never write down references on your résumé or anyplace else. The object in job-hunting or changing is to sell yourself. You may have been doing just fine until the interviewer caught one of your "reference" names and it turns out to be someone detestable or unreputable (in the interviewer's opinion)—and you're dead. Besides, it's a waste of time and energy; if someone agrees to be your reference, obviously that person is a friend or will say something good. What a high-level recruiter does is try to sound out local competitors or foes to see what *they* have to say. If they are experienced players of corporate politics, they will never say anything bad about you because the rules of team play are roaring at full steam here, and ex-teammates or ex-opponents do nothing but praise other players for whatever good qualities they can think of. Beyond the code ("You never know who will be your boss someday so you don't burn any bridges"), there is the very practical matter of a libel or slander suit. Ex-employers do not have an unfettered right to interfere with your livelihood by passing along hostile, reckless, abusive, subjective, unkind, or unsolicited remarks. If you ever hear that adverse comments which go beyond simple facts of job dates, title, and measurable performance results are being said about you, get a lawyer and sue for malicious damages.

The biggest bamboozle foisted off on unsuspecting clerical or bottom-of-the-pyramid women is this nonsense about references. To hear them tell it, there is supposedly a consortium of employers who exchange forms or letters about previous employees. Young women who have been fired are especially terrified that they'll never get another job because their "reference" will not be good. They expend enormous energy to get hold of a piece of paper from a past employer (even one they hated) on the assumption they need a "reference." Forget it. The woman corporate politician depends on herself and her growing ability to describe the job she did to sell herself. She is never concerned with selling somebody else (i.e., a "reference"); let them do their own self-promotion. If you have any doubts or qualms about this tactic, you can check it

203

very easily. Call up all your previous employers pretending you are a prospective new employer of you (or ask a friend to do it for you if you think someone might recognize your voice). Find out what they are saying about you (providing the records aren't in the basement or gone to storage so they "aren't available"). With that information, you can go ahead and play the game to suit the circumstances.

Never say you were fired. That circumstance is an *impossibility* in business because there is no such word in the business vocabulary. If there were (and it meant anything), quite a few successful men I know would have been unemployed for the past twenty years. Instead, each time they were fired (and they were repeatedly for good and just reasons), they moved on to a better job at more money. "Getting fired" is an anachronism straight out of the female language. Cessation of employment with a specific company is alluded to in the usual business jargon, such as:

Terminated: Means person is no longer in employ of that company; covers any situation ranging from the company going out of business, to the fact that the guy was a hopeless alcoholic or was rifling the petty-cash till.

Left by mutual agreement: Means your salary checks stop at the end of the month.

Staff cutback: "We don't have any work we want to give to this person."

Reorganization: Similar to "staff cutback." Means they reorganized that person out of the organization.

204

Laid off: Means we have eliminated all women, minorities, and young people due to bad business conditions or because our top management is colossally incompetent in running the business profitably but they won't fire themselves.

Personality conflict: Covers a multitude of sins; the most frequent one where women are concerned is that some slob kept making passes or suggestive remarks and fired her because she wouldn't sleep with him or kiss him.

The game of corporate politics for women is endlessly fascinating as the moves become more intricate. Nowhere is this more evident than in the area of job mobility, whether it means looking for a new job or extricating yourself from an unacceptable pigeonhole. The time to start playing the game is now because every time you practice your game you learn something valuable and it improves your prowess and judgment. Every woman will play the game differently, according to her own personality style and the strengths and weaknesses of her immediate opponents. Your style of play will be your own; the principles of the game are constant.

CHAPTER
8
Warming Up
for the Tryouts
—College

To those of us who have spent the decade of the Seventies immersed in the problems of women struggling to escape from the quicksand of female cultural conditioning, one institution emerges as the major villain in suffocating women. That institution is the education system, starting with nursery school and climaxing at the university level. Higher education plays stud poker with naïve women, successfully wiping most of them out of the economic game before they enter the tryouts.

A few years back I asked a long-time good friend who heads the teachers college of a large New England university how he squared his conscience and personal integrity with his unethical profession—which I equated with luring innocent women by the thousands into four or more years of expensive training with an implied promise of teaching jobs which he knew didn't exist. His answer (strained by his controlled fury at such "unethical" bluntness) was that colleges "cannot tell" students what to take, the university's responsibility is limited to teaching whatever students want. In effect, this reputable authority was claiming that eighteen- and twenty-year-olds dictated policies to prestigious universities, a convenient if spurious rationalization for much of the irrelevant time-wasting that goes by the name of college education.

Contemporary women who look forward to a business career (where a college degree is mandatory) must be extremely wary of not getting ripped off in the college-degree poker game. Every future economic gamester should start by shrewdly guarding the $20,000 to $25,000 kitty that represents her investment in an undergraduate degree. To fritter this stake on trivial subjects or gamble it recklessly without thought of consequences *stamps a woman graduate with a big, fat "O"* for out-of-the-running. If a woman is insufficiently trained for the tryout preliminary, she is unnecessarily and possibly irrevocably handicapped because many of the decisions were within her control but she neglected to read the signals.

Watch Out for Advisory Four-Flushers

Few professionals bother to tell women the truth. Vocational guidance counselors and college advisors are no exception. Since the post–World War II period when the G.I. Bill funded years of higher education for veterans, a college degree has been equated with job success and vastly increased lifetime earnings. *But,* these economic trade-off statistics apply *only to men*—a woman college graduate today makes less than male high school dropouts! Yet women have blindly assumed that a college degree equals job opportunity for them too. Tuition-hungry colleges perpetuate the fantasy. "From the minute I got there," said one of the first women admitted to Yale in 1970, "they told me 'You will succeed, you will be a leader,' the Yale slogan—you could taste it in the air." Two years after graduation she was still hunting fruitlessly for a nonsecretarial job. Like women college graduates many years her senior, she is bitterly disillusioned. She's

207

been had by one of the sharpest male con-games around —educational stud poker.

Women of all ages get taken to the cleaners in this popular national game because they fail to analyze two statements about college:

1. A college degree is an essential requirement for high-paying jobs (what business says)
2. The more education before working, the better the job offers (what universities imply)

Both statements as they stand hold out false promises for women. Let's strip them down one at a time.

How Would-Be Rookies Get Rooked

Contrary to popular belief, a nonspecific college education has nothing to do with training for business. As an instruction medium, universities are capable only of reproducing themselves, that is creating more teachers who are trained to instruct students on various subjects in a formal academic setting. That's the last thing private industry needs. Corporations have no place in their hierarchical structures for college graduates who are learned in disciplines which foster passive teaching capability; they are looking for potential *doers*, athletes on the money-making team. Therefore a woman with a college degree per se has gained no knowledge that business considers usable, and her college degree is a total loss from a business perspective, not at all a qualification for a "better job" in private industry.

Degrees which represent preparatory training for college teaching—dubbed "liberal arts" at the undergraduate level—are useless in *both* the academic and business communities. A bachelor's degree course in the arts or humanities is a historic first step in weeding out less serious applicants for the university's original function, development of scholars. A second elimination stage occurs upon

208

completion of a master's degree, so the Ph.D. identifies the true scholars. A doctorate has become very nearly minimal to obtain a college teaching post; the B.A.'s and M.A.'s are scholarly rejects or incompletes as far as academic employers are concerned. Business employers have no alternate use for this academic overflow, so neither undergraduate nor postgraduate degrees in liberal arts categories lead to industry jobs. The fact that universities persist in spewing out exquisitely finished self-serving products for which there is no outside market only underscores the deep philosophical chasm which separates the two establishments. Business, after all, depends for its very existence on markets and marketing; academia discounts the need to market even its own human products, a philosophy that would be life-threatening to a commercial business operation. Competitive companies can't afford to take chances with such noncommercial thinkers, and the proof is strewn over the landscape in the form of unemployed Ph.D's.

What this situation boils down to is the reverse of the statement that a college degree is a passport to a well-paying job. For women, a college degree in any of the stereotyped female teaching or teaching preparatory fields is equivalent to no degree. The effort adds up to at least four and probably seven years of wasted time and money as far as upgraded admission into the business world is concerned. All women liberal arts graduates eventually come face to face with the cruel trick that was played on them but, significantly, I have never met one who recalls being told beforehand that her nonspecific college degree will have no marketable value. Who would tell her? The high school vocational counselor who never worked a single day in industry but whose job is justified by the number of students who go on to *any* college? The equally unsophisticated college advisors who consult lists of occupational shortages (*always* headed by demands for college-educated secretaries and clerks) and think it

209

would be "nice" to provide docilely trained women for these readily available dead-end jobs? The college recruiters who owe their own jobs to the number of full-tuition students they can attract with any bait? The self-serving college professors and department heads (almost exclusively male) who are as intent as everybody else on maintaining the all-male status quo? (Universities lead the pack in discriminating against women as professors and deans, not to mention women students and graduates.)

The second educational myth that women accept in trusting ignorance is the "more the better" delusion. It's easy to see how this deception follows the first. When the Phi Beta Kappa graduate with her treasured B.A. in Speech, English, History, Philosophy, Psychology, Sociology, Drama, Art, Journalism, Foreign Languages, Comparative Literature, etc., can't find a job (unless she takes a course in typing and shorthand), she naturally falls prey to further blandishments from the same self-serving academic coaches who misled her before. If a bachelor's degree isn't sufficient, then a post-graduate degree is held out as the key. More years, more money, more hard work —and the same frustration at the end of this paper rainbow. To avoid getting rooked, women have to learn the rules of college-education poker. If you don't, your college tuition stake may be the most money you will ever accumulate in your life.

College Degrees as Stud Poker Hands

Poker is the favorite card game of American men and for over a hundred years was considered unsuitable for mixed company, i.e., women weren't allowed to play or watch a game until recent decades. It's a man's gambling game where everyone plays for himself and the object is to win the pot which consists of the bets all players have made on one deal. Poker has a mathematical basis, so the value of possible holdings in a hand are in inverse proportion to their frequency; the more unusual the combination according to the theory of probability, the higher its value. Good poker players know, for instance, that a flush (the fourth highest value) is a great combination to bet on because only a few thousand higher hands can beat it, but it beats some 2½ million lesser holdings, such as three-of-a-kind or two pairs. A no-pair hand is valueless in this form of the game because everything, including one pair, beats it, and one pair can be expected in every other deal. In college-education poker, women have been gambling their chips on no-pair hands.

Skillful play in educational poker requires an understanding of the relationship between business and college. A collection of credits known as "a college degree" is like the five cards in a poker deal; the hand can amount to nothing or it can be a betting combination. Inasmuch as colleges are intrinsically geared to deal academic hands, the odds against a high-ranking business hand are astronomical. Management knows this (has always known it) and continues to deal its own educational hand through time-honored on-the-job methods (however unstructured or haphazard). To lighten its training burden, however, management does encourage preliminary formal study that provides theoretical or technical underpinning for its future on-the-job students. From a business viewpoint, a college degree is looked upon simply as a credential, a hand with some high cards; a credential for those who want to gamble on the tryouts for the business team. Clearly, a gambling credential is vastly different from saying a college degree guarantees a graduate a position on the first team. This is the crucial distinction which is never explained' to women. Nor is, the fact that college credentials are weighed in value, just like the card combinations in a poker game. If you are attending college now—or considering a return to college—the biggest favor you can do for yourself is to learn the values of the hands in educational poker.

A Full House Beats a Flush, Beats a Straight . . .

The surest way to learn which combinations rank high is to check the holdings of acknowledged business winners. In May, 1976, *Fortune* published results of its survey of chief executive officers from the 800 leading corporations in the country (only one woman was eligible, Katharine Graham of the *Washington Post*). Fully 86 percent graduated from college, and a surprising 40 percent had earned postgraduate degrees somewhere along the line. Obviously it will be a rare bird who flies to the top of a corporate pyramid without a college wingspan. But the significant question is: What kind of college credential got them into the tryout field at the beginning? More than half majored in one of two subjects as undergraduates: *business* and *economics*. Another one-fourth studied business in graduate school.

Those cards are face up on the stud-poker table and the lesson for shrewd bettors is plain: if you go to college with the intention of using it as a credential for a business career, learn what college professors have to say about business. That's the most valuable hand to begin the game. Of course the *Fortune* executives are now in their fifties and early sixties, so most of them got their undergraduate degrees in the years after World War II, some twenty-five or thirty years ago. Are these same credentials still valid? It is illuminating for contemporary students to hear what formal background knowledge these top executives say would benefit them currently, now that they are actively dealing with everyday business problems. In answer to that question, the majority named business administration, accounting, finance, law. Essentially the same subjects— business and economics—plus familiarity with law as government regulation of business increases.

These, you must remember, are the heads of leading companies who send out employment recruiters to spot promising college candidates for the team tryouts. What kind of college credentials would you bet they'll be looking for?

Raising the Ante on Specialty Degrees

So far we have labeled undergraduate and graduate degrees in all branches of liberal arts and education as the poorest hands in the deck, not worth a nickel in the business pot; and elevated degrees in business administration and finance to the value of a full house, safe enough for a maximal bet. That still leaves a goodly number of other hands in the area known as specialty degrees. It is *au courant* these days to advise women to get undergraduate degrees in special fields where men predominate, such as engineering, chemistry, mathematics, and sciences. The advice is well intentioned and based on a logical principle: that jobs will be awaiting women who have credentials in occupations that were formerly closed but must now legally seek qualified females.

That thinking is valid as far as it goes, but it doesn't go very far; or perhaps I should say it goes *too* far in the sense that a simple bachelor's degree no longer carries much credence in scientific-engineering staff specialties where advanced degrees are requisite for the good technical jobs. Women must be forewarned that the odds favor certain in-demand Ph.D.'s in chemistry, physics, mathematics, or metallurgy. Hidden on the underside of the B.S. advisory coin is a traditional pitfall for unwary women—the downgrading of once-respected professional credentials when women acquire them. I have no wish to see a young crop of women engineers and scientists replacing non-degreed men as drafters or engineering and science *technicians* rather than full-fledged professionals. The precursor of this dour employment circumstance can be seen in projections for female employment in 1980 and 1985 when women will predictably increase dramatically in technician jobs. The 1980s brand of sex discrimination will probably be justified with the argument that "real" engineers or scientists have advanced degrees.

Despite these serious forebodings, a skillful woman player can turn a bachelor's specialty degree hand into an excellent bet in the educational poker deal. An intrinsic element in expert poker play is bluffing, and this technique can magnify a minimal specialty degree into a better hand than a business administration full house. The principle in this bluff is to get a bachelor's degree in any field of science or engineering that attracts you—but *never take a job in the specialty occupation.*

For example, if you like rocks and earth formations, take geology. Plan to complete just enough courses to satisfy the minimum degree requirements, then fill the rest of your schedule with any courses you like in the whole university, from Persian Poetry to Theories of Personality. All you care about is the business *credential*—in this case a degree in geology—but the rest of your college education (which business doesn't care about) can be up to you and the university's strictures. When you graduate, do not take a geologist's job under any circumstances. Head for the oil companies, the mining companies, the nonferrous metals or fossil fuels industries, the diversified multinationals or conglomerates which have land-holding subsidiaries here and abroad. Apply for a job in the *management training* program or in the *production* or *sales* department. Your geology degree is the necessary credential to get on the management trainee team.

The identical system works (or can be made to work by the farsighted woman) with any technical subject in

214

the science or engineering fields. If you think you'd like to work for Xerox, IBM, Kodak, TRW, General Motors, General Electric, RCA, or hundreds of similar corporations, look them up in *Moody's* or *Poor's* or *Dun and Bradstreet* references to find out what technical backgrounds their five top executives have and take the relevant technical courses. With your bachelor's degree, beat down their doors to get into their management training programs or operating departments. You will have the necessary credentials for technically oriented companies where management intern programs are bound to be 90 to 100 percent short of a required female contingent. Don't get detoured into an engineering staff or support-service department—that way, you'll end up as a lowly technician.

The reason you don't treat your specialty college degree as vocational training should be clear from the discussion on line and staff jobs in Chapter 6. If you enter the engineering department or chemistry laboratory, you will be located in a staff department with all its promotional limitations and its narrow focus of activity. On the other hand, if you are sure you *want to be* a research chemist, an electrical engineer, or a working geologist all your life, then you would purposely select a staff specialty department where you will have an opportunity to work exclusively in your personal field of interest.

The Odds of Improving a Bad Hand

If you are presently in college and well along the road to a zilch degree in something as nonspecific as English or Psychology, it is worth your while to calculate the odds if you draw a few new cards. Try juggling your credits to see if you have the basis for a more directive credential in Industrial Psychology or Behavioral Psych, or anything with a remote relevance to business. Do you have enough

215

math to build into an accounting or financial credential? If you can possibly afford to extend your schooling another semester or year, it would be extremely wise to get the catalog of the business school and see what you can salvage from your completed courses to transfer over and graduate with a B.B.A. rather than a B.A. Anything beats a no-pair hand.

To sum up, women must remember that a college degree course is their own choice. Don't get ripped off by accepting traditional "women's" degrees which are always the lowest-paying and *most competitive*—the competition, unfortunately, consisting of equally misled women. Get a bachelor's degree in anything *except* teaching, nursing, and liberal arts, if possible. *Then get a job and get to work!* Business education is on-the-job training and experience—essentially you *start* the same place whether you have no degree, a bachelor's, or a doctorate. Don't invest educational dollars on a pig in a poke; find out whether you're any good in the field or like the future career path before educating yourself for futile purposes. Women who are undecided cannot go wrong if they focus their undergraduate efforts on any and all courses or programs which deal with MONEY! If you don't love money, you're not going to get anywhere worthwhile in business and you can't love something you're scared of, ignorant about, or loath to discuss.

When to Turn In Your Chips

If you have been out of college for years and are thinking of going back to school, should you? You certainly should not—not unless you know exactly what you are doing and why. The foregoing explanation of the negative relationship between nonspecific college education and jobs in business is very pertinent to the woman who thinks she should "get more education" because she harbors a

216

vague notion that additional school credits will miraculously open job doors. For older women victims of the college poker vultures, the mental devastation may be far worse than the economic losses when her unrealistic education dreams are shattered by the help-wanted pages. Nondirective education often has a boomerang effect, tagging an inexperienced woman with the damning epithets "overeducated" or "overqualified."

Betsy Hogan, one of the country's foremost consultants on equal opportunity and editor of *Womanpower*, the authoritative national newsletter for affirmative-action executives, thinks the "get more education" myth is swallowed almost universally by women in and out of the job market. "It is ironic," she says, "that this easy route, the placebo, is most often taken by those women who already have excessive education." She attributes part of this school romanticism to the fact that many women don't want to believe in sex discrimination and prefer to sit on their feminine pedestals as cheerful, ever-smiling, obliging workers. When their pedestals are rocked by glaring instances of pay inequities or closed doors in the job market, such women gloss over the real problem and immediately assume, "There's something wrong with *me;* more education will fix it." So an experienced professional woman starts night classes to get her M.A. when she discovers the janitor makes more money than she! Too often women hide behind "education" rather than face the hard realities of business and life and sex bias.

Certainly there are many circumstances where additional schooling is essential or required. If you decide to be a doctor, you must go to medical school; a lawyer must first graduate from law school, then take the bar exam; an architect needs a five-year college degree plus three years experience. In any occupation where a license is required, the formal school credentials and the test requirements are very specific. Before a woman with one or more college degrees returns to school, she must decide

217

exactly what job she is after and what credentials are mandatory. Extraneous education is wasted from a job viewpoint. You don't need a B.A. in English from Princeton, an M.S. in Counseling from Berkeley, and Ph.D. in Sociology from the University of Wisconsin to be a temporary Christmas clerk in a department store. *You don't need them for any job in private industry.*

The time to take definite action in returning to college is when you have a job and your progress is blocked because you lack a specific credential. For instance, if you quit college without a degree but are now moving up in a bank job which will subsequently require the credential "college graduate," you had better go to night school and earn the degree. A bookkeeper who is actually doing accounting work (as many do) is well advised to get a degree in accounting even though she may learn nothing new and be more informed than the teachers. She needs that crucial credential (the degree) to move ahead to high-paying jobs and managerial positions in the fiscal area—or even to get paid fairly for the accounting work she handles as a nondegree bookkeeper. Business, you'll notice, talks out of both sides of its mouth on college credentials—they're no good (only business experience counts), but fabulous performance is no good without a meaningless degree.

From Stud Poker to Corporate Politics

A management-bound woman employed by a company which stresses the importance of M.B.A. degrees (Masters in Business Administration) or any other postgraduate degree, should be playing educational corporate politics, not reverting to the preliminary practice game of college poker. That means she should be striving to get her employer to finance or subsidize her graduate education, as is routinely done for promising male executives.

218

The alert female gamester investigates the entire range of schooling subsidies offered by her company, from tuition-refund programs to leaves-of-absence for advanced degrees, to fully paid, on-salary attendance at graduate schools.

Taking full advantage of corporate education subsidies for employees is much more than shrewd economic planning, it is playing the game at a sophisticated level because management values the education it pays for more highly than the same education undertaken personally by an individual. Women who have not grasped the *psychology* of corporate gameship might veer toward the illusion that the more skills and knowledge one brings to a job, the better: "I saved the company money by educating myself, they'll appreciate that." Sure they will if you are a secretary, a library assistant, or a keyhole puncher; indeed, they will demand that you bring rudimentary skills which they can easier restructure than teach from scratch.

At management mobility levels, the perspective is extremely different. As a subordinate manager, you are in no position to pre-guess key executives about the changing needs of business, nor to perceive informational gaps of management personnel in a complex modern corporation. But these are the prime stimulants for broadening the formal education of higher executives. You didn't forget you're in the army, did you? The lieutenant doesn't decide what further education he needs to become a general; the general determines what supplementary knowledge will benefit future generals. Then there's always the team coach who may spot latent talent in a player that he wants to develop. The coach, not the player, dictates the form and duration of training.

Traditionally, continued education for management's purposes has been offered to selective men exclusively. The historic pattern will continue unless alert women keep track of subsidized educational policies and pressure

219

for equal access. The nondiscrimination statutes apply to all "terms, conditions, and privileges" of employment—and there is no reason for the corporate-sponsored Advanced Management Program at Harvard Business School to be a male preserve (a few women *have* pressured their companies successfully to crack this prestigious fifteen-week course).

When playing for subsidized education stakes, it's surprising what can be accomplished with a three-letter word: ask. Your immediate supervisor is unlikely to be a font of information on tuition programs, but it's politic to ask your boss whom you should speak to on the subject. It covers you vis-à-vis the chain-of-command rule, it can be used to flatter your boss inasmuch as you are deferring to superior knowledge about corporate contacts, and it gives you a painless opportunity to indicate that you are serious about moving ahead and expanding your options. Make an appointment with the person in charge of employee education programs and frankly discuss your reasons for investigating company schooling subsidies. Ask about procedures and approvals because there is usually a bunch of red tape to go through.

A mathematics major who landed in the engineering department of a major government-contractor company convinced her department head that the increasing complexity of contract regulations favored bidders whose contract personnel were legally astute. The company paid her way through law school at night while she retained her job during the day. Affirmative-action programs for women usually include company provisions for management preparatory educational funds. The courses may range from full M.B.A. studies to one-week management seminars to financial specialty courses to graduate science or engineering degrees. The secret of success is to ask, and keep asking.

Taking courses and earning a college degree with the highest ranking hand you can manage are calisthenics in warming up for the business team tryouts. Wage-paying recruiters look for other evidence of your athletic potential. Extracurricular activities carry considerable weight in the evaluators' book and so do subjective impressions about a person's "presence" or "sophistication" or "maturity." Men have an immediate edge over women graduates if their extracurricular activity was team sports and especially the football team. When it comes to insidious private judgments about "potential" or "suitable personality," both male and female recruiters (or personnel interviewers) are apt to be swayed by every female sex stereotype they've grown up with. To counteract these unfair handicaps, ambitious young women must move out of the book stalls and the rap rooms during college years and learn to flex nonacademic muscles that they'll need as corporate athletes. Here are some exercise tips from experienced businesswomen who are often appalled to see the flabby condition in which women appear for the working world tryouts.

1. Join a college women's sport team or compete in intramural events in swimming, crew, tennis, or gymnastics. Even if you aren't a physical champion, several years of structured team play and athletic competition will be invaluable preparation for the cooperative team-sport milieu of business. Furthermore, as an active participant in women's collegiate sports you will be exposed to a classic specimen of institutional sex-discrimination—the disparity in funding between men's and women's campus athletes. When Title IX of the Education Amendments was passed by Congress in 1972, it banned all forms of discrimination in schools that receive federal money or

grants. This equality statute has never been enforced because the male varsity squads mobilized immediately to oppose women students' rights to comparable sports equipment, facilities, and training. Title IX applies to every activity in a university from equal pay and tenure for women professors to sports—but the athletic funding is the eye of the hurricane. From Title IX in college, it's an easy jump to Title VII in employment—you can always measure bias in dollars and cents.

2. Select other extracurricular activities for their value to you and your growth. Pick organized groups such as large clubs, student government bodies, or publications which offer you a chance to gain expertise in running for office, running meetings, running affairs, running the paper, running anything; with you trying to become the runner—the president, an elected official, the chief, the leader of the group. Eschew those extracurriculars in which you become a passive joiner or listener.

3. Travel. No matter how you do it (biking, backpacking, camping, automobile), visit as many sections of the United States as you can, and, if possible, foreign countries. Whenever you have a choice between an extra course or a trip, take the trip. Grab every opportunity to visit school friends who live in different cities and make them give you a wide-ranging tour of the town, including its industries. Take low-cost charters to Europe and meandering bus tours through America. Learn geography at firsthand from ground level, because "curbstone hicks" (people who scarcely leave their home block) don't radiate the independent self-confidence that pays off in business. More to the point, travel broadens your appreciation of the diversity of this huge country. Management thinking zeroes in on "markets" and markets are simply places or people all over this country and the world. Travel opens your eyes to "markets," your mind to varieties of needs and interests. Another reason is the entrenched stereotype which says women don't

222

like to travel—which naturally makes them unsuited for important jobs. A young woman can nip this weed early by having traveled widely and being eager to travel more. A paragraph at the bottom of your résumé headed "Travel" should list every city, state, geographic region, or country you've visited.

At least once during your expeditions register and stay overnight at a metropolitan hotel, please. I wouldn't have thought this last reminder necessary until I met recently with twenty-five working women in their twenties or early thirties (all college graduates) prior to a national convention. Instead of studying the convention agenda and resolutions, most of the women were transfixed with worries about how to cope with hotel reservations, confirmations, checking in and out, charging, tipping, bell captains, room service, and airport limousines. Evidently this was to be a first business trip to a strange city for them and they were as helpless as babies. Nitty-gritty self-education of this type belongs in the college period.

4. Learn to drive well. Energy crisis or no, over 90 percent of the people in this country get to work by automobile. Yet even in California and the Southwest, where cars are the only mode of transportation, I find women afraid to drive freeways or expressways. Today's and tomorrow's management woman can anticipate a lot of rented cars at strange airports in her future, so ability to read maps, drive competently, and figure out cloverleafs is a basic component of job mobility. There is a great deal of sex symbolism and power symbolism attached to cars. To gain respect, a woman must be capable of taking the wheel and driving herself where she wants to go, literally as well as figuratively.

5. Broaden your life experience. Go out with many men and women or groups whose interests are far removed from your own, people who can introduce you to different categories of experience. Discover opera or sym-

phonies with a classicist who communicates enjoyment and appreciation; watch jai alai or soccer with enthusiastic sports addicts; share experimental theater or club dates with budding performers or composers or playwrights; play chess with an expert; visit museums with an archaeologist; eat foreign food with a native; build a barn with a carpenter. Learn from your peers and try to do something unfamiliar once a month. Read? Sure, but women already read a lot. What they don't do is translate the reading to life because they have experienced so little of it. College is the time to expand your personal horizons, develop a breadth of vision from real-life experience outside yourself.

6. Work in profit-making firms. Few students can get through four years of college these days without working to supplement the astronomical expense. If you have any options, choose a job in a profit-making organization rather than a nonprofit or academic service. Dishing out food in a college cafeteria or the local greasy spoon may seem like the identical job, but it's not. The school food service is nonprofit and subsidized, whereas the local commercial cafeteria is pure private enterprise, geared to making a profit and taxed on whatever it does make. Working in the school library is not the same as working for the local bookstore. A summer job with a social agency bears no relation to a summer job in an insurance office, although you may be doing the exact same task. There is almost no carryover from nonprofit, government, or academic jobs to comparable jobs in private industry. Corporate college recruiters are wary of women whose part-time and summer jobs are all in nonprofit institutions. Nor is the work experience helpful to the young woman in her transition to the business world. It's difficult to explain the contrast in pace, atmosphere, attitude, and outlook, but it's easy to experience. In that college poker hand you're holding, part-time jobs during college years can

raise the rank of your card combination considerably. But not all summer jobs, any more than all degrees, carry equal weight. Business beginners will only get credit from hiring firms if the part-time jobs were *business* jobs, in profit-making organizations (usually excluding any family business). For your own sake, the greater the variety of business firms you work for, the better; it will give you insight into a diversity of industries.

7. Vote. Better yet, join a political club and work for candidates. This is not a treatise on civics or citizenship. This is hardnosed business advice. As an aspiring businesswoman your future is bound to be deeply entangled with government actions at local, state, and federal levels, as regulatory agencies and proliferating laws of every description impinge on the functions of business. Keep in touch with school friends who enter government service —the day will come in business when an intimate knowledge of the inner workings of government agencies and politicians may help you hit one over the fence. As for your personal development, I cannot understand a spiritual daughter of Susan B. Anthony failing to exercise her hard-won voting right, any more than I can understand intelligent women being opposed to the Equal Rights Amendment which would rectify the omission of the Founding Fathers and make women equal citizens under the Constitution.

In our sexist society, women are a protected species. Girls are guarded as children lest they learn the true facts of life; young women are shielded from experiences which are critical to full human development. Wives and mothers are draped and hidden in overstuffed suburban cells, insulated from growth experiences. Women who are conditioning themselves for an active life which includes a progressive business career must stretch atrophied muscles. Mental exertion alone will not set you free. Action —physically moving around in the world—is more impor-

225

tant than formal studies or college training in preparation for the work tryouts. Your degree is no more than a ticket to let you in the gate of the tryout field.

CHAPTER
9
The Bottom Line
—Money

As we have seen, most business jargon is borrowed from assorted male-culture vernaculars. As if to repay the favor, business is now lending one of its cherished phrases from the management patois to compatriots in the non-business world. The expression on loan is "the bottom line." As it moves into general usage, the phrase translates as "the core of the matter," the "kernel of truth," the "unchanging verity," the "irrevocable finality." If there is a semblance of religious fervor and universality conveyed in the transliteration, that is as it should be. For "the bottom line" is the management code designation for "money."

"Money" is a generic word which identifies any medium of exchange used in any society. It has existed in some form since humankind emerged from caves and it will continue to exist as long as planet Earth is inhabited. Because money is synonomous with "life" as we know it in our modern industrial society, the concept has been assigned its due reverence in the male culture. It is a deity to be revered, honored, and appreciated, and private industry considers itself the temple of divinity. The sole function of a business organization is to nurture this life-force, and to do that, every business organism must make a profit. The precise definition of the term "the bottom line" is net profit (or net earnings, or net income); it is the monetary figure which appears as the last line in the financial statement. Unless its net profit figure increases each year, a business organism will fall into a coma and die. Which is to say, the goal of any and all business organizations is profit and growth. Period.

Money Is the Scorecard

Since "the bottom line" is a measurable reference that is applicable to all corporations, it should come as no surprise that money is the basis of the scoring system in the competitive game of business. No artificial symbols are necessary because money carries the components needed to keep track of winning points. Money is also flexible enough to identify successful players because the scorecard for the organization's game and the employee's game is parallel.

Because money is the very lifeblood of business, it's easy to see why the departments and jobs which are directly responsible for increasing sales or money supply are the ones which lead to the top of the pyramid. The chief executive officer's job is seeing to it that all the parts of the organization are synchronized to implement that goal. Obviously a woman with serious business ambitions must be oriented to the profit motive—making money—because there isn't anything else! Every single job in private industry is measured against the yardstick of how much it contributes to the company's economic well-being. Every job is evaluated on a dollars-and-cents basis, *and nothing else*. Whenever a job or a collection of jobs (high or low) fail to contribute a measurable benefit, they are cut out of the pyramid (taking most of the job occupants with them). From this mercenary orientation comes the cold-blooded impersonality of business.

All the moves in the game of corporate politics are directed toward the parallel goals of income for the corporation and income for the game-playing employee. The bottom line for women is accepting the immutable fact that one works for a proportionate share of the company's money—*and nothing else!* If it sounds like I'm hitting you over the head with this emphasis on money, I am. Women have been so brainwashed by the destructive female culture that taught them to associate money with sin, evil, and everything crude, vulgar, filthy, ill-bred, crass, dirty, unladylike, unfeminine, gauche, and obscene that they cannot separate money from uteri. The roots of this psychic crippling go so deep into the historic subjugation of women that it would take an entire book to untangle the subconscious fears and incredible fantasies that the simple noun "money" evokes in most women.

I am deeply aware of these problems; indeed I share them. My own female money demons must have come gurgling out of the slime as I wrote this chapter. I found myself getting off on irrelevant tangents, wading into theories of economics, dissecting income statements line by line, launching into bitter tirades on the financial in-injustices perpetrated against women—almost anything except the gut issue of this chapter: how to ask for the money you're worth on the job market. As one woman said, "I can't do it. I can't put a price on myself!" Apparently all of us women suffer the same knots in the stomach, clammy hands, nervous trembling, and paralyzing shock when a job interviewer says, "How much do you want?" The worst symptoms develop when we think of asking for a raise. However this congenital phobia developed, it makes us silly-putty in the hands of industry. The customs of the foreign country—the Business World —take no account of taboos against money. Money is

229

the friendly deity who cures all ills, appeases all pain, and spreads joy over the countryside. Money is also an accommodating idol; it totes up the scoring points in the game.

This chapter cannot attempt to solve women's serious philosophical and psychological problems. I can only tell you how money is perceived in the big business milieu and what devastating penalties accrue to female players who haven't learned the rules. More than anything else, the game of corporate politics is a planned strategy to outwit the house and win your deserved share of the gross. The stakes are high and the payoff is huge. For women, the payoff is more than money—it is rejuvenation of their delayed growth and maturity.

Facing up to the brutal reality that the unemotional accumulation of money is a prime indicator of female coming-of-age may be agonizingly hard for many women, but every teenager can tell you that growing up is a painful process.

Learn to Add Up Your Chances

Women are beginning to understand how seriously the educational system has shortchanged them in the basic three R's; most learned reading and writing, but arithmetic was reserved for the boys. Not surprisingly, now that women are flooding into the workforce, they discover that the flour and shortening of reading and writing is not much use without the yeast of arithmetic. Mighty few women are inept at figures and money calculations, but they *think* they are because they are so abysmally ignorant. Phobias and psychological blocks feed on such ignorance, but they can be checked and overcome (not eradicated) by factual knowledge.

Working women must take concrete steps to fill in this inexcusable math gap in their general education. Before you buy another pair of shoes or go out to dinner, invest in an eight-digit pocket calculator with a percent key. The tiny electronic chips will take over the rote arithmetic and perform the more complex mathematical calculations you are likely to need. If you're so bad off you think you can't balance a checkbook (it requires third-grade subtraction), start attending lectures and workshops on finance, investing, taxes or anything with a financial base. Many are free, as banks, securities firms, and insurance companies go after the new female dollars. The YWCA night schools, and adult education institutions usually teach courses on basic personal finance; knowledgeable women experts are setting up financial or tax counseling services for other women in cities all over the country. As your basic encyclopedic reference, buy *Sylvia Porter's Money Book* (New York: Doubleday, 1975) but to get yourself off dead-center and into the heady regions of playing with money, turn to Paula Nelson's guide to women's financial freedom, *The Joy of Money* (New York: Stein and Day, 1976).

Most important of all, learn by doing and observing at work. Never turn down an opportunity to get involved in budgets, sales estimates, income expenses, overhead, costs, percentage of increase, threatened decreases, or any other profit-and-loss aspect of your job or the operation in which you are located. Pick up—and in this case, *speak and use*—the terminology of finance and budgeting as it relates to your job function. Don't ever turn down a job which offers you the chance to learn business accounting fundamentals!

A couple of years ago I frequently visited the president of a home furnishings business group. The professional women members represent diverse corporations whose business is entwined in the vast kaleidoscope of products used in the home. At that time the president got several calls a week from executive recruiters or companies looking for potential managerial job candidates. My friend passed the job leads to experienced, highly qualified women in her group, but, as she told me in disgust, the women were uniformly scared to interview for jobs which required them "to deal with figures." "I don't know anything about budgets," was the most frequent whine, followed closely by the helpless "I don't know how to figure costs or price estimates." Neither did my friend, but she accepted one of the more promising jobs, took a cram course at a technical school of finance, and learned the specifics of budgeting and estimates the same way male executives do—on the new job. Since then she has negotiated a significant promotion and is the highest-ranked woman in her company and one of the top in her field.

Everyone Plays against the House Gross

Legally the ultimate owners of a public corporation are the shareholders. Obviously if you become one of the owners, you have some insight into the operations of the house and its gross intake. Every aspiring corporate gamester should buy a share of stock in her employer company as soon as possible. One share is all it takes to give you a vote, make you an owner, and provide you with annual and quarterly financial reports and the immensely valuable proxy statement and 10-K Report (the unvarnished financial operations facts submitted by law to the federal corporate overseer, the Securities and Exchange Commission or SEC). As an employee you can frequently get those reports by asking the Corporate Secretary's office for copies.

With this data at hand you get a general picture of what the house stakes are, where they're coming from, and which pot is up for grabs at your table. To see the stakes, you have to understand the following rudiments of the financial statement (also called the Operating Statement, the Profit and Loss Statement, popularly shortened to "P and L," or the Consolidated Statement of Income or Earnings).

Gross Income Includes net sales and other revenues from services or operations; also covers interest or investment income, ergo the growing importance of financial people in the corporate pyramid. From this total, subtract—

Direct costs of producing the income, such as direct labor costs or the cost of raw materials or resources. If you are a production or manufacturing employee, your stake is included here. Your wages rise and fall in direct relation to the volume of goods or services produced and sold. This is union territory.

Gross Profit is the amount of income after deducting the basic cost of production or manufacture but before deductions for business expenses or taxes. The percent of gross profit to net sales is computed industrywide so that individual companies, investors, and smart female employees can compare any company against its industry norm. Rising costs and falling markups are reflected in these figures. From the gross profit is deducted the—

Expenses This is a big item because most of the monied play in corporate gaming takes place in this area. There are three general categories of expenses. (1) Fixed indirect production expenses such as equipment, tools, supplies, rent, repairs, and depreciation; (2) Sales expenses, such as sales department salaries, commissions, advertising, storage, shipping, distribution, and other marketing costs; (3) General or administrative expenses, including salaries of corporate officers, sal-

233

aries of staff department employees, phones, insurance, interest on bank loans, and all other general administrative expenses. The stake of professional employees and administrative personnel is located here, which includes the bulk of aspiring women who are slotted into staff positions. The quickest way to raise the figure on the bottom line is to reduce this one. That's why women's jobs are often the first to go in economic downturns.

Profit before Taxes is the amount left after subtracting all the Expenses from Gross Profit. After that, you subtract Federal income taxes and you end up at the bottom line—

Net Profit As you can see from this bare-bones skeleton of a corporate financial statement, "the bottom line" is a residue, the leftover, the balance remaining after all the players in the corporate politics game have won their share of the house stake.

If you still labor under the delusion that demanding an equal salary or requesting an appropriate raise has anything to do with your personal self-worth, go back and review and digest this economic game board. The stakes in corporate politics go to the best players, the ones who set out to get their legitimate share.

House Tricks Help Preserve Its Stake

One inviolate rule of management is to never give away money, which is understandable when money is the lifeblood of the organism. Players have to trick them out of it so the game is eternal between employer and employee. The overriding rule for all players is *get as much*

234

as you can because that's the objective of the game and it's taken for granted that all players know it. Most women don't.

I've always considered myself lucky because the first full-time job I ever had was a high-precision grinder on an assembly line in an airplane parts factory. For almost three years I was paid on a piecework basis. All finished products were checked by inspectors who credited perfect ones, returned defectives for repair, and scrapped those totally damaged. In such a job, performance is objectively measured and salary is direct compensation for quality and volume of work produced. The monetary rewards were tied to superior performance, hard work, perfectionism, and efficiency, right? Absolutely wrong. Here's why.

I loved machinery and metals, and polished steel sculptures flew off my machine so rapidly that operators in the line behind me couldn't feed through the rough pieces fast enough. I'd help the others at their jobs to process the work through to me because I was making fabulous money for those days. This financial bubble burst in a few weeks when the efficiency engineers descended like vultures to recalculate the piecework rates on my operation. Management's response was quick; if I could produce so well and so efficiently, then the job was obviously overpriced and I should get paid *less* per piece! My indoctrination in the Protestant Work Ethic was demolished instantly. In the real world if you work too hard and perform above average, your work and ability are devalued, not appreciated and rewarded.

What really happened was that I didn't know the rules of the game (which, by the way, is not exclusive to white-collar office workers). I was a dumb kid who thought you should work as hard as you can for your money and do the best job possible for the company, and you will be suitably rewarded. In this particular game, the management rate-setters understood that experienced men

235

machinists deliberately slowed down their work pace when efficiency engineers were observing because the longer it took to finish a piece, the higher the rate. Naturally, rate-setters had adapted a formula to compensate for the relaying tactics—say 20 percent. Not knowing the slow-down game, I operated my machine at peak performance speed (to show how good I was?), but the raters automatically calculated that output at a maximum of 80 percent of my real capacity. And that's how they lowered my per-piece rate. I now had to turn out 20 percent more pieces than I was able to produce at peak performance so my earnings dropped a whopping 20 percent for top work.

After that, I made it my business to figure out the salary compensation game. When I played it expertly, I got my working time down to two hours out of eight, the other six hours I goofed off. I collected hefty bonuses and overtime when they needed my excess production and were willing to pay heavily for it.

Performance is not so easily measurable in professional or white-collar jobs, but the byplay on pay is equally merciless. Women who demonstrate exceptional ability are gradually overloaded with additional work demands without added compensation. It is assumed that if they can do so much extra, the job tasks were overpriced initially. Your only countermove is to ask for a raise every single time you are told to do anything beyond your original sphere of operation, or to absorb additional responsibility. Your boss's return move will be something like this: "Let's see how well you can do it first, then we'll think about more money." Your move: set a time limit for the test period, maximum one to three months. Then remind the boss of the salary increase—or drop the assignment. If management needs the job done, you'll get the raise; if it's not worth money, it's not worth doing by you. From the boss's viewpoint, this was an attempted bluff which didn't work with you (so it will be tried on another sucker). Meanwhile, you have not lowered your rate, which is precisely what will happen when you accept more and more work without asking for the money. They will never voluntarily give you the money because the management game is to get as much work as possible for nothing additional in pay.

Rules for Requesting Raises

Most women I talk to admit reluctantly that they "never asked for a raise in their lives." No wonder they're not getting paid. They aren't playing the game, they're just watching it on TV. Asking for a raise is the visceral tactic in the game of corporate politics. The full arsenal of management tricks, ruses, feints, and faking is brought into play during the classic confrontations between employee and boss. Everybody who is worth anything is *expected to* play in this game. In other words, if you never ask for a raise, you are classified as an inconsequential player on the team and dismissed from mind. A harried boss (who hates to talk about raises as much as you do) is concerned with deflecting or minimizing the requests flying into the lifeboat; those in the backwater who aren't making waves are blessedly forgotten.

Every so often, company policy dictates a review of salaries with an eye to minimal merit increases for those who are plodding along and patiently doing their work—a group composed heavily of women. Most companies realize that an occasional "token of appreciation" is necessary to keep turnover down, motivation up, and salaries in line with competitive companies. But any across-the-board increases immediately increase costs (the "Expenses" line in the financial statement), so the objective is to keep these mandatory raises as low as possible. Thus, a gratuitous raise will always be minimal, never reflective

237

of your real value to the company or the monetary contribution of your work. "Waiting" for a raise is low-echelon thinking. Ambitious achievers who have confidence in their own ability, plus respect for the job they're doing, indicate this by asking for raises at appropriate annual intervals and whenever else their output justifies a monetary reward, regardless of job level.

To psych yourself into the proper frame of mind to ask for a raise, your CEO perspective is critical. You must subtly dovetail your request with the overall goals of the corporation (improving the bottom line figure), but you must also think about the subject from the viewpoint of your boss. A division head or manager or whoever has responsibility for granting raises in your situation is working within an overall budget and is forced to play games with the figures. Usually a specific percentage is set aside for raises but the allocation of this amount affords considerable leeway. No rule says everybody is entitled to equal raises (or indeed, any raise), so the pot is really up for grabs.

Try practicing your management-perspective role pretense in these two typical situations wherein salary decisions are made:

Annual Automatic Raises. As the manager in charge of the salary kitty, would you evenly dispense all the money available? Or would you assign the smallest amount to those who won't complain, no matter what, and larger amounts to the ones likely to raise a ruckus? Would you reserve some of the fund as a backlog, just in case a valuable subordinate unexpectedly threatens to leave and you'll have to match a big offer to keep the person? And what about principals such as a hard-working assistant manager who wants (and deserves) a healthy raise? Not much of the superior's time is devoted to this money manipulation because the manager's decisions are sandwiched between everyday work demands. The allocations are more off-the-cuff than carefully considered.

238

The "automatic" aspect of annual raises is the timing, not the amount per person.

As an employee, fit yourself into this picture. Are you one of those who tensely wait for the company to "reward" you? Are you one of the nonentities known to never complain, at least to the boss who holds the purse strings? If so, you can be positive that you receive minimal raises and the amount has little to do with your ability or performance. More likely, it is a reward for being a nice girl and taking what you're offered like an obedient daughter or wife should.

Salary Review Committees. Visualize yourself as a member of such a group, which could be comprised of a department head and a couple of key subordinate managers. You are going through the detested chore of assigning (or withholding) dollar amounts of raises to the entire list of employees. The conversation could go something like this.

> *"John Adams? Very mediocre; doesn't deserve any more than he's getting, but I suppose we have to give him a couple of hundred." "Come on, that's an insult, he's got a big family; better make it $500."*
> *"Mary Barnes? Steady, conscientious, hard worker. Very willing and pleasant. Would be grateful and satisfied with $250."*
> *"Bill Colin? Oh, yeah. I've had a couple of discussions with him, as you know. He wants $5,000. That's a little rich; what if we split it up, $3,000 now and $2,000 in six months? Wonder how he'd take that?"*
> *"Look, let's go through and see how many other big ones we have in here. If we dispose of them first, then we'll know better what we have left for the rest."*

Now back to yourself as an employee. How will you appear to the "impartial" salary review crowd when your name comes up? How well do they know you and your work? Do they know of any special assignments you undertook? Do they know how much you expect as a raise? Do they know what you'd consider an "insulting" amount? Have you ever complained afterward and requested a re-evaluation?

This technique of reversing your perspective on raises —seeing yourself as you will appear to your boss or boss's boss at money-juggling time—helps clarify why you must *always ask* for a raise. Otherwise you are like a puppy dog sitting there with pleading eyes waiting for a crumb. It's not businesslike. It's certainly not gamesmanship because it leaves the perfect opening for men who are making hard decisions about the department budget to rationalize that, "She deserves more money but obviously money isn't important to her because her husband has a good job and she doesn't need it," or, "She doesn't have any responsibilities beyond herself, and a young, single girl doesn't need any more money."

Needing the money should have no influence on your decision to ask for adequate pay for your work contributions, nor should you use such an argument when mentioning the subject of a raise. The only valid reason for getting an appropriate raise is that you are *doing the job you were hired to do* with superior or exceptional competence. (Doing a different or enlarged job is grounds for a promotion and accompanying salary upgrading, not simply a raise.) Focus your request on the value of the job you are doing and its contribution to the goals of the department or company. If you've never before asked for a raise, your first approach may be a casual reminder to your boss (or whoever has responsibility for salary decisions) that you are measuring your work in monetary terms. "When I accepted this job for $9,000 I knew the salary was quite low, but it gave us both a chance to evaluate my expertise and competence. Now I can see that my work is worth at least $12,000 and I hope you agree because the annual review seems like a good time to reconsider the salary on this position." Don't belabor the point, just drop it in the hopper to give your boss something to think about.

Many women seem to harbor an irrational fear that asking for a justified raise means they have to quit (or might get fired) if they don't get the raise! My guess is that they have allowed themselves to be underpaid and exploited for so long that they finally erupt in angry hostility, saying "Give me a raise or I quit!" Never hand down ultimatums in raise negotiations; what you are really doing is bartering—your demonstrated performance against management's need to fill that hierarchical job hole with an unknown quantity (somebody else). If your work is valuable and well done, even a stupid manager is ready to talk money as opposed to interviewing, hiring, and training a newcomer and hoping the choice turns out as well as you did. It's not the manager's money, it's the company money, and allocating raises is, again, impersonal. It becomes personal to the manager or supervisor when losing a good employee raises the demands on the boss (i.e., replacing and training a new employee). That's *your* leverage when dickering on raises, how much you ease or simplify your boss's job. Note the verbs above: negotiating, bartering, dickering. Those are the keys to successful and nonhostile raise reminders. Always remember it's a game move, not a bitter confrontation. If you don't win this time, you can try again.

Good Timing Pays Off

Corporate gamesters learn early that substantial raises have little to do with ability or achievement and nothing to do with personal self-worth. In the corporate realm, giving raises is a matter of dividing up the available dollars in such a way as to hold down the overhead but

241

assure peace on the local labor front. Certainly the squeaky wheel will get oiled soonest, and explicit dollar requests will get priority consideration.

A periodic schedule is the most popular management game ploy in the raise contest. The time interval is designed to keep the majority of the animals quiet for a whole year. Such an inflexible, rigid policy might be accepted by all-female groups but no experienced male player falls for it. An undeviating salary policy would turn private industry into civil service; such an automatic salary increase pattern is anathema to competitive industry where good men are expected to demand payment for their productivity. Consequently, the knowing female game player is not impressed with restrictive schedules or timetables. Raises can be negotiated at any time during a year, or a couple of times within a year, whenever the outlook is propitious. This is important to remember because good timing in successful raise tactics depends on striking when the iron is hot.

Always ask for a raise when things are in your favor. Move fast when your star is ascendant because the whole situation could change tomorrow. Act: when results come in on a successful business project; when your workload is high and you are producing visibly more than teammates; whenever you are asked to take over for an absent or vacant position and the boss needs you and your output. If you are ever responsible for an extraordinary bit of business which makes the entire group or team shine, ask for your recognition in the form of a raise. Should you be singled out professionally in a complimentary manner, as getting elected president of an important trade association, or having a bylined article published in a respected business paper, or if you are cited and thanked by upper management for some contribution (running the Red Cross solicitation drive?), inform them that you know the market value of plaudits by bringing up the subject of a raise.

Management, incidentally, will expect to see you coming with your request because this is the way the game is played. You can anticipate your boss's countermove which is almost automatic, it's used so often: "Let's see how things go for the rest of the year and we'll talk about it again; I've certainly got you in mind." "In mind" isn't money in your pocket; these delaying tactics and procrastinations are classic bluffs from the management player. The expert gamester doesn't fall for the bluff but suggests that now is much better than later—who knows what later will bring? If you are really in a strong position, the gentlest intimation that you might not be around later can call that bluff. The actual words you use to broach the raise subject will depend on your style, your relationship with the boss, and the details of the situation, but the moves and countermoves in a salary negotiation are quite standard. The two of you are batting a badminton birdie back and forth. In other words, a boss's countermove is not a rejection; it's part of the game, to see who outplays whom.

A friend who read part of this manuscript held her head and moaned when she realized the chances she missed in her jobs. "Most women don't take advantage of power positions they inadvertently get into because they don't recognize an open door when they see it; they don't know that you walk right in and collect your share of the loot." She recalled one vivid instance which almost made her sick in retrospect. She had brought to management's attention an imminent regulation by the Food and Drug Administration which, if undetected, could have had a disastrous effect on the company's pharmaceutical business. She was included in the emergency top level meetings and invited to ride on the company's private jet—a privilege reserved solely for top management. When word leaked out about her unique honor, she played it down, saying "it was nothing," and never mentioning it. Her executive superiors treaded around her warily for a while, but when she disparaged her distinction and made no move to exploit it with a big raise and promotion, her job slid back to its normal supervisory rut and she didn't even get a raise, although her alertness had saved the company millions of dollars. "When I look back, I realize they were all waiting for me to make the logical move. At that point I could have asked for anything I wanted and got it! To think where I'd be today if I'd only known how the game was played!"

A Raise in Salary Is a Number

Salaries and raises belong to the financial arena of business, so the communications medium is numbers. Anytime you talk about money in business, talk numbers. Vague statements like, "I haven't had a raise for a long time," or "I've been here for more than a year so I thought it was time for a raise," don't communicate anything where the spoken language is financial. The word "time" is especially incomprehensible since time bears no relation to merited raises. Good performance as a dependable team member or contribution to "the bottom line" is the correlation for salary increases. A request for a raise is always expressed in dollars per year. For instance, if you make $200 a week, don't go in and say you think you should be getting $215 a week; you will reveal your amateur standing in the game and that will be the hardest $15 you ever got, if you get it!

To fit the game rules and financial terminology, your discussion should flow in this direction. "I've been thinking a lot about my job in the last few months and I hadn't realized how critical my work is to the smooth functioning of this department. As a matter of fact, I'm convinced that job should have been paying $13,000 a year instead of $10,400. Since I have considerably enlarged the scope of the work during the last year, I would say that an accurate assessment of its value to the department is now $15,000. To reach that level, my salary would go up $4,600, but considering the importance of the work in the overall picture, $15,000 is not unreasonable. It's still on the low side, but I foresee several areas of expansion and I expect my operation will be seen as progressively valuable as time goes on."

In game terms, you have served the birdie into the boss's center court; the salary negotiations are now set up to go back and forth, back and forth, as the two of you try to outdo each other. Every dollar the boss chops off your $15,000 figure will score as a management gain; every dollar you obtain above your present $10,400 will score in your favor. Since you've left $4,600 to play with, the odds are you'll settle at some midpoint where management gains $2,000 and you gain $2,000, with a $600 leftover that could go either way or be divided. By playing the game, you not only get considerably larger increases but you create the illusion that both sides won a victory. Contrast this setup with a bitter wrangle over a measly $15 a week where nobody can win graciously. You can see why an experienced male player at this game much prefers to have another skilled player in opposition. Never assume you know the final score (how much of an increase you can get) until you play the game. How else will you know?

Some Tips on the Numbers Game

To launch a salary increase game you must make the first move by pitching a solid dollar figure to your managerial opponent. But how do you arrive at the figure? Your preliminary calculation borrows some techniques from football planning (analyzing the variables of immediate departmental budget, the job market in the industry or profession, the significance of the job in the

245

company hierarchy, the abilities, tenure, and experience of the employee, and the personalities or relationship between the opposing players); some from simple arithmetic (adding up the figures or estimating percentages); some from advance scouting (collecting salary data).

A minority of women are in jobs which can actually be measured in dollars-and-cents contribution to the profit picture. If you are in some branch of sales or production where you can say "my work was directly responsible for this company earning $100,000 this year," or "saving $50,000 over two years" or "gaining a customer worth a million over several years," you are in good shape from a salary viewpoint. Hard data on dollar contributions can be immediately translated to a raise, as in "I hope to see this reflected in my salary at $10,000 a year"—or $50,-000 a year if you are in a position to walk away to another company with your customers, expertise, or financial know-how. In some volatile industries, entertainment for example, doubling your salary every year is not exceptional for executives who are "hot" that year and are responsible for best-sellers of one kind or another.

The majority of working women, unfortunately, do not yet operate in corporate profit centers. They are members of staff departments or support services, which may or may not be susceptible to profit-and-loss calculations. (If you are unhappily responsible for a loss some year, keep a low profile as they say and don't mention raises during that period.) Some staff employees *can* translate their work into budgetary figures by connecting it with the money-making operation they support. A researcher, for instance, could use the sales figures for a successful new product with which she was involved; or a personnel official might calculate the savings she initiated by holding down turnover or negotiating less expensive recruitment methods; advertising or publicity writers can claim a share in larger client fees to their employers resulting from satisfaction with the agency's output. Secretaries who work for

246

a suddenly successful boss should expect to request a percentage of that windfall. Any method you can figure out to measure your job contribution in literal increased dollars (reducing expenses always raises the bottom line, remember) should be utilized when measuring the gamble on numbers in the raise game.

Translating a raise request to numbers becomes trickier when your output or job contribution lies in the intangible areas of general administrative expense. Intangible factors are also important to a corporation or it wouldn't be bothered with its image, customer relations, employee communications, or cafeterias, but it's almost impossible for lower echelon people to put a dollar figure on this contribution. Under these circumstances, women must look outward and upward in the company, industry, or local job market to arrive at an initial figure to start the raise game going.

Women must include special considerations which apply to their history of unequal treatment in the employment area. No matter what figure you settle on as a "fair" raise, you should probably double it to be talking in elementary game terms. Obviously there can be no pat answer or fixed formula to determine every woman's salary increase pattern, but here are some benchmarks that may help in your private calculations.

1. Start with the assumption that you are underpaid compared to equal male co-workers. All women are, and you are unlikely to be the sole exception which proves the rule. Even Barbara Walters, who has been shamefully maligned primarily for trying to get equal pay for equal work, ended up with a contract which calls for her to do twice as much work as comparable men for the same money. (When you see her annual compensation reported in comparison with all network news anchor*men*, let me know!)

On a national average, women are paid half men's salaries. In specific categories such as college graduates, or professional and technical specialty jobs, women get two-thirds of what men get in their paychecks. If you make $10,000, you can safely assume men doing your job are getting nearly $15,000. If you make $15,000, comparable men will be earning $20,000. If you earn $18,000 or $19,000, male colleagues with less experience are getting $25,000 and up. My next-door neighbor, who has long headed a small department in a large corporation, meets monthly with men and women who head the same operation in other major corporations; she just discovered that one of the men (who handles her identical job in a similar corporation) makes $60,000. She makes $18,000. Never underestimate the underpayment of women by the "nicest" corporations.

2. If you haven't asked for raises but merely accepted whatever was offered, your increases have been minimal compared to men who've been playing the game all along. Depending on how long, the differential could be thousands.

3. Inflation reduces everyone's salary but women frequently ignore this income-eroding percentile. Just to stay even with last year's salary, you must get an increase to match current inflationary losses. For example, if inflation is running at 5 percent, you need an annual increase of $500 on $10,000, or $750 on $15,000, before you can begin to calculate a meritorious raise. To get an exact figure applicable to your city, look for regional consumer prices statistics or follow local union negotiations, especially in regard to cost-of-living factors included in the settlement.

4. Try to collect salary data for men doing substantially the same job as you. Asking outright is one method, but men are either secretive or inaccurate (they lie), so the information is unreliable. If you have close friends with access to salary records (payroll, accounting, personnel, executive secretaries), ask them what they know. Mainly, read want ads in newspapers and trade publications and maintain records of salary ranges for similar jobs. Talk salary and pay scales all the time to acquire a feel for the job market.

5. Watch your company's "bottom line," as reported annually and quarterly. The figure you want to notice is "percentage increase in earnings," that is, the amount by which the net profit increased from last year to this. Say your company's earnings were up 20 percent, use that percentage as a guide for your personal calculation (after the inflation factor). In a diversified corporation or conglomerate, see if the figures in the annual report are broken down by division because someone in a booming profit center can request larger raises than a person in a flat or unprofitable operation.

6. Save the corporation's proxy statements (the announcement to stockholders of the annual meeting). This legal pamphlet is loaded with goodies, including salaries of the top officers. Note by how much they are increasing their own salaries, being mindful (and the proxy statement notes will alert you) that upper level income increases may be buried in deferred compensation arrangements, stock options, and assorted other "fringe" benefits.

Aside from helping you reach an intelligent figure for an increase, close attention to dollars-and-cents values in the job market will expand your horizon on money. Women have spent so many years saving a few pennies here and there to stretch inadequate living budgets, they extrapolate this penuriousness to big business. Never lose sight of the fact that the company you work for is thinking and talking in millions and billions of dollars. Aspiring women must also learn to talk authoritatively in substantial amounts of money. When it comes to salary increases, never talk anything less than thousands of dollars annually in regular raises. Although I said formulas were impossible, my own conviction is that no woman should settle for less than a 25 percent raise. In order to get that under the game rules (where it is assumed that your first figure will be much inflated over what you expect), you will have to ask for a raise in the neighborhood of 50 percent. If you think that's an atrocious figure, you are a typical woman—naïve about salaries.

While you're at your salary research, if you discover that a man who held your job previously got paid more than you or that a man doing substantially the same work as you (never mind his title, the job functions are the key) is getting paid more, don't go home in fury and frustration. Pick up the phone book, look under U.S. Government, Department of Labor, Wage and Hour Division. Call up and ask about the simple process to file an Equal Pay Complaint. No one will ever find out because this agency, which enforces the Equal Pay Act, operates in secrecy and confidentiality. Don't confuse the Department of Labor with EEOC (Equal Employment Opportunity Commission), which enforces Title VII; these agencies are as different as a boa constrictor and a puppy dog. The Equal Pay Act is your friend, but like all government agencies its procedures take time. In the meantime, work on your boss, practice your skills at corporate politics, and try to get your salary up to a respectable level.

Despite your game-playing skills, there will be times when a salary increase is out of the question. To be ready for such impasses, suggest a solution which will satisfy you until there's more money in the corporate kitty but will not cost management a cent—a new or better job title for the position you hold. Words and titles are free, and, as we know, new levels can be inserted into the hierarchy for convenience. A more prestigious title conveys status (which can later be parlayed) or a title more descriptive of the work you perform can give you room to branch out in your contacts or operations. Don't mistake title change for promotion and accept more work— you're trading *words* only. Visualize how the new title will look on your résumé (which you will immediately reprint when the title comes through). If you pick title requests brilliantly, you may double or triple your salary on your next job.

Fringes Are Free Points

As you must know, not all salary is reflected in your take-home paycheck. Most companies estimate that the standard "fringe benefits" add 25 to 30 percent more to each employee paycheck. The standards such as health and disability insurance, group life insurance, pension plans or stock-purchase plans are available to all employees. There's another category of "fringe benefits" which are enjoyed very widely by men executives but so rarely by women executives that many women never heard of executive "perks" or perquisites.

Perks come in a variety of styles and shapes and they are often dispensed by whim, a kind of superior's largesse to favored subordinates. So guess why a lot of women executives never heard of them? Although most perks are not officially listed anywhere (and they can be withdrawn at any time), their existence is not a secret; an observant female gamester can smoke them out rather easily. The point in such ferreting is to make sure you get the perks that go with your job title. Many companies and bosses have a positive reluctance to extend perquisites to women, but these are among the "privileges" in "terms, conditions and privileges of employment" as defined by Title VII. The management-oriented woman keeps a sharp eye out for any status privileges that are withheld—and promptly requests equal access. One accumulates perquisites as one goes up the hierarchical ladder, so different privileges are extended at various job levels which can vary tremendously depending on the company.

Usually an alert woman will discover that, conveniently, no one ever told her about the perks men at her level routinely enjoy. When she brings up the subject to the authorizing superior, he'll be so surprised—"You mean no one told you! I can't believe it, that's terrible." He'll authorize the telephone credit card with grand apologies—and refrain from mentioning that she also has a chauffeured limousine at her disposal! Here are some of the more common perks for executive women to watch for and *claim* whenever one applies to men at her job level.

—Lavish expense accounts (including at-home parties and entertaining).

—Reserved space in the parking lot.

—Charge cards of all varieties: telephone, airplane, restaurant, general.

—Chauffeured cars and limousines. Top officers have

their private mobile office. Lesser executives may be picked up and driven home, or driven anywhere on request to the company pool.

—Private automobiles, usually very expensive models, leased by and fully insured and maintained by the company but the executive keeps it as his personal car.

—Season boxes at ball games, concerts, theatrical productions, etc.

—Memberships in country clubs, golf clubs, athletic clubs, private dining clubs.

—Dues and expenses for professional and business societies, including convention travel.

—Use of permanently rented corporate hotel suites and apartments; sometimes homes.

—Use of corporate hunting lodges, resort facilities, executive retreats, yachts.

—Fully-paid expenses for a wife to accompany executive husband on trips worldwide or local.

—Lump-sum "bonuses" for vacation trips or personal use.

—Use of the corporate private jets and helicopters.

—Quantities of free products or installations, depending on what the company makes.

—Stock options (if the stock goes up, an executive can

buy shares below market; if price falls, he doesn't pick up his option).

—Et cetera. Perks can add up to 100 percent extra compensation to top executives.

What's a Job, Anyway?

That's my favorite question to ask women at job seminars, workshops, or my Womanschool classes. So far, I've never gotten a reasonably accurate definition from either long-term or beginner working women. Yet all one need do is look in the dictionary. A job is a piece of work of a definite extent or character done for a certain fee, especially one done in the course of a profession or an occupation. In short, an agreement: specified tasks for a specified salary.

A job, as all senior executives know, is a contract. They know because they draw up a written document after negotiating the details with their new employer (or renew one with an existing employer), and have it legally witnessed and signed by both parties to the agreement. The job contract generally spells out the area of responsibility, the level of authority, the title or officership, the direct salary, the deferred compensation, the stock options, the percentage of increase in compensation, the pension rights and anything else employee or employer wants stipulated. A job contract runs for a specified length of time, commonly five years, and if the new executive fails to produce as promised or is eased out of the job for any reason the salary contract remains in force and the ex-employee continues to collect.

Women who are being sought by companies which have no token woman (as is happening frequently today to the comparatively few available female executives) should be negotiating written job contracts with anxious new employers. Any woman at the $20,000 and over level, when making an upward job change, should probably be discussing a written job contract. Whether you get one or not is largely dependent on the company's need for your services or your ability to persuade them that you're so in demand they ought to tie you up with a legal document—which, of course, you negotiate for your best advantage, with the help of your lawyer and accountant. The point to remember is that any job is a contract between two principals, you and the employer corporation. It's a cold-blooded business arrangement, whether written or unwritten.

The vast majority of jobs are unwritten oral agreements wherein you promise to perform certain tasks for specified monetary amounts. If you don't look out for your own interests and renegotiate the terms of your contract regularly throughout your employment—ask for raises and promotions—you will not get them. It's really that cut-and-dried. One woman who just got another raise, bringing her salary to $40,000, laughed nervously last week when she told me, "It's unbelievable what happens when you start asking for raises; often you don't get any flak or argument, they just give it to you!" The interesting thing about her situation is that she's in a bad job from her point of view. She is being held down and sidetracked and is making little headway in getting transferred to an operational management position. She says her job in an auditing firm is a glorified clerical position, but as long as the firm apparently wants her there she decided to insist on the salary equivalent of men who are moving ahead in the line positions. A couple of years ago she started asking for specific raises and has kept it up steadily. Her job hasn't improved one whit, but at least her salary is multiplying rapidly.

Keeping your eyes and ears open to salary education is most important for women. We just don't have the background and experience in business to know the facts about

255

annual compensation. We're all learning about money and salaries with a kind of ga-ga astonishment. A young woman in her thirties told me how ecstatic she was less than two years ago because she was earning $20,000 a year as the only woman trader in a Wall Street brokerage. She loved the job and the company and was very proud of her annual gross and manifest success. Until one day she found out accidentally that the young man trader at the next desk, who goofed off most of the time and did almost no work compared to her eager efforts, was earning $30,000. She didn't want to make a fuss, so she quietly began looking for another job, that is the same job in another firm. Her boss heard about it and called her in. She explained that she loved the company but figured she must have started so low, being the only woman, that she'd never catch up to men's earnings and felt in all fairness that she should get equal pay. He asked her if she'd stay if she got equal pay and she said, "Yes."

Two weeks later when she opened her paycheck envelope she almost fainted in disbelief. Her income had jumped to $50,000 a year! In her business, annual earnings depend on commissions and bonuses; it had never occurred to her that she was making a smaller percentage on her own sales (i.e., that this figure was negotiable), nor did she know that commissions and bonuses can be earned on total sales, of the entire group of sales people, or the entire department, of the entire company. The man who did little work was getting paid a percentage of the hard work of others, including herself, because he was shrewd and knowledgeable enough to negotiate a better deal. She was making a lot of money for other people but was very naïve about her personal renumeration. She is naïve no longer. This year she moved to a larger firm, negotiated her income provisions, and will clear $100,000. She has upped her salary from $20,000 to $100,000 a year while doing the exact same work!

Both these women started out to "make it in the man's

256

world" on the basis of their personal confidence, willingness to work harder than any man, and conviction that they could overcome all those "crazy women's lib complaints" by their own exceptional talents. Both are turning into rabid feminists, anxious to "help" and "inform" other women about salary discrimination and how managements succeed in keeping women out of the economic sweepstakes.

If you're an ambitious working woman, stop fooling around with pennies. Keep your eye on the bottom line and get into the salary game.

PART
3
Symbols, Signals, Style, and Sex

CHAPTER
10

The Game Site
Is Resplendent
with Symbolism

To awestruck sightseers in the land of the business hierarch, the architectural grandeur is overpowering and impressive. Stately edifices dominate landscaped vistas of suburbia and mighty skyscrapers silhouette the profiles of major cities. Flowering gardens, soaring plazas, ample parking, vaulted lobbies, air conditioning, musical elevators, carpeted lounges, spacious dining rooms, and hundreds upon hundreds of linear offices bathed relentlessly in fluorescent brilliance dutifully impress gaping tourists.

But all this structural munificence does not divert the expert gamester who looks beyond the steel and concrete public visor of the corporate persona to identify the heraldic markings painted on the battle armor. Like the shields carried by knights of legend, the modern corporate building reeks with symbolism. Far from being a mere architectural wonder, every pane of glass, slab of marble, and foot of carpet performs a dual function in identifying the tournament site. The buildings are impersonal monuments to the power and wealth contained therein. Space itself, in both the exterior and interior layout, is weighted with abstract significance. Just as a heraldic seal reveals a great deal about the one using it, so spatial divisions reveal important information about the modern-day knights.

Today's business building, especially the corporate headquarters, is a physical representation of the hierarchical pyramid. It is the tangible game board. A walk through a large office, from floor to floor, is like threading a course through the hierarchy. Trappings of rank, position, and power are spread around the place like icons in a cathedral. They identify the important players and signal their positions in the game. Neophytes must grasp the design of the game board and learn the initial placement of the pieces before making any irreversible move.

Very often businesswomen approach the game of corporate gamemanship as if it were a throw of the dice which pits their future against pure chance, or luck. The real game for women more nearly resembles chess, in which one of the sixteen playing pieces is a strong female (the Queen) and the object of the game is to "check" the adverse King. Chess is an intellectual military exercise based on a combative attack against equally matched opposing fighting units. The descriptive play language of chess is indistinguishable from that of war "games" or football or business—lines of attack, defensive systems, infiltration, onslaught, sacrifice, control (territory or foes), power, weakness, strength, strategy, tactics, maneuver, surrender, challenge, conquer, win. Each pawn, rook, knight, bishop, queen and king in the chess set is endowed with specific agility to move only in certain directions and for stipulated distances. Each piece is made clearly identifiable so that players and observers can watch the game progress and know exactly what moves have been made. Unlike cards, chess is a public game spread out for all to see.

So is corporate politics a public game. In business the so-called status symbols serve to identify the playing pieces and reveal their positions on the board. The masculine pecking system, regardless of the all-male activity, is replete with emblems and shared identity signals, many of which speak louder than words and obviate the need for verbal communication. If you've ever wondered why your boss pays inordinate attention to "silly" objects or personal privileges, very likely these are crucial business status symbols. Few of the customs and practices of business life are meaningless. They only look that way to women who have not learned the fundamentals of the game.

How to Tell the Players Apart

Status symbols are two-way communications. If you can interpret them, they tell you where a co-worker stands in the ranking system, and they tell others where you stand. For that reason, women cannot afford to ignore these ubiquitous symbols because each tiny accumulation of visible status is an increase in power or advancement. Indeed, as the game plays out, a woman often needs her power emblems more than a title or salary increase to effectively use any authority she acquires. It is difficult if not impossible for a pawn to behave like a bishop or queen if she doesn't have the mitre or crown that differentiates the chess pieces.

Most of the common status differentials can be perceived at even the lowest levels. As employees move up the hierarchical ladder, the emblems are gradually emblazoned with additional symbols or sophisticated refinements of the basic seal. Here are some of the categories of rank insignia which help you tell the players apart and prevent you from being bluffed by someone at your own level who tries to "pull rank" on you without justification. Conversely, a familiarity with the status symbols protects you from being duped by management if you are offered an empty promotion or promise which carries no visible authority emblem.

How You Are Paid. Not how much, *how*. Cash in a brown envelope indicates the lowest rank. A check thus becomes a status symbol, a sign of progress. If the wage is figured on an hourly basis or a weekly basis (the non-exempt jobs which are subject to overtime beyond forty hours), it has a lower status than jobs which are exempt from overtime. I remember a junior writer who tried to lord it over her friends with a claim that she had been promoted to professional ranks. She lost all respect and admiration when it was discovered that she still filled out "the little green slips" which were required for weekly time sheets. She thought she was a "writer" because she was allowed to write; her shrewd co-workers knew she was still considered an hourly clerical worker by management because that's how she was paid. An annual salary paid out in the standard semimonthly equal installments is a symbol of the supervisory and professional ranks. Very high levels of management often have options to tailor payment methods to suit their own convenience. Many executives don't get a check at all; they have it sent directly to their banks and deposited to their personal accounts. Corporate officers almost all arrange to have big portions of their high salaries "deferred," that is, not paid to them until some later date or in some other form. It pays to keep an eye on how superiors receive and cash their salary checks. Incidentally, some executives send their secretaries to the bank with their checks; these secretaries are worth wooing if you're trying to collect salary data.

What Time You Report to Work. Flexibility in choosing one's own working hours is a clear mark of distinction. The lowest degree of status is reflected in punching a time clock or being "signed in" by an overseer, the sure tag of a manual or clerical job. The time-clock insignia also extends to lunch hours and coffee breaks

264

which are strictly regimented to the prescribed minute. As one moves upward into supervisory and professional ranks, *it is taken for granted* that you have a degree of autonomy in fixing your work hours and lunch times or breaks. Women frequently don't seem to recognize that they have this status privilege, or else they are afraid to display it, and use it. I'm often jarred when I have lunch with an apparent "executive" woman who suddenly bolts her lunch and dashes away because she'll be "late" getting back to the office within an hour. This is the time-clock thinking, lowest-level clerical insignia. If her boss is what she's afraid of (as many have told me), she is being treated as a time-clock employee and allowing herself and her job to be thus degraded. No brownie points accrue to a game player who refuses to wear her status symbols. You establish rank privileges simply by taking advantage of work-hour freedom according to the local department pattern.

Freedom to determine your own working hours does not mean you work shorter hours or ignore the working timetable your boss adopts. Some women consider it wise to dovetail their hours with their boss's—so they are always in the office at the same time. Others work more independently and arrive at the hour most convenient to their personal schedule and vary lunch periods to suit personal or business commitments. One woman executive I know has remained at the same job level for twenty years although a more astute gamester with her options would have progressed several steps. Her problem is low-echelon thinking; she still acts like a time-clock secretary. Even though she travels on business regularly, she schedules her trips for one-day, eighteen-hour commutes and gets home after midnight to appear in the office before nine the next morning. Bedraggled and exhausted, she complains about her terrible schedule, but neither her subordinates nor her superiors have any sympathy; they've long since chalked her off as lacking management potential. Men who progressed from a duplicate position scheduled their trips over two or three days each time; they knew better than to ignore status symbols. If you'r uncertain about your status entitlement in time flexibility watch what male colleagues and bosses do. Then go ou and do likewise! Don't, for heaven's sake, complain abou men who proudly display their ranking privileges an wonder why your hard work isn't appreciated after you'v thrown away your own equality symbol.

Where You Eat. Not only when but where one eat is a status distinction. The lowest indication is being re stricted to the premises as are many plant and factor workers. Freedom to leave the work premises (whethe you do or not) is a step upward. Voluntary on-site lunching in large corporations is usually stamped with clea status distinctions. Lower-echelon workers go to the general cafeteria; middle-management dines in the executiv lunchroom; and top officers eat in the private dining room Senior executives can always drop into the general cafeteria if they want, but it takes a symbolic ID card to get into the executive dining halls. Anyone who is eligible to eat in the executive dining room but eschews the privilege to continue lunching with friends in the genera cafeteria is pretty sure to be knocked out of the game very soon. If, for example, you had a boss who did that, you'd know it was time to look for a transfer or new job because you're stuck with a dead-head. See how attention to visible status emblems can tip you off?

In some companies even eating at your desk can reveal status. Did you get the food yourself from the friendly mobile vendor? Did a secretary order it from a good delicatessen and have it delivered? Was a complete hotplate sent from the executive dining room? Or did you bring a sandwich from home in a brown paper bag?

Are you beginning to think all this is silly, like who cares? That's just it; nobody cares—if you're a woman. All your male colleagues and co-workers will ignore your eating habits as long as it keeps you out of their favorite rendezvous. They've already decided you belong with the brown-baggers (low-paid secretaries and clerks who bring their lunch), so it won't surprise them one bit to see you ally yourself with lower-status lunch groups. As an ambitious woman you have to care. It will never do for you to exclude yourself from the semisocial lunch and cocktail gatherings where more business is conducted, more information exchanged, and more contacts made than during the regular working hours. If you can't worm your way into a suitable lunch group, go to a movie or go shopping for a couple of hours, but definitely exercise your status prerogative.

The Mail You Get. Mail sorters, if they were so minded, could diagram the organizational chart by noting the incoming mail for various individuals and the routing pattern on memos. One of the first status symbols is an in-box on your desk. The next improvement is denoted by an out-box. Increasing status is determined by the style of the containers, utilitarian metal being at the lower end and hand-woven straw, hand-painted wood, or other elaborate designs being better. Perhaps because this symbol is so widely distributed, some statusy types dispense with this common denominator and have incoming correspondence neatly piled on the center of an empty desk (they probably have little of significance to do and hope their status symbols will carry them through to retirement).

More important than the box is the incoming contents. Daily deliveries of the *Wall Street Journal* and *New York Times* or regular copies of *Business Week, Fortune, Barron's, Forbes, U.S. News and World Report*, or economic newsletters are distinctive emblems. Company-paid subscriptions are status symbols in general, but the more management-oriented the publication, the higher the status rating, *Harvard Business Review* outranking the Gizmo trade journal by far.

267

Outgoing mail also has status value if your name is imprinted on the corporate letterhead, either by itself or as one of the partners or officers of a firm.

Your Working Location. In a factory, the operator at the end of the assembly line has more prestige than one near the beginning because the product is more valuable in its finished state. The principle of increasing value of work follows through to the top of the hierarchy where the office of the chief executive is obviously the ultimate in status and power and the choicest in location. Proximity to the power generator exudes status, with the office adjacent to the CEO being the most prestigious but the entire floor sharing in shadings of top rank. In a suburban complex with several buildings, the one with the executive offices is the power generator and a poor location there is superior to choice space in any lesser building. In short, physical locale is a status symbol, so the location of your office is one of the most telling emblems in revealing your rank in the hierarchy and your favor with the boss. It's an important piece in the game.

How Space Confers Status

The "executive floor" is known to most employees by virtue of the fact they have never set foot on it. This is the true inner sanctum, and the power emanations are so strong that minor employees are afraid to get near. I've seen adult men literally shake in their boots at the prospect of answering a call to the executive floor. For those who are physically located "in the boondocks," "over in the boneyard," or "out in the sticks," (i.e., distant buildings or branch offices), a move to the headquarters city or building signifies a boom in status long before anyone knows if the shift was accompanied by a change in title or a better salary. Geographic and internal physical office moves can track an executive's path through the hierarchical labyrinth more clearly than a title change. A company may have hundreds of vice-presidents or divisional managers but the really important ones are distinguished from titular peers by that prime emblem of status—the office location.

Within the physical boundaries of every corporate department or operation much the same pattern of office locale identifies the ranking of subordinates and superiors. Most department layouts are square or rectangular. The corner offices, which are larger, brighter, and most secluded, are choice spots and the highest ranking executives naturally choose them. The remainder of the outside walls are customarily divided into small offices so that each has a window or a portion of plate glass. These are known universally as the "window offices" and have much higher status value than non-windowed offices. Size is also an emblematic factor, so a large window office is more valuable than a small window office, but a small window office is superior to a much larger "interior" office.

The internal space in a typical office floor layout can be left wide open and filled with rows upon rows of desks (generally populated with clerical women). Here employees work in the wide-open area with no privacy and where they can be easily observed by the supervisors. Another solution is to partition the vast internal space with one or more rows of "interior" offices, each of which has walls to the ceiling and doors; these are real private offices but have no windows. The third alternative, and a highly favored one, is to erect movable partitions which enclose the desks of individuals in the interior sector. These tin or plastic partitions are waist- or shoulder-high; they block the view of a person sitting at the enclosed desk but allow any passer-by to look over the top and see the occupant at work. These constructions are well known to all working women as cubicles. Status-wise, they are a step up from the wide-open clerical or secretarial pool pattern (often referred to as "paper factories"), but not as prestigious as a fully enclosed office which carries more symbolic value even if it must be shared with another. A "window" office is generally considered an "executive" or supervisory symbol.

Symbolic Meanings of Windows and Walls

Since window offices can be roughly defined as officers' quarters, the position of rooms "weights" their relative values. Proximity to the corner offices carries the most weight, then comes view. An unobstructed view of the skyline or gardens is far more prestigious than a window on the ventilating shaft or one overlooking the parking lot or delivery entrance. An office located on the traffic lanes, one in the center arena of business activity, represents higher status than one hidden away in an isolated nook or placed near the nonstatus "public" areas, such as cloak rooms, bathrooms, lounges, elevators, or storerooms.

Offices in the middle of the outside walls, that is, those that are equidistant from either corner office, are least desirable because the occupant's connection to either corner power generator is weak, tenuous, and not immediately identifiable. Michael Korda, the best-selling folk etymologist of sophisticated male business mores, attributes this midcenter office weakness to a power dead spot. In his book *Power: How to Get It, How to Use It*, he asserts that power flows in a X-shaped pattern from each corner office to the one diagonally opposite. The center of the space (where the X-lines bisect) represents the point at which the authority of the corner person peters out. Under his theory, the center of the floor layout is equivalent to a power blackout area and outer offices parallel with the center of the room are thus located in power dead-spots.

I've seen office setups where enclaves of competing

270

executives use the X theory to amass power. With their cronies and subordinates flanking them, they set up hostile camps in each of the corners. Newcomers or nonaligned workers invariably floated to the nondescript center offices. In firms where several executives have equal rank, for instance partners in auditing, law, or brokerage firms, they can apportion the corner offices by a coin toss and the power flow runs as easily down the sides as across a diagonal. Even so, the central offices are less prestigious because ranking executives like to have their closest allies physically near them. Proximity to a superior is undoubtedly the best gauge of status within a team group. Watch carefully when offices get switched around. It means that status symbols are changing hands and the rank of the movers' is being visibly altered although their titles and salaries are unchanged.

A lot of women may think this game of musical chairs with office locations is also silly and unnecessary. It may be, but the accretion of status symbols is very serious business to ambitious businessmen. They know that a display of status symbols means as much in the corporate hierarchy as a chest full of medals does to an ambitious officer in the military hierarchy. If women are to function equally in the action arena of business they must be able to decipher the code and demand the proper rank insignia for themselves as they progress haltingly up the corporate ladder. To disregard the value of preferred office location is tantamount to selecting a rhinestone ring over a diamond because the first one looked "prettier." Refusing to wear epaulets which identify your business rank because you don't appreciate the genuine value is a disastrous mistake.

Don't Garble the Locality Message

Judging from my personal observations during the past

five years that women have begun moving ahead in corporate jobs en masse, it seems safe to say that many have ignored the status code. Which is to say that they get a better title but they seldom get the visible emblems of rank. If you believe you are making progress on your job, count the number of times you have changed offices. A meaningful promotion almost mandates an office change; a token title and slight salary increase does not give you the necessary authority to handle the new job unless subordinates and outsiders see that you were issued the appropriate rank insignia.

By and large, women are oblivious to rank symbols because so few working women have *any* office privacy that a room of one's own is—in comparative *women's* terms—the ultimate achievement. As long as it's private and "workable," women are inclined to "accept" any office offered them and make the best of the disadvantages that inevitably appear. I know women who have sat in the same office for the past twenty years. I don't know any men in that category. In the industry circles I travel, men who are that immobile were fired or quit years ago.

If you had trouble back in Chapter 6 in diagraming your department's organization chart or evaluating your own advancement potential, try a different tack. Make a floor plan of the office layout and see who's sitting where. This floor plan will guide you in determining which of several people on the same job level are the more favored or powerful—they will have offices very near the top-ranked superior, or they will have established a power enclave of their own in one of the opposite corners. Then locate your own office in relation to these authority areas. You should get a pretty good idea of what your superiors think of you and your potential according to the office they assigned you. It may be more than adequate by your personal comfort standards, but if it doesn't translate into appropriate status according to the male heraldic seal, you are being symbolically downgraded or dead-ended.

Reluctance on management's part to dispense money in the form of raises is understandable because of manifest business concern but unwillingness to issue women their status insignia is propelled by pure male chauvinism. A female corporate politician must be alert to this subtle form of sex discrimination and take steps to alleviate it. Specifically, *ask* for and fight for your office emblem. Before making a final decision on a new job offer, ask to see the office that goes with the job. If you get a promotion, inquire immediately about the new office that you'll get. If you discover you have a lesser status office than your job indicates, ask for the next vacant office in the area you decide you belong in. Keep your eye on possible office vacancies and ask for a more desirable location before they put a newcomer (usually a man) in a higher status office than you have. Keep asking.

One woman I know who was an analyst in the research department of a large investment firm reacted instinctively and volubly when her company moved to elegant new offices in a beautiful skyscraper. She was the only woman in an all-male group and the covey of expensive industrial designers, office planners, and management consultants had settled her in a noisy isolated corner next to the coat room and elevator banks and off-kilter from the rest of the section. "I didn't know anything about office sites," she told me, "but I felt like I'd been slapped in the face. My intuition told me there was something seriously wrong and I refused to take the office. A young guy who had just arrived was settled in an office I liked, so I demanded that one on the basis of seniority. I loved the job, but I refused to appear at the office until I got the right accommodations. They put up a terrible fight, until I was mentally prepared to quit over the issue." Her determination paid off and she got the office space she selected. Later that year, one of the firm's partners brought his wife in to meet her, saying proudly, "I'd like you to meet the only woman in our research department." My friend pointed out that there was now another woman in research but he brushed that aside, saying, "I forget about her. I consider you our only woman because you are the only one who fought for your office!"

By contrast, a lawyer I know got a very good job in the corporate counsel's office of a huge industrial corporation. She's the only woman on the executive floor and since her first day's pro forma expense-account lunch with a few of the senior attorneys she has been totally ostracized by her colleagues. That was easily accomplished because her office (with a spectacular view from the top floor of a Manhattan skyscraper) is on a corridor on the opposite side of the building from the legal department. For all intents and purposes, she is physically as well as psychologically isolated from the counsel's team! Asked why she accepted that office she exclaimed, "Oh, it's beautiful! Carpets six inches thick, anything I request in the way of furniture and equipment, and that astronomical view. They originally apologized for it, saying nothing better was available, but I told them this was perfect. How much better could you get?" But when visiting executives from divisional offices and subsidiaries regularly take her for a temporary secretary, it's partly because she has no rank insignia, no team identification.

Watch Out for Female Ghettoes

The retailing industry and fashion merchandising are typical of businesses where women predominate at lower levels and have moved upward in restricted areas to executive levels (a handful are getting close to the top).

These industries are nevertheless dominated by male status symbols, and clever corporate politicians must analyze the patterns and play the game by classic standards. Many women who have "made it" through the twisted paths of historic blatant discrimination have had no opportunity to learn the game rules in entirety. They are particularly blind to status emblems or to be more precise, they were furnished garbled emblems intended to ghetto-ize them and they now have difficulty unscrambling the hodge-podge.

I will be watching the progress of an executive friend who just began playing the corporate game in the retailing field. Helena has been floating on a relatively high plateau in specialty fashion retailing for the past several years. She's spent her entire career—close to twenty years—working with women colleagues whom she likes and admires. But once she was alerted to the broad ramifications of the corporate politics game, she recognized that her advancement opportunities were nonexistent in the retail complex where she was employed. She found a new job with a national consulting firm, using her expertise in fashion retailing as the wedge to negotiate a 50 percent salary increase. In her new firm all the employees and executives are women except for the vice-president in charge of merchandising, who is a man.

"After doing the same job for years, this offers an exciting new opportunity," she told me. "The company is dynamic, the vice-president, my boss, sounds very progressive, and the other women executives are tops in their fields, stimulating people to work with. Everything about the job seemed perfect—until I evaluated the status symbols, especially office location. I drew diagrams of the layout to analyze where my office was situated. The picture prompted me to reopen negotiations although I had accepted the job. I realized I'd be stalemated again if I didn't insist on the right office locale. I got it changed before I started."

275

Helena's analysis was perceptive gaming. The male vice-president had the most prestigious corner office. She had been assigned a large office next to the corner in the diagonally opposite area. All the women in that area were fashion specialists, too. Each of the corners held clusters of women experienced in various retail specialties. Helena is cognizant of the categorizing which restricts women executives to food, fashion, home furnishings, fabrics, domestics, cosmetics, accessories or whatever gave them their start. "When men start in ties, they don't end up tie specialists—they branch out to merchandising executives. When women start in dresses, they don't end up dress specialists—they're catalogued as high fashion, budget, sports, evening, lounge, or boutique. They are constricted by experience, not broadened to become merchandising generalists." This was the pattern she saw duplicated in the office layout at her new firm—women segregated according to narrow specialties. Since her goal was to break out of overspecialization, she perceived correctly that an office located in the midst of fashion specialists would lock her into the very trap she was escaping.

"I didn't explain *why* I wanted the particular office I chose, after all I'll be working closely with the fashion group at the beginning. But my career plan demands some proximity to the vice-president and a door on the traffic lane to his office. I'll use it for visibility and getting to know the types of merchandising clients who visit the V-P. I intend to move toward merchandising management, and my first successful game move was getting myself dissociated from all the specialty enclaves."

Office location is invested with good and poor status insignia. Office positioning has a direct relationship to job advancement. Certain office locales have high status value precisely because ambitious, aggressive people fight for them in order to get close to the central action area. Once again, watch how progressing men move closer and closer

276

to higher superiors with every promotion. Careers and office insignia move in tandem.

When Status Emblems and Stereotypes Collide, Move!

Not much is known yet about potential boomerang effects when classic male rank symbols are acquired by women. One danger area is already evident—the office adjacent to a male senior executive. Sex, sexism, and female stereotypes can rear up to cancel out all the job benefits and rank status that traditionally accrue to men who achieve this enviable geographic site, which frequently has the invisible logo "next in line for the top job." When a woman earns that status locale, the invisible logo shifts to "she's sleeping with her boss," or "she's a glorified secretary (who's sleeping with the guy)."

Over a lunch, a female officer of a subsidiary company of a financial corporation explained how her advancement was nearly jeopardized because she occupied the office adjacent to the president. "I'm not quite sure how I got assigned to the office since I was one of several vice-presidents who were eligible for it. Probably a misguided attempt to prove they didn't discriminate against women, a laugh considering I was the only woman executive in the entire firm at the time. Take it from me, token women are more to be pitied than censured; like the first child of nervous parents we suffer from the ignorance of our elders." At any rate, she occupied what male colleagues looked upon as the most enviable office in the company, but it slowly turned into nightmare alley for her. "I had an important and demanding job but I was interrupted constantly. Executives from our own company as well as all outside visitors marched straight into my office, left messages for me to relay to the president, explained their problems to me, or dropped in for idle chats if the president got an important private phone call during their appointment."

At first she tried directing the men to the private secretaries and assistants, but each day there were other strangers who made the same automatic assumption—that the woman closest to the top executive was naturally his private secretary or assistant. "I foresaw the end of the line in my career if I remained in that close proximity to the chief executive. I was becoming identified with him and his work, not my own operating responsibilities. My authority was rapidly eroding as I was stereotyped into an 'assistant' or 'helper' to the great man. I decided I *had* to get out of there and I'm absolutely positive I'd never be where I am today, a functioning administrator and top management, if I'd allowed the implied tie-up of superior male–subservient female to continue."

The educational aspect of her story was how she made her moves to solve the problem. She assayed all the male vice-presidents who were equally eligible for the office. From the group she picked the man she disliked the most and who returned the feeling with a vengeance. He was also the one most envious of her position and most blatant about his raw ambition and his disparagement of her qualifications. When she invited him to lunch with her, he was wary and hostile. "He almost choked to death on a piece of fish when I asked him if he'd like to trade offices. He couldn't believe anybody would be so stupid as to give up the ultimate status symbol, and it took a while to convince him I was serious. Once he saw that (swallowing my story that I really *liked* his office better for its afternoon sunshine!), he joined the conspiracy with me to get the trade approved without any flak." Between the two of them they arranged the transfer smoothly and she regained her independence as a line executive. Her male accomplice gained his most cherished desire. "He was in seventh heaven in that office and the

278

superior rank symbol pushed him steadily ahead. My freedom from that office allowed me to grow and develop on my merits and demonstrated performance; we both benefited. Best of all, he turned from an enemy into an ally. He is one of my strongest supporters and advocates."

Porcelain Insignia That Won't Flush Away

Toilets seem to be the major obstacle to women's equality. If you don't think so, you haven't heard the nuttiest arguments against the Equal Rights Amendment (i.e., the ridiculous fear that public restrooms will be co-ed). Or you haven't been faced with employment problems which evolve from the superior status symbolism of urinals. The good news is that women aren't entirely alone trying to revamp this physical hallmark of sexual supremacy; management is a nervous wreck as working women demand equal facilities and senior executives in many institutions expend as much energy on the dilemma of bathrooms as they do on the next Quarterly Earnings' prediction. Porcelain status symbols are proving to be non-biodegradable.

Some companies try to evade the entire subject. To this day, the J. Walter Thompson Company advertising agency refuses to recognize indelicate functions. Its dozens of bathrooms hide decorously behind plain unmarked doors and nary a discriminatory word such as "Men's" or "Women's" sullies its pristine halls or executive offices. Pity the new male client or supplier whose initial contact is a woman executive (if any); the prime executive-to-executive bond has evaporated into embarrassed agony.

Some companies treat the subject like a huge, salacious joke. They are apt to be institutions that have given urinals the most visible priority status. One of the country's largest utilities (hardly the only offender in this category) left no doubt where its sympathies lay by installing men's urinals in spacious rooms off the well-lit hallways. Women's facilities (patronized by vast majorities of the working population) were jammed into dingy, cramped quarters on the unused stairway landings. Female complaints were dismissed cavalierly even though several women had been frightened or molested by rapacious public freaks who crept up the abandoned stairwell. The enraged women got together and organized a pee-in in the men's bathrooms until their class status was upgraded and the bathrooms were switched.

Some companies are just plain scared as women edge closer and closer to a highly prized male status symbol —"the key to the executive bathroom." One of the few women who arrived at this eminence insisted on her executive token and demanded her status key. She promptly ordered the sign changed from "Men" to "Executives." Every so often she pretends to use her key (of course she's the first and only women to collect this rank emblem) just to see what male executive comes bounding out of his office to "check if it's clear." Privately she admits to gleeful friends that she'd never really use it. "I'll never give up my privilege to use the Ladies Room. For one thing, I hear all the juicy gossip that doesn't get on the grapevine, or I hear things before any of the men at my level. But most of all because I'm in a position to help other women. I can get to know women from several departments and keep an eye on the progress of those I admire. Already I've pulled one promising young woman into my department simply from meetings in the bathroom. I'm anticipating the day when the women's bathroom becomes just as powerful a focal point as the men's urinals when it comes to internal political manipulation."

The Queen in the chess set (in case you don't know) can move any number of clear spaces in *any* direction, backward, forward, sideways, or diagonally. A lot of visible status symbols can be collected with that maneuverability.

CHAPTER
11
Deportment at the Gaming Table

The ability to play a game, whether team sports, individual athletic contests, card games (except solitaire), gambling games, board games, or the game of corporate politics is a *social* asset. To become a successful and proficient player you must be popular at the gaming table, you must be someone that others like to play with. When it comes to competitive—that is, social—games, the only way to learn and master the skills is by playing with better players or by getting accepted on a team that plays other teams. This kind of popularity depends on your manners and deportment, much more than technical skills.

Women in general have been exposed to so little in the way of life-preparatory games that they don't know how a popular competitor *acts*, they don't know how to create the impression that they can be interesting, challenging, exhilarating, respected, admired opponents. The social graces that earn one competitive popularity in the gaming world are sometimes called unwritten rules. They are only unwritten because serious players (exclusively men until recently) know them and consider them so basic that no one with common sense would expect to get into a game without observing them. These manners have to do with such things as your posture at the table, the way you handle the playing pieces or equipment, your conversation during play, and your attitude in general. For instance, a bridge player who slouches all over the table, carelessly disturbing the playing surface, would be unwelcome in any foursome. A chess player who didn't know which end of the board was which and couldn't set up the pieces properly would not get another chance to play even with a serious beginner. A football or poker player who didn't understand that a player can (and should) do anything to fool opponents as long as it's not outright cheating would be silently excluded in the future, as someone who doesn't really want to play. Game etiquette has nothing to do with "proper" manners à la Emily Post, it comes from observing the demeanor and attitude that other players find comfortable. In that respect, all game players seem to agree on one unforgivable sin—displaying nervousness or fear, or getting upset. Nobody enjoys playing with someone who can't conceal nervousness and uncertainty. *Doing something wrong* is highly preferable in all forms of gamesmanship compared to agonizing with indecision, holding up the progress of the game, or commiserating with losers, including yourself when you are losing.

In the working game, your office (or worksite) is your seat at the gaming table. It contains all the playing pieces and gear, plus much of the training and practice equipment you need. It is where you display your grasp of the behavior that is looked upon favorably by other players. It's where you practice the etiquette of play which should become so automatic that you observe it as unthinkingly as brushing your teeth. It's not easy for women to learn this social grace because it's often the opposite of everything they've been taught or told. Try to wipe your mind clean of irrelevant preconceived ideas and

approach the task and learning experience for what it is—
a new game you never heard of but want to become an
expert at playing.

Office Decor Is a Tip-Off

The interior furnishings of an office speak volumes
about the current rank of other players. Decor is second
only to physical locale in establishing the relative seating
at the game table. Large companies have administrative
staffs who do nothing but decorate offices, establish
standard models for various levels of importance, and
maintain lists of allowable items down to the finest
detail. Such necessities and amenities as draperies, carpets,
desks, chairs, couches, bookcases, pictures, carafes, wall
colors, or telephones are much more than efficiency or
comfort conveniences. They are also Morse code messages
rapping out player positions.

The slightest changes in office decor can telegraph im-
pending changes in an employee's relative position or
favor. Draperies of better-quality material or exclusive design signal an upgrading as does a carpet or a pushbutton
phone or a solid wood desk in place of veneer imitations
or plastic-topped steel. At high levels, corporate offices are
veritable living rooms, or complete apartments with
private baths, bars, refrigerators, couches, upholstered
chairs, coffee tables, art collections, plants, light dimmers,
television sets, stereo—you name it. Different companies
develop different signals for player identification so that
an elegantly decorated office in a lavish company might
indicate lower ranking than a sparsely furnished one in a
penurious corporation. Decor symbols vary considerably,
so you have to check out your local gamesite to discover
some of the decorations which are unique to your company. In one corporation where I worked, the tip-off to
mounting managerial status was the appearance of the

building carpenter. The aging office layout was a legacy from a long-dead chief executive who believed in unfettered employee communication, so no offices had doors. A later breed of executives, to whom privacy denoted superior position, installed doors as soon as they reached the requisite level of authority. In that company, an ordinary office door became a telling signal that this was a high stakes table.

Your Private Office Is Your Public Game Seat

As I said in the preceding chapter, women are at such a beginner's stage of corporate politics that a private cell barely large enough to contain a desk, a chair, and a visitor's seat represents substantial progress to them. However small, it is up four degrees, a considerable advancement, from the wide open clerical spaces to cubicles, to shared space, to a private office. Not surprisingly they treat it as a peaceful spatial enclosure in which they can work undisturbed in solitary splendor. They look upon it as their personal working oasis, blissfully unaware that a private office is their first visible symbol of player status. Whether they know it or not, their office is sending out signals and these silent signals are informing other players whether they know enough about game etiquette to be allowed to play. Most do not.

An after-hours stroll through any office layout is sufficient to identify female locations. These will be the private offices where windowsills, shelves, and desktops are stacked with papers, folders, magazines, and work in progress. Cardboard boxes, display boards, fabric swatches, samples, print overruns, old clipping books, and similar paraphernalia related to their field overflow the office. Much of the accumulation bears the invisible message "Better hang onto this just in case." By comparison, most men's offices in the same sector will be neat, orderly, and antiseptically free of clutter.

This predilection for saving junk undoubtedly has a historic origin. Traditionally, the "responsibility for detail" has been given to women workers because they are supposedly so "good" at minutiae. (Strangely enough, this female talent for detail work emerges most forcibly when the work doesn't pay much; as soon as exacting tasks are extravagantly compensated—say brain surgery, trial law, or corporate auditing, women miraculously lose their gift and males acquire the facility by osmosis.) Consequently, male superiors are in the habit of turning over their leftover files and business residue to a female subordinate. The female recipients don't question the value of the material to be "kept" nor their duty to keep it; they have been indoctrinated at clerical levels with the importance of filing, never mind what the files contain.

When women enter business at professional ranks, their jobs usually involve paper-producing activities. Writers, editors, copywriters, artists, publicists, customer relations, personnel, fashion coordinators, researchers, and many others generate paper records and background source materials as prime components of their task. Small wonder their offices overflow with evidence of their production. Especially since many have no permanent private secretaries to take care of "the details." But when the deportment of women professionals and executives becomes indivisible from those in a lesser job classification—clericals—the signals emanating from the private office are confused and scrambled.

The aspiring executive woman is engaged in a perpetual battle with hangovers of past discrimination as well as the renegade troops of continuing discriminators. She must take extraordinary measures to insure that her player status signals are registering on the same wavelength as

286

those of comparable or superior men, *and that the message is, "Yes, I'm ready to play."*

Good Officekeeping's Seal of Approval

A private office signifies "executive" in the sense of "potential game aspirant," but the use and condition of the office tells whether the occupant is adopting the stance of a serious player. Game etiquette requires that the playing area be neat, orderly, and free of extraneous items not related to the game. The more you treat your office as if it belonged to someone at a much higher level than you, the more surely you will convey the image of a well-mannered participant. Clerical workers are never allowed to be active players, so it goes without saying that any resemblance to a clerical catch-basin must be avoided.

To find out what experienced players consider proper office decorum, treat yourself to some extensive walking tours around your company. Start as high as you can and travel down the hierarchical ladder checking the appearance of men's offices. As a rule, the higher the status of the executive the neater his office, to the point where it almost looks unoccupied. If the man is not in his office, see if you can figure out whether he is at work but has merely stepped away for a few minutes, or whether he is out to lunch, gone home, or on a business trip. Chances are his office will look the same no matter where he is —uncluttered. That simple exercise shows how little the silent message ever changes, the message which says, "I am so efficient, well organized, and competent that I'm always on top of the work of this office; I am prepared to continue the game from this seat, or to move onward at any moment to a more challenging table."

Years ago I had a friend who was a very successful trade association director. His work took him around the country meeting with corporate presidents and he said he made it a point to schedule his initial meeting in the man's office. "Lunches, dinners, and cocktails are fine once you know a person, but if I have an important business mission I want the chance to size up my man first, and I can do that very rapidly by observing how he handles his office," he explained. Many of his impressions were visceral and subconscious, but he also judged from the obvious.

"The desk of a good executive is clear of papers except for a folder of notes on the subject we are discussing. He's relaxed and at ease and acts as if I am the one person he's wanted to meet. He listens attentively, asks incisive questions, and makes a decision. If he wants more time to think about it or consult associates, he tells me what day to expect his answer and if by phone or letter. I trust that kind of decisiveness and have never been disappointed. The type I've learned never to trust is the harried executive who's obviously overworked. This is a guy who acts surprised to see me although the appointment was made weeks before, or can't remember why I'm here. He keeps shuffling papers around and makes calls on his intercom for more records or just to tell his secretary to do something he forgot earlier. He tries to give the impression that the place will collapse without his vital decisions every minute of the day. Maybe it will, but I can bet he won't make a decision about my topic. Almost invariably this type requires half a dozen follow-up calls or letters before I'll get an answer."

At the time of this conversation my friend was sitting in my little office. I glanced furtively at the double-decker in-box flowing onto a foot-high stack of unopened magazines, at my desk top completely covered with letters to be answered, lists to be checked, mail to be signed, phone calls to be answered, while my ongoing project littered the typewriter table. "Well," I said defensively, "if I had a couple of full-time secretaries, an executive assistant, and hundreds of subordinates, I could get rid of some of this clutter!" He laughed and said he doubted it because I evidently didn't have the knack. Why not?

"There's a trick—or perhaps I should say a rule—that good executives use to keep pace with the daily influx of material that demands their attention. All the *good* top executives I've encountered rely on the same principle irrespective of the number of assistants they have." The trick is: *Never let a piece of paper go through your hands twice.*

Getting the Knack of Expert Shuffling

As with most aphorisms, this statement sounds simple enough—but wait till you try it! What appears to be a routine paper-handling system turns out, in daily practice, to be an endless self-training course in decision-making —the foremost skill demanded of successful management executives. Facility takes time, effort, and constant drill to develop, but the results are immediate; you can measure your improvement by the neatness of your office, but the important changes are taking place in your work habits and your thinking process.

The following suggestions may be adjusted to suit the specific conditions of your job, but the principle applies to any kind of job assignment and any materials. The trick is to practice daily, as speed and accuracy increase with repetition.

Incoming Mail. Try to keep your in-box empty by disposing of its contents after each delivery, but in such a way that no piece of paper ever goes through your hands again. The objective is to read it, act on it, get rid of it, without procrastination and without retracing your decision later. Scan the letter or announcement and if the subject is irrelevant to your activities, throw it straight in the wastebasket. If the information may be pertinent to someone else's job (or if you want to impress a superior or colleague with the quality of mail you receive), route the printed piece to them with a short comment. If the letter demands a response that can be handled by a subordinate or secretary, delegate the task to them.

For responses you must undertake, use the fastest method possible. Answer by telephone if feasible and discard the letter. Or hand-write a short note on the original and return letter and answer to sender. When a formal answer with an office copy is essential (watch this "necessity"; if the topic is legal, money, or authorizations, copies are important, otherwise probably not), write or dictate the answer to be mailed the same day.

Your Desk Calendar. Use your daily or monthly calendar as a schedule reminder. Transfer appointments, invitations, meeting details to your calendar on the appropriate day and throw away the paper announcements. If phone calls are uncompleted, jot the name and number on your calendar for follow-up and toss out the phone slips. Your wastebasket is a major efficiency device.

Periodicals and Publications. Don't be tempted to save dated material. Cull what is immediately pertinent to you and get rid of the publication. Read the table of contents of newspapers, trade magazines, and routed publications. Pass along any which you don't need; skim the few articles that may be important and take notes, clip or reproduce essential material and re-route the bulky remainder. Do not become known as the department's librarian or reference room; utilize your wastebasket or your out-box. If you want to read some publication thoroughly, put the copy in your briefcase or hide it in a bottom drawer for later—but get it off your desk. Whip through employee publications and company announcements immediately, noting especially items on promotions, reorganizations, new policies, retirements, or any information that is vital to your career plan or future advancement. Keep those which may be personally useful, but throw away the rest.

Your Personal File. The only work file worth your attention is the one that concerns you. On the subject of *you*, save everything—but bring it home, don't leave it in the office where you may lose it if you're suddenly fired or quit. Make a copy of everything you do or produce so you can build a portfolio for job-hunting. Keep the original or a copy of all letters, memos, or complimentary notes which reflect favorably on your performance or ability. Write acknowledgments or thank-you letters recapitulating verbal compliments or conversations so you have a record for your personal file. (This technique is known as "covering your ass" when used in business matters that have dangerous ramifications unless the record is straight.) Your at-home personal file should be a documentary exhibit of your successful working history, the source for an impressive sample book to demonstrate your capability and experience.

Corporate Files. Saving company records is not considered a modern management virtue. Executive secretaries today are often appalled at new men bosses whose first order is to clean out and throw away existing files. Male executives who discard or "lose" important documents rarely falter in their climb up the ladder. Those of us with broad experience in Title VII court cases learned years ago what Watergate investigators more recently discovered—that industry records disappear like magic when the contents may be incriminating. In sex-discrimination cases, material favorable to the women (good evaluations, praiseworthy memos, complimentary reports, personnel records) no longer exist; but reports of a deleterious nature have been carefully preserved, just as auditing records document every legitimate $25 lunch but reflect no sign of millions of dollars in illegal bribes or political contributions.

The point is: don't hesitate in discarding material that clutters up your office files or makes your office look like a mess. Conscientious women employees often believe, mistakenly, that keeping accurate reference files is a plus,

291

whereas executive thinking requires discriminating judgment in separating the important nucleus from the discardable chaff. So, once important items are acted upon, the original letter becomes obsolete or outdated—and usually unnecessary.

Neatness Is a Top Social Asset

Maintaining a neat, efficient, and organized office has serious implications for the corporate politician. Its significance is traceable to the basic military mentality of corporate life, to the passion for orderliness which so characterizes military procedures. Remember, your top boss is supposed to be running a precision operation which could pass muster by the management review officers, so any team member who is addicted to spit-and-polish perfection subtly transmits the message that she *understands the system!*

Working Habits. A universal characteristic of office work is comparable to housework—it is never "done." Job tasks could be graphically illustrated with flow charts as a steady or irregular stream of duties. The best executive can only keep pace with current or daily requirements, based on priority decisions. Watch higher executives at work and notice how they approach large tasks without looking overwhelmed. Many, you'll find, are addicted to three-ring notebooks which they keep in closed cabinets. The notebooks contain essential records or references, budget figures, and projections. A supplementary file folder, maybe a computer printout, the notebook, and a yellow legal pad may be the only materials in evidence on the desk. If interrupted, they can close the book, push the files aside, and appear unharried and unperturbed. Women whose daily tasks require accumulated referral materials might well revert to this schooldays system of organization. Otherwise, try to work on only one project or part of a project at a time. Assemble only the tools necessary for the immediate task.

Looking Unbusy. If you manage to get your assigned work done promptly and efficiently while maintaining an aura of relaxed confidence, colleagues and superiors will be intrigued and slightly suspicious. That's good for the practicing gamester because a minor air of mystery is advantageous to a good card player. At the same time, co-workers are apt to drop in to visit you thinking, "She doesn't look too busy." You can practice your executive deportment by giving them your undivided attention for a few moments and making them feel welcome and conversational. Women executives are cut out of so many networks of informal discussion and interoffice gossip that every bit of unsolicited conversation is helpful.

Personal Artifacts. For the ambitious woman, an office should be more like an overnight motel than a permanent residence. As such, its main furnishings will be those provided by the owners (which do double duty as status emblems). Be sure to acquire all furnishings, draperies, pictures, and other accouterments that go with your rank. Check with the office manager or whoever handles such things when you're in doubt. Proudly fill and display such insignia as a water carafe even though you never use it (trips to the water fountain can be invaluable sources of office gossip). Don't dilute the power symbolism of your office with home-decoration goodies. A professional army officer or football player doesn't encumber himself with personal mementoes, nor should an active business game player. Certainly a plant, a gift desk-set, an elegant ashtray, an interesting vase as a pencil holder, a clock are allowable. Family photographs are iffy—if your superiors set the tone, okay; if not, consider it in light of the signals you'll be sending. From women, the messages can be self-protective—"I'm married with a family so keep your distance." Or the message received may be—"She's not a serious businesswoman, her husband and kids dominate her life. She doesn't care about getting ahead."

Clothes, umbrellas, extra shoes, makeup kits, and other personal paraphernalia should be carefully hidden. Although men executives frequently keep a clean shirt or electric razor in the office, you never see these items strewn around in full view. If necessary, take another after-hours tour of your building to observe the acceptable personal belongings for offices. Copy the successful executives at levels above you, not the occasional slob. These observation trips are very helpful to learn the status-symbol codes; soon you'll be interpreting the signals as clearly as your superiors.

Your Boss's Junk. If male superiors try to dump their junk in your office, promptly claim that you have no room for it, no matter how much empty space you have. Tell them *you* cannot foresee any future need for it, or suggest that such valuable materials should be properly guarded by master storekeepers or the general file personnel. If you can't avoid taking it, hide the stuff so well that nobody can find it again. Better yet, throw it away some night after work and be prepared to say "the cleaning people must have accidentally picked it up thinking it was trash." If you don't dare be so ruthless, pile it obtrusively in a corner of your otherwise neat office with a huge sign identifying it as "John Smith's materials."

Promptness Is Good Deportment

Appear for all meetings right on time with a relaxed, confident air, to extend the image that you are so well organized or that your work is so easy for you that it takes no visible effort. This is easier said than done if you have an engrossing job or many demands on your time. A clock in your office may help, but a timer is even better; one of those kitchen cooking timers that can be set for five minutes to an hour, or one of the keyring types that are sold to keep track of parking-meter time. Try to find one that doesn't tick too loudly, but you'll probably have to keep it in a drawer in any event.

If time allocation is a real problem for you, set the timer to clock how long it takes you to do something so your time estimates will become more accurate. Overwork is often self-induced by underestimating time requirements. Use it to remind yourself when to stop working and leave for a lunch date, a meeting, or the end of the day. If someone happens into your office and hears the "ding" go off, you can explain, "That reminds me, I must make a long-distance call now to catch the St. Louis people before their lunch hour." When necessary, the timer can be used to inoffensively get rid of bores and pests with just such an excuse. It may be a while before you acquire a secretary who keeps track of your schedule and reminds you of appointments, but in the interim your personal timer can serve as a mechanical substitute. "Time is money" in the lexicon of upper management, so discovery of your little device will not produce disfavor— only amazement that you are practicing game players' deportment.

Office Memos Are Playing Pieces

Interoffice memoranda are versatile communications instruments. Their surface messages are underlaid and overlaid with symbolism and secret signals. You have to figure out what memos mean in your organization, and then interpret the wig-wag code of the sender before responding. Memos demand individual attention before jettisoning them from your in-box. Some companies breed memos like hamsters. Others bestow them like knighthoods. Some employees write lavish memos in place of working. These boring communiqués from unimportant memo-glorifiers can easily be dismissed with a scrawled note near your name ("Good idea," "Very interesting," "Keep me informed") and returned to the sender who will be satisfied to think you read it. Some bosses demand floods of memos to make them feel important. They ask for a memo on every little thing, which is both annoying and time-consuming, but you have to structure your work to their priorities. The silent message alerts you to schedule one hour after each thirty minutes' productive labor to write a glossy memo about what you did. Such bosses aren't interested in results per se, they are impressed only with performance that can be dramatized in memos.

All companies and most employees play games with memos. The more a company or a manager is concerned about "communication" with the team members, the more likely memos will proliferate. Sometimes everyone gets every memo on every subject under the guise of keeping everyone informed about what everyone else is doing. When the topic does not concern you, these can usually be jettisoned with impunity because once you're "informed" that's all there is to it. In more selective distribution cases the names of the memo recipients are revealing and significant. Seeing your name slide to the bottom of a memo list can be a warning that you're out of favor; or it can mean that a new secretary typed the list any old which-way. Memos, in short, are a powerful corporate communications medium, but the information in the body of the letter is the least important message; what counts is the implied meaning and the direction it is traveling. Who sent it, who got it, who was on the "CC" list—and what kind of response does the sender expect or request?

As a corporate politician you have to figure out the memo game in your company. Don't take the substance literally; combine it with all you know about the various individuals involved and their interrelationships. And don't forget those who are left *out* of the memo; that can sometimes be more revealing than who's on it. When it comes to initiating your own memos, be very careful to cover all your own bases. Never write a memo in anger or disseminate information that could backfire. Once you've put an idea or suggestion into a memo, it becomes the recipient's property and can be appropriated—unless you, the author, carbon interested parties originally. Watch out that you never write anything in an official memo that may haunt you when you request a promotion or raise.

Memos are commonly used by management to initiate plays in the game of corporate politics. "Confidential" information or rumors may float to the grapevine via planted memos which are calculatingly used by management. Usually several executives work in collusion. All decide what information they want to disburse, and the one with the least "reliable" secretary (she who can be counted on to whisper this highly confidential news to a friend, thereby activating the grapevine) is chosen as writer of a "confidential" memo to his management collaborators. Popular subjects of planted memos have to do with projected losses in a quarter (i.e., looks like no raises will be possible) or "plans" for staff cutbacks (i.e., everybody better start humping it lest they be the first to go).

New managers may use memos offensively for a variety of testing purposes. One of my friends got caught in a veritable memo typhoon that almost drove her from her job before she grasped the implications. She's one of fifteen editorial executives (female and male) in a smaller division of a large publishing combine. For several years her section operated rather placidly under a general manager whose idiosyncrasies were well known. All knew, for instance, that the easiest way to sidestep a sticky decision was to write a long memo to the general manager outlining the problem. He took so long to respond that he was viewed as a friendly mortician by savvy executives whose lengthy memos guaranteed interment of any subject they wanted to avoid or postpone indefinitely. Naturally they never wrote memos on matters they favored or acted upon every day.

One day corporate headquarters went on a reorganization binge. A new general manager who was unknown to any of the division staff arrived from another company.

"This new guy went through the place like a dose of Epsom salts. He deluged us with memos; they came down like rains during a monsoon and flooded us all. None of the executive staff was used to this, to put it mildly. We were terrified trying to figure out what was up, but since most of us are ex-writers we had the technical competence to get into the act. Soon the entire place was shitting memos and the tide mounted higher every day. The truly unnerving aspect was that the new manager appeared in your office forty-eight seconds after you sent him a memo! In one cloudburst I found a memo by a woman colleague which had been forwarded to me without comment from the manager. She was criticizing my work and my department! I was absolutely furious and started to answer in kind to justify my operation. Fortunately I was so busy by then trying to get some work done for a change that I put off writing the memo. After some sober thought, I decided I'd had enough of the Holy Memo Crusade if it had degenerated to backstabbing, and thereafter I wrote a memo only if I needed immediate approval for something. That episode occurred months ago and a lot of heads have rolled since then. I'm still there, functioning well under the new management, and finding the innovations very stimulating. I can't be sure, but I'm willing to bet that the Memo Monsoon was a deliberate tactic by the new manager to get a fix on all the strangers he inherited as his key executives. My own fortunes changed for the better when I stopped writing unnecessary memos, including an answer to the nasty one."

Telephone Manners—a Whole New Set of Rules

In most matters having to do with status symbols and game etiquette, aspiring women are well advised to follow the patterns established years ago and faithfully observed by indigenous males. By and large, these symbols and customs grew out of a presumed business necessity and have acquired a mystical property which gives them special meaning today—they are signs of increasing power and authority. Not so with the telephone. The telephone has been treated as a toy by businessmen and only lately is it being recognized as an essential (if not *the* essential) business tool. Consequently, there is no significant business symbolism attached to telephone practices, only an incredible array of time-wasting nonsense that seriously interferes with efficiency, aggravates everybody, and contradicts common sense.

Emerging businesswomen are free to develop their own standards of telephone behavior. There is no reason to copy men's pompous games, which is fortunate in a way because the oneupsmanship mentality (for example, making the other person wait) doesn't work with women executives—they are taken for the telephone operator or secretary anyway, not the imperious executive. Managing the telephone intelligently is a business skill that few executives below presidents have mastered. At top levels, efficient executives install two lines; the first may be the company toy, the second "private" line is the instrument they use as a business tool, the one on which all important calls come and go, the one they answer themselves and dial (or push-button) themselves.

As a long-time heavy user of the business telephone, I am acutely conscious of initial impressions conveyed by phone-answering habits. Most of them are worse than bad, they are insulting and infuriating. After thousands of calls to every manner of business firm, I have discovered that the real status and competence of business executives is in inverse proportion to the number of people one must go through to reach the party. The president of a large company tipped me off years ago on what to watch for. "Always call the highest-ranking executive possible, preferably the president because he'll answer his phone. The minor functionaries are the ones who set up elaborate screening systems; they think it makes them important."

Low-echelon women executives should consider the long-range advantages of perfecting common-sense telephone manners:

—Answer your own phone, identifying yourself with your full name. Callers will love you (or you'll find out which ones resent a woman being in the executive position). You will free your secretary (if you have one) for important work; if you don't have your own secretary, your calls are being screened by a clerk who is uninformed about your job and performs no function except wasting three people's time—hers, your caller's, and yours.

—Call yourself up. When you're out of the office, try calling at several times of day and on different days. Find out what reception your callers get and whether they are put through the idiot's catalog of "Who's calling? How do you spell that? Does she know you?"—all before the caller finds out you aren't there! Leave explicit instructions that in your absence only one question is allowed to those who answer your phone: "May she call you back?" Otherwise your callers may be asked, "Can someone else help you?" as if your job and you are needless extravagances.

—Direct lines. The growing popularity of direct-line extensions is creating a new problem when the individual is not there to answer—passing employees pick up the phone even if they don't know whose line it is, much less where the person is. Apparently the ringing gets on their nerves or perhaps they have orders to answer, but few casual answerers seem to relay messages. That kind of answering is the supreme time-waster and it would be much wiser to let the phone ring till the caller hangs up. Long before direct lines, I worked with an unorthodox executive who treated his extension as a private executive line. He waged a long, witty campaign with the departmental telephone clerk, secretaries, and other employees to convince them he was serious when he said no one was ever to answer his phone. If he was there, he said he'd "talk to the devil if he called" but the intermediaries "would scare the old boy (meaning the devil!) off." If my irreverent friend was not at his desk (and he frequently was not), he left orders to let the phone ring because "anybody who can't figure out I'm not here and doesn't have brains enough to call back" wasn't worth talking to in the first place. I've come to appreciate his philosophy in the past year with proliferating direct lines. At least two executives I call use his system (wittingly or unwittingly) and I much prefer the swift certainty of no answer to delivering messages to strangers who don't transmit them anyway.

—Making calls. There's no logical reason not to dial your own calls except for the time-wasting stupidity you're apt to encounter on the other end. On balance, having a secretary place your call (and getting you on the line after the other person answers) is bad business for women because the called person is in a put-down position (waiting for mighty you to deign to talk). Men use it frequently as a petty power ploy according to Michael Korda's *Power!*, but serious businesswomen can scarcely afford to antagonize outside business acquaintances. However, if some man pulls that stunt on *you*, a woman executive is obliged to retaliate in kind.

—Note to women secretaries of male executives: the telephone is a marvelous instrument to sabotage a boss who expects you to produce in quantity and quality while interrupting you repeatedly to place his phone calls, screen his callers, or relay his messages. By procrastinating sweetly and dumbly, you can delay his picking up the line for several unnecessary seconds on each call, thereby irritating the other party beyond apologies before the conversation starts. You can ask innumerable questions of incoming callers, pretending you never heard of the company or the person (also infuriating the caller). You can calmly tell every caller he's "in a meeting and can't be disturbed unless it's terribly important" even though he's sitting around talking football with some crony (the implication being that the caller is "not important"). Or you can buzz him repeatedly when he *is* in a meeting, asking if he wants to accept a call from so-and-so about such-and-such, meanwhile keeping the caller waiting on the line. Then go back and explain that you asked your boss but he's "too busy" to talk to that caller right now. All this is done with grace, charm, and innocence, of course, but the aggravation quotient of put-down telephone practices is so high that it doesn't take much to put your boss on the defensive trying to mollify important telephone contacts. Meanwhile keep accurate per-minute count of all the time you spend screening or placing his calls in case he complains that you're not getting his typing done. You'll be surprised how many hours a week of your time are devoted to his little game of Telephone Tyrant.

Women executives should remember that skilled phoning is one way to reduce the flow of unnecessary material to your in-box. Use verbal communication to settle, solve, or decide a business matter without engendering follow-up letters. Accepted etiquette requires an initial pleasantry and a sentence or two of polite health inquiry ("How's everything?" "Been to any association lunches recently?"), but the object of a business call is to conclude the business at hand as expeditiously as possible, then hang up. Practice is the best teacher of brevity on business calls and of manners to conclude a rambling conversation— "Yes . . . I'll call you next Tuesday with my answer," or "Thanks for the information, I'll get back to you if I have any further questions."

Unlike internal relationships with colleagues and co-workers, your telephone calls open up the outside business world to ambitious women. Every phone acquaintance is a potential helper at some point in your upward climb. Unsolicited callers bring a wealth of information with no effort on your part, and businesswomen cannot afford to pass up any new contacts or general business information. Keeping control over your own telephone has a further advantage unique to women. You can create the image you want in the office by blocking your personal affairs from the office grapevine. The calculating corporate politician may find it very useful to prevent others from knowing how many times your children call, or your husband, or teachers, or nursemaids, or lovers or doctors, or male friends . . . or executive recruiters.

Entertaining Visitors (Little Ones?)

The protocol for nonbusiness office visitors is obeyed so stringently by working women that they often seem afraid to invite *anybody* to their office. A confident player can be looser than that with adults, but children present a special problem.

In most corporate operations the very thought of chil-

303

dren coming into the business environment is enough to set male management's teeth on edge. No matter how much they gush or pretend, most men hate the sight or sound of children in the office. The place for children (their thinking goes) is home with their mother whose sole reason for being is to take care of the kids and keep them out of father's way as he pursues his world-shaking business affairs. A woman executive sets this anti-female time-bomb ticking each time she reminds male business associates that she is a mother ("Why isn't she home where she belongs instead of butting into men's business?").

Nevertheless, full-time working mothers have a compelling reason to violate this "no-kids" stricture once a year—peace of mind for the children. In a society where some 50 percent of mothers do stay home, young children of working mothers can feel lost or excluded from the family's activities; they have no way of knowing where or what "work" is, although both parents go to this mysterious place each morning. A visit to their parents' offices (but especially their mother's office) can calm their fears, let them feel grown-up and respected, and give them something to brag about to their peers. For her part, the working mother will find it much easier to explain to children when she has to work late or go out of town on business trips, or why she can't be bothered with innumerable phone calls during the working day; they can visualize "busyness" as clattering typewriters, ringing telephones, bustle and activity as people walk about an office and talk to each other or operate fascinating machines.

Ideally you should plan your children's visit to cause the least amount of friction but accomplish all your aims. Quite a few companies let down the bars against children on Christmas Eve day when little work is expected and all employees are encouraged (or not *dis*couraged) from bringing their children to the office and leaving early with them. Obviously this is a situation to exploit because the anti-mother attitude is at its lowest ebb and most colleagues are relaxed and receptive to admiring or amusing children. Of course the children may get the idea that "work" is akin to a big, exciting party, but they also see their mother's office, know where she sits, play with her office equipment, meet the secretaries or assistants whose voices they know from telephone calls, are introduced to co-workers and bosses whose names they've overheard in discussions at home. Thereafter they can picture their mother in a real-life situation surrounded by friendly people instead of imagining that she disappears into a lonely black void.

If your company has no comparable children's day, you'll have to set your own. An hour is more than ample, so plan the children's arrival within the last half hour to hour of quitting. Bring them into your office while you pretend to continue working and answering calls. Control their behavior by impressing them with the seriousness of "work." Their presence will be no secret and the novelty will draw co-workers (especially other women) to your office to see them. Introduce your children to co-workers and your immediate boss (whether he likes it or not, he will be normally curious and feel rebuffed or rejected if you deny him the recognition you have given lesser employees). The top boss need not be included in this "family affair" unless you deem it wise under given circumstances.

Someday in the future, reactionary management may understand that the poor "image" of business in the public opinion polls will never be successfully counteracted as long as children in their most impressionable, formative years grow up with the idea that a business work site is an unfriendly, repelling, and sinister place which refuses to accept them until they are over twenty years old. (Notice how fiercely business opposes child-care facilities on its grounds.) For the time being, individual

305

women are too new and powerless in business to change the indigenous customs.

Once you have grasped the principle that working toward an executive or management job is truly a game, you are better able to understand why successful men *enjoy* their jobs and how they can become so deeply absorbed in the day-by-day byplay. Hard work is part of everybody's job, but women will always work harder than men colleagues if they continue to bend all their efforts toward the technical skills required and pay insufficient attention to the more important elements required of the social competition. Learning the game skills *must* come first for ambitious women because mastery of business technical skills is only gained through playing with and against more accomplished players. To get the chance to play with them, you must look and act like the rest of the team and the recognized experts.

CHAPTER
12

Take Charge
—Assuming the
Habits of
Command

Somewhere along the line, women must develop the habits of command if they hope to advance into positions of real responsibility. Exerting control and authority easily and naturally is a new experience for most women. Like any other skill, it must be learned and practiced. Obviously women have special problems in learning how to be authoritative and self-confident because they must first overcome the disabling effects of female upbringing. Without belaboring the point, which has been well covered by other authors, it is manifest that a woman who has been taught the "typically feminine virtues" of being sweet, helpful, helpless, agreeable, sentimental, loyal, obedient, and self-effacing is going to have more than her share of troubles getting recognized as a competent leader in a business group.

The popularity of assertiveness-training workshops for women as well as the proliferation of books on the subject testifies to women's willingness to rehabilitate their crippled psyches. Shifting from nonassertive to assertive behavior is becoming a current fad. The phrase has been picked up quickly by the Business World, and a favorite management platitude these days is, "Women must learn to be more assertive." Once management hands out free advice to help women get ahead, anyone who is familiar with the corporate politics game gets very leery—there's a catch in here someplace.

The catch isn't hard to find. Assertiveness is a valuable personal trait for women to develop (like motherhood and apple pie, it can be lauded), but it's not much of a threat in the business game. Assertion, after all, means to insist on recognition of oneself, or to maintain your right to legitimate feelings, needs, and ideas by making positive statements. As now taught to women, assertivness means to "express yourself to get what you want but don't make anybody mad in the process; be nice about it!" Especially, warn the assertiveness trainers, don't slip over the line and become aggressive. Assertive is nice, aggressive is naughty. If you are aggressive you are disposed to vigorous activity and are inclined to start an attack or encroachment. Management will buy that trade-off with no qualms—be as assertive as you want, as long as you're not aggressive and pose no threat to established players.

For some unknown reason the personality trait "aggressive" has become identified with the word "hostile" in the female vocabulary, whereas "aggressive" in terms of competitive sports and individual games is distinctly nonhostile. The football or baseball team which plays an aggressive winning game is admired and respected by the opponent team; many fierce competitors on the links and courts and chess tourneys are close personal friends. Champions like other champions. They are worthy opponents. They are aggressive players who are out to win. Aggressiveness is a positive trait for game players.

Nervousness Is a Gaming No-No

As noted earlier, practically all game players despise

308

evidence of fear or nervousness in another player. Anxiety is a communicable disease and if all the players become infected with the jitters, the game will not go well. What this tells you is that other players feel just as uncertain as you, but they cover it up. They will attack and abuse any player whose weakness might shatter their own façade. It stands to reason that women who want to be accepted at the gaming table must put on an act just like the others; they must conceal their nervousness and do their best to *appear* calm, confident, and collected. You don't have to *feel* self-assured to inspire confidence and be in control —you just have to be a good bluffer. A commanding appearance starts by playing a role, a part in a play. Familiarity with the role develops gradually over time; self-assurance comes by practicing before every available audience.

Once again the problem of women's overdependence on intrinsic knowledge or technical competence comes to the fore. You don't assert control over inanimate objects such as skills or technical know-how. You take charge of situations in which other people are involved. Thus, the habit of command concerns the impression you create in front of others. It is a facility which becomes very important as you move up into supervisory or responsible positions where you are playing the game with many other players. Inattention to the impression you create can have a debilitating effect on a woman's advancement because the opinion of other people in the game environment is far more important than your own opinion of what you know or are worth.

When Lynn was promoted to account executive in a large advertising agency, she suffered the inevitable nervousness of a new player in an unfamiliar place. She discovered that her working milieu altered drastically when she lost the anonymity of being one of many women in the creative services and became a frighteningly visible novelty as the only woman in a group of eight male account executives. She couldn't hide behind her "work" any more; she was pinned in the merciless glare of the game-table spotlight. "The temptation to pull back and blend with the wallpaper is psychologically overpowering," she said. "You feel the pressure as everyone seems to be staring at you, literally or covertly. At my first meeting I kind of slunk into the room and took a seat as far from the moderator as possible, in what I hoped was an inconspicuous spot where I could listen unobserved." Luckily for her, she found out immediately that her mousy, self-effacing tactics boomeranged uncomfortably and interfered with her performance. "When I did speak up at one point after our boss directed a question at me, every one of the eight men turned, moved their chairs, and craned their necks to get a look at me. The physical commotion on top of the psychological anxiety drove ideas right out of my head. I couldn't think straight under the intense scrutiny, and I realized then and there that there was no way I could be invisible. A new woman executive is in an exposed position, like it or not, so I decided to stop fooling myself."

At the next meeting Lynn acted more aggressively. She arrived early and took a prominent seat between two men who had no qualms about seeking attention. They had long since figured out which seats were easily visible to other group members without physical contortions. Once Lynn accepted her visibility and capitalized on it, her performance improved. "Just sitting where I could be seen easily got me used to the spotlight, so to speak. Instead of concentrating on being inconspicuous, my energies were freed to pay attention to the business at hand. I felt like a member of the group, not a guilty intruder." Later, when Lynn had to take over as moderator and run staff meetings herself, she discovered that her automatic visibility could be used to gain control of the meeting from the outset. "The time to start a meeting is immediately after you walk into a room or soon after you're seated at the head of the table, when everyone's attention is on you."

Men, incidentally, are often outspoken in resenting this automatic visibility that today's businesswomen have. They fantasize about how well *they* could exploit such a favorable situation. When they see a woman downgrade her advantage, they have ambivalent reactions. On one hand they welcome it—"I told you so, women don't know how to act in business"—but on the other hand they get angry while watching a woman dissipate an advantage they envy. In the game of business only the uninitiated fail to capitalize on natural advantages. It would not occur to an ambitious man to downplay an inborn resource, whether it's height, good looks, or family connections. Today's pioneer women can begin taking command of situations by merely accepting their unique position of being in the spotlight. As they develop expertise and self-assurance they can gradually become more aggressive in exploiting the situation.

Quarterbacking—Taking Control of a Managerial Position

When a woman achieves a promotion that puts her in charge of an operation that she must supervise and manage, she is physically and psychologically exposed. All eyes will be riveted on her, those of her new subordinates and those of superiors who will be watching to judge her in action. In essence she has been given the chance to play quarterback and her future potential will be predicated on how well she calls the signals and how well the team functions under her control. Women entering supervisory management jobs are quite aware of their new responsibilities, but many fail to perceive that their priorities have changed. They often plunge headlong into the task itself, desperate to prove their worthiness and intent on demonstrating their ability. They don't realize that their task has changed—from doing the work to getting others to do the work for them.

Superiors are often more hindrance than help in affecting the changeover. Managers often turn into protective, possessive "mommies" when it comes to promoting women. They act like emotional, overanxious nannies watching their small charge climb the monkey bars, as they wring their hands distractedly and call out: "Be careful; hang on tight; watch your head; don't slip; oh, dear, oh, dear, I'm so afraid you'll get hurt!" This kind of reflex from grown men is too uncharacteristic to be believed. One must assume it is a deliberate pose. After all, an experienced coach (which they all claim to be) knows better than to undermine a player's self-confidence at game time. As a matter of fact, a comparable male who's routinely promoted gets merely a ceremonial coach's slap on the fanny which serves as an indication of support and a boost to morale. Any woman who gets promoted with much hoopla and concern might be well advised to take a skeptical look at the "great opportunity" offered her to make sure she knows who has the ball. Overprotectiveness is a subtle method of undermining one's authority.

Accustomed as they are to being in subordinate positions (and with those unnecessary admonitions ringing in their head), women are apt to look upward when they take over a manager job, intent on proving themselves to superiors. In corporate gamesmanship terms this is known as losing sight of the ball. You can't be looking toward the coach and keep track of the action on the field. In other words, your immediate concern is the action going on with your teammates, your new subordinates. As a supervisor, you are the one calling the shots because the coach has delegated some of his authority to you. Before all else, you must size up the other players and figure out the logistics of the play in progress. The worst play possible is throwing the ball wildly without seeing that someone's there to receive it.

My friend Sharon is one of the most proficient players I know. She has honed her skills at corporate politics in a hot-shot conglomerate, parlaying three successful moves in five years, bringing her to an operating vice-president level. If success is the criterion, she certainly knows what she's doing, so her advice is worth listening to. "I'm a rotten loser," she admits. "I only go in to win, but I've learned that the knack is getting started on the right foot.

"The first thing I do—real quick—is find out if someone who is my subordinate wanted the job I got. That person is going to hate you and can easily destroy an outsider. It's a very delicate situation, but I take him to lunch within the first six weeks. At the beginning I have casual conversations with everybody, trying to find out where the bodies are buried. I'm very noncommittal, leaving a wide-open field for others to make their little moves. I let people bully me—just to find out who they are. I leave plenty of loopholes to identify the slightly mean or pernicious characters. For instance, I'll give an instruction verbally rather than in written form and pretend not to follow it up—just to see if the person remembers it accurately or twists it around to distort my intention, or decides not to follow my order at all.

"I absorb all the personality information coming my way like a sponge, soaking up office gossip, listening to 'helpful' comments by and about various individuals, reading all memos and notes flowing to my office from colleagues and subordinates. You have to get the lay of the land, take the measure of people you're working with. I try to figure out who is allied with whom, who I can probably trust and who probably can't be trusted. Eventually you're going to have to make friends, but not before you've sized up the situation.

"As a manager, the next thing to do is find out how they all work together. Long before you ever set foot in

313

the place, certain norms and customs were established by those already there. How do they address each other? Is everyone on a first-name basis or are there distinctions? Is it the kind of place where the listing of names on a routing slip has enormous significance? How are memos circulated—to everyone or just to those who need to see them? How do the working-hour patterns shape up? Is everyone prompt or do they dribble in late? Are lunch hours strictly observed or is there laxity and flexibility?

"I try to look into their system and find out these little things without rocking the boat too much, in case I have to rock it later with major things like restructuring. If you get people uptight on silly things, you'll never get done what you have to do because they can easily band together against a new supervisor and obstruct you at every turn. There are lots of little quirks in every company or department—just everyday habits—that may seem inconsequential or ridiculous to you, but I found out they can have the most influence on your ability to manage the department, so I spend the first couple of weeks trying to find out what they are."

Sharon has learned to be unusually perceptive and circumspect because her last two moves put her in charge of departments full of men who had never had a woman superior and were none too thrilled at the prospect. She did not make the mistake of barreling in to prove how smart she is or how efficiently she could whip out the work. Many other women, unfortunately, have not learned that lesson, and their experience invariably includes horrendous reports of how one or more persistent enemies frustrate the work production or just make life miserable for the woman supervisor. This common female miscalculation of what's important reminds me of playing jump-rope. You had to concentrate on the task itself to reach a peak performance of 100 jumps without tripping, but there was no question you had harmonious, cooperative turners supporting your endeavor. That's what made it "nice" as a girl's pastime. If jump-rope were a competitive sport, the skilled jumper would be pitted against the turners who would have a certain leeway to foil the jumper by unexpectedly slowing the rope down, speeding up, or whatever. In that case, jumping skill alone couldn't carry the day; attention to the turners would be equally important, as it is in supervisory jobs.

Management men describe the acclimating period immediately after a manager takes over a new job as "getting your feet under the desk." For the first two weeks at least, the only query from a male superior to a new male supervisor is, "How's it going? Got your feet under the desk yet?" meaning, "Have you sized up your subordinates yet? What kind of a team do you have? Are you working out the human relations problems?" It's understood that a successful supervisor is much too busy in the early weeks getting what Sharon calls "the lay of the land" to sit down at the desk ready to concentrate on major tasks. A new woman manager must follow the same rule: deal with the people around you first; only then can you know what you're doing, and what you can count on them doing.

Guard Against Personal Fouls

Despite their best intentions, advancing women cannot escape being victims of personal fouls committed by businessmen who cannot get beyond the stereotyped thinking that relegates any female in their vicinity to old-fashioned roles. The seemingly ineradicable tendency to treat all women as secretaries or servants also has an intended purpose in business (it's not entirely subconscious); by undermining the job or ability of an advancing woman, resentful men can push her backward and interfere with her progress. These are deliberate fouls. But whether such moves are unwitting or purposeful, women must guard against them and be ready to deflect the perpetrator.

By far the most common foul is expecting executive women to take over chores which fall into the secretarial or clerical category. To guard against these moves, women must divest themselves of all equipment that is normally associated with secretarial work. That means pencils, notepads, typewriters, files, and records. To eliminate those ordinary working tools takes planning, but a football player can't carry his play book of diagrams onto the field so he memorizes and studies the plays until he carries them in his head. Ambitious women must do the same.

An exceptional memory is the foremost protection for women who can't bring their recording tools to meetings. Learn to rely on your memory (or pretend that's what you're doing) until you can rush to the privacy of your office to jot down your notes. Never be caught with a pen and notepad in hand. In this case, don't copy male equals who may be scribbling like mad, but take your cue from your boss or whoever chairs the meeting. Watch how they listen, nod, and *remember*—any note-taking is done by their secretary or assistant, not them. Fighting stereotype classifications is more important to the practicing woman gamester than getting the information straight. If you forget a point, you can ask your boss or a colleague to refresh your memory; but if you are thought of as a nonstrategic clerical addition to the staff meetings, you will have constant difficulty being respected as a business equal.

As a practical matter, the elimination of the requisite writing tools helps deflect the immediate glances toward you should the automatic question come up, "Who's going to take the notes at this meeting so we'll have a record?" You can't. You don't even have a pad or pencil. If the situation gets sticky and you are literally ordered to do it, you have to start playing corporate politics in return and try to outfox the fouling player. Make a cheerful (but disruptive) project out of wheedling a suitable pad and pen from one of the men. Discover that you can't write with the proffered ballpoint and must get up to sharpen a pencil. Sweetly ask people to repeat what they said so you can get it down accurately; since you are such a neophyte at this note-taking task, you don't write very fast. "Bill, I'm sorry but George interrupted you so I didn't hear the end of your sentence; what was it?"

If they ask you to be recording secretary, show them how you jump to the task with eager enthusiasm. Interrupt constantly "to keep the record straight." Pretty soon the focus of the meeting will have shifted to the conscientious note-taker; the leader will gradually lose control of his meeting. Precisely. Your objective is to scuttle stereotyped ideas that you are a meek, subservient secretary-steno. You outplay the chairman by raising the status of note-taking to the most important activity of the meeting. This is one job you want to do as lousy as possible, that is, as *unlike* the way any trained clerical would do it. When writing up the notes, make them so long they are meaningless, scramble a few items, and "forget" some important conclusion. Clever game-playing can be much more productive than stubborn resistance in these cases.

Aside from the secretarial connotation, aspiring businesswomen should avoid note-taking because it interferes with their ability to grasp the nuances at the meeting. Most of the significant communication at a business meeting is carried on with voice tones, body language, facial expression, implied suggestions, signs of tension, hostility, or anxiety among players. A change in facial expression can completely alter the meaning of the word spoken. A quick exchange of glances can endorse or dismiss a statement without a word being uttered. All this interplay and human interrelationship are lost to a recording secretary who is forced to look down at a notepad and concentrate on actual words in a string. An ambitious woman can ill afford to lose the *real* conversation under the words; she has too much to learn.

The enduring immediate association with secretarial duties is a typewriter, of course. The executive woman must develop an aversion to typewriters that borders on the paranoiac. Practice your handwriting so people can read your longhand comments and communications. If you must have a typewriter in your office (many women in the writing crafts can't even think without one), make sure it's a little portable perched on a rickety slide-out shelf of your desk. The classic secretarial association is tied to a standard office model typewriter, preferably electric, bolted to a stand. You can get away with an unorthodox portable because the visual reminder suggests college term papers or would-be novelists.

Best of all, don't let them know you can type at all. (If you want to type something personal, for heaven's sake go to the office on Saturday when none of your colleagues is around, or buy your own machine for home.) Women are so careless about this reversion to low-status jobs that some companies warn male supervisors that they may have to wean promoted women subordinates away from secretarial and clerical duties which they continue to perform! Exhibiting proficiency at the typewriter (or shorthand or filing) shows that you don't know the difference between a clerk's job and a potential management position.

The file-clerk stereotype is another one to disabuse. Men automatically assume that a female will "know" where extra copies can be found or lost papers retrieved. Remember the advice on office deportment—if your office looks like a paper blizzard hit, they might realistically expect that you "kept" old records they discarded. Never know anything more than male colleagues about files and records. Pretend you don't know who the file clerks are (though they may be your best friends in the office). When questions come up, call on your memory to contribute to the discussion ("to the best of my recollection, we decided to postpone the project"), but don't produce a single piece of paper that male colleagues can't produce.

Office-wife duties usually take the form of serving coffee to the men assembled for a morning meeting, or calling out for the lunch order, or cleaning up a conference room after food service. Like taking official notes, this mechanical duty must be avoided wherever possible or sabotaged as sweetly and cheerfully as possible. Never volunteer to serve the coffee and don't remind anyone that it is available if none of the men is getting his own. When you take a cup, take your own and blithely sit down; do not be polite by asking a man if you "can get him a cup." Assume these are strong, capable men who can walk a few steps and lift a little cup. Let other men do the obsequious duty of serving the top executive or elderly curmudgeon at the meeting. Those trying to ingratiate themselves will do just that. If a woman copies such ingratiating techniques, she's just another waitress; from her it's *expected*, not treated as a special favor or politeness.

There are times when an available woman is implicitly ordered to do the honors as hostess, wife, and waitress. When you can't avoid it pleasantly, do it carefully—but do it terrible! Turn into the nervous, fluttery, oversolicitous hostess. Slop coffee into saucers and onto tables by overfilling cups, forgetting sugar, putting cream in the wrong cups. Make a big commotion as you clean up the mess and offer to get a properly unseasoned cup for the non-sugar man. Rattle on with insipid comments. "I'm so sorry about the milk, I'm not very good at this sort of thing," or "You sound just like my husband, he won't let me touch the coffee at home because he doesn't like the way I serve it." They may not say much, but they will eventually get the idea that (a) you don't want to do it; (b) they are putting you into a subservient role unrelated to your job; (c) it's more trouble than it's worth to have you mess up the conference table with the goddam coffee.

Sometimes women are afraid to act incompetent and flighty for fear they'll create the impression that they are equally incompetent at significant, responsible tasks. That sounds reasonable and it would be true if women were actually accepted as viable business partners on the active team. They are not yet in that psychological position and this is a game. The pitcher or first baseman does not gain his credentials by substituting as the best water-boy or bat-boy the team ever had. Nor does the bat-boy get to be pitcher because he's so terrific at handing out bats. Never forget that team positions are specific assigned duties, highly restricted in function. The symbolic impact of diverting your concentration from your explicit responsibilities to minor tasks tends to classify you as an undependable teammate—who can be sure you won't run off to pick up trash on the field instead of concentrating on your team assignment?

Smart Players Promote Themselves

A woman who sits in her office doing a marvelous job will be noted with appreciation by one person—her boss, who will probably be taking all the credit for her excellent work. This, of course, is his right by virtue of his superior rank. Essential as it is to develop a compatible working relationship with your immediate boss, that classic situation puts you in a dependency position because your immediate supervisor is in legal control of your future. If he or she is a good player who is moving ahead steadily and bringing you up in the vanguard, that's fine for a while, but you must realize that tracking another executive always means that you are in the subordinate, dependency position. It takes an exceptional executive to "cut loose" a capable assistant or collaborative subordinate at higher levels. Each woman has to gauge the dangers and advantages of such situations for herself.

If, on the other hand, your immediate boss is a clear loser, the ambitious woman's problem is to make herself and her work visible to others besides her immediate boss but *without breaking the chain-of-command* commandment. That means you can't go over your boss's head directly to impress the boss's superior. But you can go sideways in the hierarchy at any level without breaking the rules and indirectly impress higher bosses. Working women should make deliberate efforts to expand their personal and working contacts to people in other departments and divisions of their company; you never know where a new job may open up. There are few jobs that don't dovetail with the work or functions of another department. Capitalize on these to make yourself known to others in the corporation, to find out how various operations fit into the overall picture, and to create cooperative ventures when the situation warrants or can be so stretched. If your immediate boss is a real dunderhead, these lateral departments may be having trouble getting cooperation from your sector. You might serve as a conduit for them to reach your ineffective boss if you can help them manipulate work through your department. Just watch that you don't infringe on your immediate superior's area of authority while doing it.

The way to gain visibility at corporate levels far above your departmental rank is by watching for opportunities to volunteer on corporate-wide do-good projects. These must be *policy* projects which are the baby of some top officer. Things like the Blood Bank, the United Funds collection, the Red Cross drive fall in that category. Some top executives have private philanthropies that they push, and many chief executives put the whole weight of their company behind selective community affairs. These are the places to "volunteer" your eager efforts because the drive will be coordinated by an officer of the corporation and you'll work together with existing or upward-striving executives (mostly men) that you have no other opportunity to meet. Granted that the task you perform will probably be menial and rather clerical, but it opens the door for you to meet all kinds of people legitimately, outside your boss's orbit. (P.S.: If your boss volunteers for the drive and attends all the meetings but then orders you to do the thankless clerical collections in your department, revert to your brainless idiot act; do as lousy a job as possible to make your boss look bad because *this* is a personal favor you're asked to do, not a part of your team responsibility. It is outside the hierarchical chain and the deference rules don't apply.)

As a general rule, women must be extremely cautious at "volunteering" to do anything in the business milieu because of the stereotype that women love to be volunteers just "to help other people." All your volunteering must be accompanied by an ulterior motive: what will it accomplish for *you*. With that in mind, stay miles away from volunteer projects that are employee-initiated and don't require a corporate policy decision. Collecting dolls for orphans at Christmas or taking handicapped children to the circus are typical. These smack too much of "women's work" and the motivating force behind them is supplied by humanitarian employees, not the corporate big-wigs. Donate to and support such activities but don't offer to help with nitty-gritty details; they don't need you anyway; lots of employees enjoy doing these things, so let them.

Public Appearances Build Prestige

All practical career plans must focus outside your present company as well as within it. To become known in your industry or trade, it's important to join professional societies, trade associations, or local industry lunch groups. If your company won't pay for it, pay the dues yourself and consider it an investment in your job future. Of course, the contacts can be very important, but you can extract much more than friendships from an organized group: you can use it as a training ground for practicing your management skills. This is possible because a professional or trade organization functions as a loose, rather sloppy hierarchy. You should join such societies with the express intention of becoming president of the organization. The effect may be time-consuming and frustrating, but it is a cheap way to learn the problems inherent in managing a group of people, motivating and persuading them to do something you want, and manipulating the entrenched officers and power figures in the group as you work your way in. Pick an organization that is job-related so that your activities reflect favorably on your corporate employer while your local "fame" reflects only on you.

Many people complain that their jobs are dull, repetitious, and unchallenging. To be honest, most jobs are exactly that. To keep a job interesting, you have to keep on the move, aiming for a long-range goal. As long as women were excluded from the upward mobility track they were rooted to one spot, literally buried to their necks in the shitwork of corporate life. But now they have a chance to participate in some of the fun of working—getting into the limelight of the game. As the game expands to larger playing fields, the player too faces new and interesting challenges. Fresh vistas open up as people and human relations become factors in the game. Playing different parts in a repertory theater group is great fun, but the deep satisfaction comes when the public audience appreciates the play. That facet of the game of corporate politics which plays to the grandstand prevents a job from settling down to a dull routine. All you have to do is assume the habits of a star player. Women are experts at playing roles; as they learn this game, they should be great at outwitting the pros.

CHAPTER
13

The Uniform
—What to Wear
as an Active
Game Player

If you were a comedian or cartoonist you'd probably have at least one sure-fire joke in your repertoire based on women's clothes. Unlimited mileage seems possible with variations on the "She didn't have a thing to wear" theme. Lampoons about women's indecisiveness and procrastination when it comes to selecting an appropriate costume for an important occasion are rampant, as are satires on women's flights into shopping expeditions to cure depression and loneliness. Masculine audiences are hugely entertained by visions of women making fools of themselves cavorting in ridiculous getups that are annually ordained by fashion moguls. Yet men never protest too violently except for expressing mock horror at the outrageous bills for these female fancies. As men see it, women's fashions are like trips through the fun house at the amusement park— harmless diversion for the fickle sex.

By alternately encouraging and disparaging women's interest in clothes, men gain a feeling of superiority, as much as to say, "What else can you expect of silly women? We men can't be bothered with such fashion frivolity; we have important things to do in this world."

Let me tell you, nothing could be further from the truth. Men are *much more* attentive to their clothes than any woman. For centuries men have deluded women that clothing styles mean nothing to them. But if you look around you'll see that men can't pursue the most ordinary of their male-exclusive activities without just the right clothing. Look at policemen, garbagemen, doormen, clergymen, jockeys, firemen, Shriners, or the Ku Klux Klan to get a slight appreciation of the importance of clothes to male bonding.

Business executives—the proprietors of the corporate hierarchies—are the most clothes-conscious of all. They are the acknowledged arbiters of men's fashion and they accept that responsibility with utmost seriousness. It is no accident that dressmaking is treated as an inferior craft to men's tailoring, nor that clerks who sell women's dresses are paid less than men's department clerks. The pay disparity is not solely due to sex discrimination; department store management insists that the items sold in women's dress departments are less prestigious and valuable than items in men's haberdashery (even though prices may be higher in the women's section).

Men's Clothes Are Identifying Uniforms

For more than five years during my promotional career I plunged headlong into the Loch Ness of men's fashion hoping to disgorge the mythical monster of organization conformity. My client was a quality men's suit manufacturer who distributes under his own label but is also a private-label manufacturer for leading specialty and department stores across the country. (Private-label manufacturers produce the suits that are sold under designer or store names.) The effort was professionally fascinating (only two other women were connected with that field), highly educational (I'm just realizing how much of my

326

business knowledge was gained during that stint), but thoroughly frustrating from a marketing viewpoint—the more things change in men's fashion, the more they remain the same.

The truth is, in the male business world there is not and can never be any serious interest in fashion as women understand it. That's because male business garb is nothing more than a standardized uniform. It is no more changeable as a matter of individual choice than the daily uniform of military personnel or the team garb of baseball, basketball, or football players. You can easily see why, now that you understand the underlying military and team sport foundation of business hierarchies. In every branch of the armed services, the team of officers is distinguishable from rank-and-file troops by the style and design of their uniforms; further gradations in rank and authority are visibly announced by tiny ornamentations added to the uniforms, the insignia. In business, men's clothing performs the same function. Your male boss's and colleagues' everyday work garments are loaded with symbolic and psychological import.

A young friend is one of two women management interns in the corporate headquarters of a large chemical company whose nonclerical employees are almost unanimously male. When riding the elevators with her fellow trainees she noticed that the men would occasionally stop talking business when certain other men were on the elevator. Mystified, she asked, "Who were they?" Her associates' response was, "Who cares? But they don't work for our company." To her the men were indistinguishable from the thousands of male company employees, so she suspected her co-workers were putting her on. It was possible to test their convictions because the company had sublet several floors to other business tenants. She was astounded to discover that the men her associates singled out invariably got off on one of the tenant floors. She is learning to spot the subtly different "look" about the

327

strangers, but she can't articulate what makes the difference. Nevertheless, she is far ahead of other women in business, most of whom are oblivious to the panorama of class, job, and corporate distinctions passing before their eyes daily in the costumes worn by male business associates.

If you have any doubts that men's business suits are team uniforms, you can test for yourself. Follow my friend's system if you have a similar situation in your bank of elevators. The idea is to decide upon entering which men will exit on noncompany floors. This is not the easiest way to start off because departments within the same corporation can adopt subtle variations of the main uniform to distinguish local team groups. For instance, men in accounting might have a different "look" than men in advertising or sales. You will see many styles of men's dress, ranging from dark, conservative suits to well-tailored high-fashion outfits to loudly patterned noncoordinated sports jackets and flamboyant ties. Low-echelon or unambitious men are apt to be those who take a lax attitude toward their clothes symbols (as noted before, not all men are equally ambitious or intelligent). Executives, however, and perceptive junior executives will be noticeable for their neat, uniform look. Lobby-watching is a better exercise for beginners. You can try it in the morning when people are coming to work, any noontime when men are leaving for lunch, or after work when employees are going home. Stand or sit wherever you have an extensive view of the passing parade and watch how the men are dressed. Judging only from their wearing apparel and the impression it makes on you, try to guess what their job title or occupation might be.

What you'll discover after one or two sessions of lobby-watching is that you can quite easily distinguish top-level executives from lower-status men. You won't have to check your observation; you'll *know* you're right when you decide, "*That* man has a very important job." The

328

status symbols will be pulsing loud and clear from his costume even though you don't know how to decipher the code. If you lobby-watch in a small office building which houses several companies in different industries, you may find yourself able to distinguish male employees of one company from those of another merely by scrutinizing their clothes. Should you be located in a suburban complex where all men obviously work for your company, you can try a sophisticated variation of the same exercise. Station yourself near the parking lot and try to separate those men who work in one building or department from those who walk toward another building; which men work in the executive suites, and which in the test labs? A further refinement of this exercise is to scrutinize visitors in a main reception room and try to guess who in your company they have an appointment with. It may surprise you how perceptive you are. If you are familiar with your own executives you're apt to find that their visitors "look" like them in costuming.

Now try any of the above exercises with passing women and see what happens if you try to guess job status and team affiliation from their clothing!

Deciphering the Uniform Code Symbols

When you consider that the entire male sex wears the identical basic business outfit—suit, shirt, tie, shoes, socks —you can appreciate the exquisite care it takes to turn these stark modules into meaningful code symbols that spell out class, rank, team, and star status. Male players *must* pay inordinate attention to minuscule details, and successful men do! As a result, a male business outfit is a virtual hieroglyphic tablet composed of tiny picturegraphs, every one of which contributes to the overall message conveyed by dress. Seemingly innocuous details in a suit, such as a fractional narrowing of lapel width, a minute

329

identation in seam or dart tapering, an inch difference in vent height, a smidgen less shoulder padding, the stitching on buttonholes, a fingerbreadth variation in jacket or trouser length are enormously significant. Tremendous import is conveyed by color and fabric, each of which trumpet signals through almost imperceptible gradations of hue or shadowy suggestions of stripe or plaid designs. Proper fit is crucial, and men's suit manufacturers are graded for "quality" according to the amount of hand-tailoring they put into the finished garment which insures that the shaping will hold up. In effect, quality workmanship consists of sewing as many sacred hieroglyphs as possible into the business uniform. The suit is the master power symbol, but the rank message can be distorted if the caste marks are not painstakingly reinforced by matching emblems in shirts, ties, shoes, and socks. All five elements must be expertly coordinated to achieve the total symbolic effect. The wrong shirt or tie can make a disastrous mess of a perfect suit.

Women have been brought up in total ignorance of this male hieroglyphic dress code. Inasmuch as women were previously denied access to the realms of money and power, the only place where rank symbolism in clothing is used, their ignorance didn't matter. But women who intend to move forward into the executive levels of business must be able to read the heraldic seals of the business knights and understand the role of clothing in the socioeconomic game. Fortunately for aspiring women, these secrets have recently been made public by John Molloy in a revealing book, *Dress for Success* (New York: Warner Books, Inc., 1976). Because this is a book by, for, and about aspiring men, it is a revealing distillation of business initiation rites in the male culture. It is a veritable dictionary of symbolic dress terminology translated into everyday lessons on how clothing emblems are displayed and manipulated. From it, women can learn how businessmen judge each other, and recognize equals, by

330

their uniform dress insignia. It is noteworthy that one of the dress rules for success explicitly warns men: "Never wear any item that might be considered feminine." Under the male rules women have a long way to go to learn how to modify female fashion into an acceptable uniform for the corporate game table.

Women Don't Appreciate the Seriousness of Fine Points

Everyone in quality menswear retailing knows that serious businessmen shop carefully and buy their own clothes. They fanatically repulse any input from wives, girl friends, or any other women. Women don't know anything about men's work clothes despite their own lifelong concern with fashion and their intimate relationships with men who worship status-identification clothes. They can't know because they have not been privy to the upper reaches of the corporate hierarchy where an executive's competence is judged as much by the insignia he wears as by the work he performs. Female influence in a man's wardrobe can be spotted instantly by attentive men and it is always a subject for derision and put-downs.

A high-status corporate wife told me that her twenty-year marriage to a successful, ambitious executive literally exploded over a button. One evening her husband came home in a rage and threw his white shirt in her face. He viciously accused her of tampering with his clothes (which she had been forbidden to touch for years), specifically flailing her stupidity for sewing a button on his button-down shirt collar. The replacement button had only two threadholes instead of the mandatory four holes and his boss, the chief executive officer, had noticed and maliciously twitted him about it all day. In point of fact, she was not responsible for the terrible deed since his shirts were always done in a Chinese hand laundry, but his violent reaction to such an insanely trivial item started her

331

on the road to divorce. Despite twenty years of exposure to him and his business peers, she could not comprehend the significance of the episode nor the reason for her husband's fury.

She is not alone in her inability to perceive the gravity of quasimilitary dress conformance. All women who persist in buying gift ties for men, or fancy colored shirts or "pretty socks" or even accessories such as belts, wallets, or jewelry, are running a terrible risk that the loving presents will be hidden or given away. The male recipients may appreciate the sentiment, but you can't give a corporate colonel a set of lieutenant's bars and expect him to wear them on his tour of duty; he would demote himself symbolically. Physical rank symbols such as office locale and furnishings are issued by the management, but each officer and team member is personally responsible for his uniform and its ornamental insignia. An executive's work clothes are not guided by comfort, looks, attractiveness, taste, or novelty—they are responses to the dress orders of the day. His voluntary compliance can be crucial to his success. Upcoming women are also being judged for future potential on the basis of dress. The trouble is, nobody knows what criteria to use— not men or women, not management policy-makers nor functional team coaches. So far it's been much easier to avoid the issue by saying "She doesn't have the temperament for management" than to admit that corporate officials progress literally by the seat (or anyway the fit) of their pants more surely than by their ability or brains.

Women's Apparel Is a Badge of Servitude

Men's clothing is not unique in assigning attributes to its wearers; women's clothing is historically symbolic, too. As far as I know, no contemporary feminist has researched the subject (no nonfeminist would care), but women who are moving into the male world of work must begin to pay attention to the symbolism of clothing.

Why are men's and women's clothes so different? Why, as a woman, do you wear what you wear? What is your conscious or subconscious motivation each morning as you dress for work? Why not just wear your bathrobe?

The phenomenon of sex differential in wearing apparel intrigued Lawrence Langner, a prodigiously successful businessman who was also an erudite scholar, a popular playwright, and a perceptive social observer. His many-faceted talents led him to the theater where he founded the Theater Guild and the Shakespeare Festival at Stratford, Connecticut. The importance of costumes to theatrical productions and the social significance of costumes impelled him to study the meaning and psychology of clothing throughout history. In 1959 he published his remarkable psycho-history of clothing through the ages, *The Importance of Wearing Clothes* (New York: Hastings House). Several years before the current wave of feminism erupted, his studies led him to the following conclusion about the marked dissimilarity between men's and women's clothes:

Contrary to established beliefs, the differentiation in clothing between men and women arose from the male's desire to assert superiority over the female and to hold her in his service. This he accomplished through the ages by means of special clothing which hampered or handicapped the female in her movements. Then men prohibited one sex from wearing the clothing of the other, in order to maintain this differentiation.

Langner traced his hypothesis as far back as Spanish Levant rock paintings, circa 10,000 B.C. and followed the evidence through subsequent ages, civilizations, and cultures. He found the primary purpose of women's dress throughout history was to prevent them from running

333

away from their lords and masters. The ancient Chinese bound the feet of growing girls to hopelessly deform the adult woman's feet; African tribes weighted women's legs with up to fifty pounds of "beautifying" nonremovable brass coils or protruding metal disks; in Palestine women's ankles were connnected with chains and tinkling bells; Moslems swathed women in heavy, opaque shrouds from head to toe; upper-class women in Venice and Spain had to be assisted by pages when they walked in their gorgeous gowns because of the fashionable chimpanies or stilts attached to their shoes—some as much as a yard high!

The only exception to foot crippling was found among nomadic tribes where women were forced to keep up with their men during the seasonal migrations. In these groups, the women were the beasts of burden, walking with the animals and loaded almost as heavily with household goods. They could walk but could not run far.

In Western societies the ubiquitous hobbling device for women has been skirts, usually accompanied by dysfunctional stilted shoes. Although skirt styles changed over time and in various societies, skirts of all kinds served to encumber women. Skirts that consisted of long robes reaching to or below the ankles hampered movement by entangling the legs in layers of heavy textiles. In more "modern" times straight fitted skirts effectively bound the knees or ankles together to impede free stride and enforce an awkward, staggering gait. Whatever the society, skirts for females were characterized by their impracticality, inefficiency, and uncomfortable designs. Not only walking but sitting, bending, stooping, and climbing were totally enjoined via "female" dress. Utility, comfort, ornamentation, or sexual attraction has nothing to do with why females wear skirts or other distinctively "female" articles of clothing. These garments were invented thousands of years ago by men to label females as dependents and to "keep them in their place." In consequence, "female" apparel carries a universal symbolism of servitude—the badge of subservience.

In contrast the exclusive male clothing in every society where women were constricted consisted of divided garments—trousers or knickerbockers—which permitted free, unrestricted movement while protecting the wearer's extremities. Men exerted superiority over women by laying exclusive claim to clothing which gives the greatest mobility, freedom for action, and self-protection.

At all times, from earliest societies, women were prohibited from wearing the clothing of males—and vice versa. The penalties for breaking the strict laws against transvestitism ("a morbid craving to dress in garments of the opposite sex") were (and are) severe. In Deuteronomy, the Old Testament thundered the "moral" imprecations which many women feel bound by even in the twentieth century. "A woman shall not wear that which pertaineth unto a man, neither shall a man put on a woman's garment."

Despite these savage laws and vicious punishments, women have periodically rebelled against their enforced clothing shackles, especially skirts. Early American feminists of the 1850s took up the issue of women's dress reform. Amelia Bloomer is the best known of the many who took to wearing short skirts or tunics over loose trousers gathered at the ankle. "Bloomers" became the derisive term for any divided skirt or knickerbocker dress. One optimistic feminist, Helen Marie Weber, told the Women's Rights Convention of 1850 in Worcester, Massachusetts that, "In ten years time male attire will be generally worn by women of most civilized countries." She was at least a hundred years off in her prediction; it has taken until the 1970s for women to dare to flout the age-old inventions of man to keep her inferior and immobile.

There are still corporations that issue edicts to keep women employees in their place by forbidding women to wear slacks or pants suits to work. Such a company

335

policy is telling women employees that they are inferior beings whose only status in the corporate setup is to serve their male masters. The clothing symbolism says: "You have no mobility in this corporation." No woman who understands the significance of corporate status symbolism would be caught dead working for such a company. Displaying a blatant badge of servitude is no way to progress in the male corporate milieu, but that is exactly what "female" dress codes dictated by men set out to accomplish.

Dressing for Success—Female Style

Given all the historical, psychological, cultural, and social factors that impinge on the personal dress habits of women, there is, as yet, no clear-cut solution to the problem ambitious women must face in inventing a suitable costume for their business role. (Anything goes outside of business situations for both women and men; our concern is limited to work costumes.) Given my personal orientation in male business fashions, plus my lifelong abhorrence of "feminine" fashions, I am convinced that the most important consideration for women is the underlying symbolism of clothing. There is no question in my mind that many women are held back in their job progress because of their inattention to dress. Or rather, their introspective evalution of what they wear. In business you are not dressing to express personal taste; you are dressing in a costume which should be designed to have an impact on your bosses and teammates. If your clothes don't convey the message that you are competent, able, ambitious, self-confident, reliable, and authoritative, nothing you say or do will overcome the negative signals emanating from your apparel.

My personal observations of women at work, plus my own experiences over many years, plus the opinions of increasingly successful women at work today are all I have to go on when proposing the following suggestions for guiding women toward a female business uniform style. I pass them along not as definitive rules but as the genesis of a practical, symbolic movement toward revitalizing women's perspective on "proper" attire for management executives, female.

Be Aware of the Uniform Concept. An amazing number of women dress wholly at variance with the "uniform" of their male associates. Your first prerequisite is to study the attire of men in your department or company. For instance, if the important men wear dark, conservative suits with white shirts and rep ties, you do not "fit in" if you are partial to busy prints, exuberant colors, extravagant hats, mod fashions, or lacy, frilly blouses. You may be a genius at that business but I guarantee you will never make it far up that hierarchical ladder. On the other hand, if you work for a go-go company where hard-driving male executives have adopted high-style Italian jeans, expensive leather boots, and suede jackets as a trend-setting uniform, you are an eyesore if you appear in inconspicuous navy knits with sedate pumps and a string of pearls. You may have exceptional talent but you will be "hidden away" far from the male executives in a dead-end service job, kept away from the gaming tables.

Keep an eye on the costumes of *superiors* to ascertain the "tone" or "look" that is voluntarily adopted by upward-moving men. Be very careful not to dress in conformity with lower-echelon jobs. If your company has a written secretarial dress code, executive women must *never* obey it. They will instantly ally themselves with the clerical ranks rather than executive or supervisory ranks. One woman told me how the point was accidentally brought to her attention, although she was thoroughly confused when the incident occurred.

She had continued to wear what she described as "attractive, feminine dresses" when she was promoted to her

337

first true executive-level job. She did a certain amount of traveling and decided she could be more casual and comfortable on airplanes. One day she joined her boss at the airport wearing a navy pants suit. When her boss came toward her, he too was wearing a navy suit that looked almost identical. "I blushed in embarrassment," she said. "We looked like the Bobbsey Twins and all I could think of was how angry women get if somebody else has on the same dress. I think I was afraid that he'd be mad at me." But her boss didn't react that way at all! Quite the reverse; he approved of the way she was dressed although he never said a word. "I could sense a change in his attitude toward me. For the first time in two years he was relaxed and comfortable traveling with me. It was as if he finally accepted me as an executive with the firm and not some secretary he was forced to accompany. The only thing different about me was the clothes."

Dresses versus Suits. Instinctively for most of my working life I preferred two-piece women's suits to one-piece dresses. For reasons I couldn't explain there was a feeling of defenselessness or nakedness about dresses when all the men in the room wore jackets. When you think in terms of symbolism, it seems quite obvious that a man's jacket is his "mantle of authority." The first thing a man does when preparing for a business meeting or visiting his boss is to don his suit jacket. Many women executives unconsciously adopt the idea in their favored work clothing. Some wear dress costumes with a matching or contrasting jacket. Some wear sleeveless tunics which seem to serve the same purpose. Others use sweaters by wearing twin-sweater outfits or merely carrying a jacket sweater over their shoulders. The current fashion in "layered looks" is possibly a recognition of this authority-mantle concept. At any rate, a separate jacket or shoulder mantle of some nature (a shirt over a T-shirt or turtleneck sweater has somewhat the same connotation) gives a feeling of strength and control to women's appearance.

338

A woman who hopes to manage affairs, control subordinates, and exert authority must avoid any kind of dresses which portray her as weak or indecisive. Any taint of the "little girl" look is anathema—pinafores, ruffles, bows, cute prints, flouncy skirts, clinging fabrics, or distinctively "feminine" frills will contradict any effort to be viewed as forceful.

Skirt Suits versus Pants Suits. As far as I can see, there doesn't seem to be any difference whether a woman chooses skirts or pants to go with her jacketed costume as long as the skirt is appropriate for her daily activities. That means the skirt must be pleated or flared enough to allow a free stride. Walk around in your skirt before buying it to make sure you can get into a car, mount the bus steps, climb stairs, or get on the commuter train without looking awkward, ungainly, or inept. A clumsy or mincing gait suggests that such a person may be clumsy or inept in other ways.

Pay particular attention to the skirt when you sit down. Test it in a mirror and see if it rides up above your knees or otherwise disturbs men, who all have an innate impulse to look between your legs. Assume that you will be seated on an open stage or head table at some point in your business rounds, so check that the skirt will not force you to concentrate on pressing your knees together or otherwise protecting your genitals from male peeks. If the shoeshine man comes around and you don't dare put your foot up to join in the ritual because of your "immodesty," that skirt is no good as a work uniform. On the other hand, voluminous skirts which get caught in doors or overhang chairs are equally inappropriate. In short, if your skirt distracts your own attention and observers' attention from the business matter under discussion, it is not acceptable as a work uniform.

Pants suits are booming in popularity with women for good reason. Once a woman starts wearing pants suits she finds it very difficult to go back to skirts and dresses. Pants serve the same function for women as they do for men. They give absolute freedom of motion, allow you to sit, stand, run, or bend over without worrying about how much "shows" or adopting all the female contortions that impede physical movement. But pants suits alone don't add up to a team uniform. There are many other details to watch when adopting this once forbidden male apparel.

Attention to Fit. Many women think they look terrible in pants (and many do) because they don't know how pants should fit. They must fit perfectly, just as men's do (or should). Relatively few women can buy a pants suit without having one or both the pieces altered. Women's pants should have a fitted waistband (not an elastic stretch which fits everybody and nobody), and the creases must fall straight to the floor. If you have acquired a lifelong habit of walking in a typically female knock-kneed position, pants will not hang right. Watch men in jobs above you to see what length they wear their trousers and lengthen or shorten yours to conform. A "high-water" look (i.e., so short your socks show) has always been the sign of a hayseed.

Suit jackets, too, must fit perfectly. Men notice those things even if you don't. I vividly remember my initial encounter with a clothing executive when I first entered the men's fashion promotion field. I was wearing a good-looking tailored woman's suit which I thought was very appropriate. The first thing he did was grab my jacket at the back of the neckline and say, "This thing doesn't fit you at all! What kind of a tailor do you have? The collar should lie flat with no bulges. Also, that shoulder seam hangs over a half-inch too far." I had never thought about such "minor details," but I immediately found myself a men's tailor, and that dear little old man gave me invaluable lessons in how clothes should fit, and can be easily altered by an expert, preferably one who tailors men's suits, until they feel as comfortable as a second skin.

Watch Your Fabrics and Finishing. A big part of achieving the "uniform" look is matching the fabric and quality of male colleagues' clothes. If your boss wears $400 wool suits, you are nowhere near the "uniform" concept in a $69.95 suit of polyester. One woman executive told me that the first thing she did when getting a promotion to a managerial position was go to the bank and make a $1,000 loan which she immediately spent on clothes. She recognized that her previous limitation on clothing expenses made her look dowdy and unsuccessful. An appropriately expensive wardrobe is likely to be a better investment in your future than a college course in some technical subject. Try to match the price and quality of your superior's uniforms, but don't surpass them. "It is not nice," one corporate wife was told, "to outdress the president's wife." The same holds true for bona fide team members. Men are inclined to understand immediately that they match but never overshadow their boss's clothes.

Remember the Function of Uniforms. Whatever else they represent, executive clothes are first and foremost appropriate to the demands of the job duties. By quasi-military standards a uniform must appear as fresh, unwrinkled, and sharply creased at midnight as it did that morning although it was worn for a full day at the office, was drenched in a rain shower, traveled 5,000 miles by five modes of transportation, and had to be presentable for a late dinner and possibly a nightclub. Executive uniforms must be sturdy and versatile.

In this respect women executives' clothes must be equally versatile and adaptable to all business exigencies. If women travel with men, they must be able to take everything they need in hand luggage that can be carried on and off the plane, just as men do. The first truly great woman's commercial I've ever seen is one by United Airlines showing a woman executive deplaning in an efficient, self-confident manner, with the comment "The boss is on her way." To be so well organized and efficient she

341

had to pay attention to the functionalism of her wardrobe. Fabrics that wrinkle, rumple, sag, or wilt have no place in a woman executive's wardrobe.

Pay Attention to Coordination of Parts. One well-dressed woman executive who flatly says, "Most women dress terribly," confines her shopping to a single shop where she gets the full attention of the owner each year when she buys her standard $1,000 worth of replacement clothes. "By giving all my business to one shop I can be sure that everything matches and parts can coordinate with other things. The shop owner orders the right color blouses or accessories so that all of my clothes are quite interchangeable. The new outfits always go with the previous year's leftovers because we select compatible fabrics, styles, or colors."

Colors Are Ambivalent. Most successful corporate businessmen find that dark blues, grays, pinstripes, and subtle plaids convey the symbol of authority most effectively. With women I do not believe the same effect is achieved. Women executives can probably exert a stronger impression with distinctive colors or patterns that men cannot get away with. Navy, black (let's raze the "little basic black dress"), dull grays, or very subdued solids do not impress me as symbols of strength in women's clothes. They smack too much of "blending with the wallpaper" and taking a back seat to the powerful men. No man could wear a red suit, for instance, but a woman dressed in the red color spectrum has a definite air of confidence and assurance. Any such powerful color must be counteracted with blended and softening blouses or scarves, but strong colors may be the one male dress qualm which women can interpret to their purposes. Women by their very nature are not "conservative" in the business world. By their very presence they are breaking the establishment rule of no-females. Since women do have great fashion sense, the best way to judge is to examine yourself critically in the mirror and ask, "What

342

impression does this outfit convey to others?" You are after a "strong" and "self-assured" look, not a mousy, timid, unassertive, impression. Whatever costume creates that impact is probably right as a business uniform.

Never Wear a Man's Tie. Never, never, never. A man's tie is a penis symbol. No woman with any self-respect wants to walk around advertising "I'm pretending I have a penis." It was this article of men's clothing above all else that probably created the stereotype of the butch lesbian look. (No self-respecting lesbian would ever make such a mistake today, either, even in the gay bars.)

Wear shoes You Can Walk In. As we have seen, foot-crippling shoes have been a favorite method to keep women in their place. The day is centuries off when "serious" business can be delayed because an executive's feet hurt. Urban businessmen do a lot of walking around city streets, and women executives must be ready to join them and keep up with them.

Buy Clothes with Pockets. One manufacturing detail sets off women's clothes (even man-tailored clothes) from men's clothes—the lack of pockets. When I used to complain about this to buyers years ago, they insisted that women didn't want pockets because it would "spoil the fit" of their clothes, which presumably were supposed to be skintight over the torture-racks of girdles and padded bras. That's nonsense. Women's clothes don't have pockets because men like to reserve these essential and handy devices for themselves. I think women should insist that all their clothes have functional pockets, not cheap imitation flaps. No-pockets is an inferiority symbol.

Dump Your Burdensome Handbag. One favorite accessory of women deserves special mention—the ubiquitous carryall handbag. There's no denying that women need handbags to transport keys, money, checkbooks, glasses, makeup, cigarettes, credit cards, notebooks, and assorted sundries between home and office, but there are powerful reasons not to drag such an encumbrance all over a business office, especially to meetings. A purse or handbag is so uniquely a female article that it arouses a host of subconscious connotations among men. The typical male outfit contains an average of nine pockets, while women's clothes usually have none or no adequate ones, thereby forcing women to carry a hampering weight in the form of exterior hand baggage.

I once asked a woman track star if she practiced her running to beat traffic congestion during the day. "You can't," she said, "because of the handbag. It's impossible to run while carrying a purse in hand or on your shoulder —it slows your speed by half and throws you off balance." A woman vice-president in an all-male group says she's noticed that men "hate the sight of a woman settling a handbag under a conference table." Many bosses I've known in business consider it a sign of subservience to carry anything except vital business papers which they are entrusted to deliver to another executive. The image of messenger, errand boy, or beast of burden is avoided as much as possible by men. Symbolically, women are the burden carriers.

Both the physical and psychological handicaps of a handbag were exposed to a skeptical member of my Womanschool class when she tested the principle during a business luncheon with three male executives. "The difference was unbelievable," she reported. "I slipped a credit card and a few bills in my jacket pocket (and a comb and a lipstick, I must admit), but carried nothing in my hands or on my shoulder. We walked a couple of blocks to the restaurant and for the first time I kept apace with no trouble. I hadn't realized how often my big shoulder-bag bumped into people and forced me to zigzag or keep manipulating it. The men, whom I had lunched with a few times before, sensed something different but didn't know what it was. One said approvingly, 'You must have new shoes on today, I see you're keeping up with us.' At the restaurant I sat down freely and gracefully without shoving chairs or tables around to accommodate a spot for my usual luggage. I didn't have to warn waiters not to trip over it nor divert my attention repeatedly to check that my bag wasn't stolen or something. I can't explain the sense of freedom and equality I felt. And somehow it was communicated to my male companions—as if I really *belonged* in an expensive restaurant having a business luncheon with co-equal executives."

Be Careful About Uniquely Female Accessories. There's one cardinal rule: Don't wear anything that jingles, wiggles, clanks, or glitters. Executive insignia are silent, understated and unobstrusive—never sexy.

Jewelry—Dangling earrings, charm bracelets, metal bangles, chain collections, novelty pins, or garish, attention-getting items that distract listeners from what you are *saying* or *ordering* will dilute any woman's authority image. Take your cue from successful men in your organization. Their idea of jewelry will be reflected in their watches, possibly cufflinks, belt buckles, rings, and tie clasps. They seldom have a wardrobe of decorations; they stick to one or two favorites that look (and are) expensive, and wear them repeatedly. Never forget that money is the scorecard in this game so executive women's jewelry no longer acts as costume decoration but as a *symbol of success*, i.e. expensive and real, not junk. Women should probably limit themselves to one or two jewelry items at a time, such as a ring and a necklace. Neck jewelry indeed may become the female equivalent of men's ties so each piece should be selected with care and be what the jewelry trade calls an "important" design, one that stands alone as a distinctive, powerful emblem. The exception to expensive elegance is when you work for a company where the *men* wear extravagant jewelry; in that case your rule is probably "the funkier the better."

Perfume—Save it for after-work hours when it can perform its function of making you a desirable sex object. The lingering odor of the most expensive perfume is overpowering and headachey in the confines of a small office or closed conference room.

Makeup and Hairstyles—Women are no different than men in wanting to look their best when they are in the public eye, as they are at work. Just remember that your makeup and hairdo must hold up under all the exigencies of a business day without excessive attention. It goes without saying that all touch-ups, including lipstick, must be done in private. Naturalness, as opposed to painted artificiality, is the aim.

The development of a "superior" or "high status" uniform for female management executives must come from women themselves because men's reactions to female dress are highly suspect. Conscious and unconscious male attitudes toward women's dress will be skewed in the direction of reducing women to their traditional weak and dependent roles. A strong and authoritative costume is apt to be criticized by men when a woman wears it. That may be the best sign you're on the right track—if you can scare a pewter-gray pinstripe into a worried comment about your bright green velvet blazer, you've accomplished something. Men will seldom tell women their clothes are inadequate to their job; they'll gladly let women make the wrong moves in the game. Some male comments can be tip-offs.

* "I see you're wearing a dress today—you look so pretty." If a man says that to you at the staff meeting, never wear that outfit again. Any time you look "sweet" and "pretty," you are in trouble; some fast-moving gamester has just captured your pawn.

* "I don't remember what she said, but she sure has great tits." When I heard this male summation of a brilliant woman's contribution to a prestigious government-business conference, I had visions of her in a neat brown-and-white print jersey V-neck dress which accentuated a generous bosom. I wasn't there; I don't know;

346

but whatever she wore, it's obvious that her costume did more for her figure than it did for her career.

* "You have a good job. You ought to dress the part." If a man says that to you, adopt him as your mentor. He's the best business friend you've run across. It may sound like he's insulting your taste in clothes, but he's telling it like it is. He's trying to help you get ahead in business.

CHAPTER
14

Sexy Games, or Playing Around in the Hierarchy

Women, I've discovered, are deeply reluctant to talk about sexual relationships on the job. Introduction of the subject in career workshops raises the anxiety level visibly. When women seek help because they are caught up in a distressing emotional work relationship, they nevertheless become cagey, embarrassed, and evasive about details. Most of the women I tried to interview for input on this chapter were elusive or less than expansive. They could tell me about situations going on in their office with *somebody else*, or relate troubles they have had because some woman was sleeping with a boss or client, but generally they had little or no personal advice for other women.

Obviously women are all screwed up when it comes to facing the pervasive and inevitable sexual byproduct of females and males working in close proximity to each other for eight hours a day. Some are confused; they hadn't anticipated the heady atmosphere of sexual tension that exists in most business offices. Some are excited; they love the fun and games, the flirtation and teasing, the free-and-easy opportunity to find willing sex partners. Some are depressed; they feel left out and unattractive if excluded from afterhours social drinking parties. Some are disgusted; they have strict moral or monogamous principles and disapprove of playing around. Some are calculating; they figure the fastest way to get ahead is to sleep with the right men. Some are in love; they refuse to think about anything but being close to their office paramour as much as possible. Some are repelled; they are lesbians and hate the necessity of pretending they are interested in heterosexual come-ons. Some are bitter; they have been burned in the fires of office passion and spend their time criticizing other women who are similarly trapped.

None are blasé or neutral. All readily admit that sexual affairs are a fact of life in the working environment. But most believe that resulting problems are personal, individual matters which each woman must learn to handle by herself. A very few recognize the pattern; they see that business sex is guided and directed by a set of conscious and unconscious rules that are invariably beneficial to men and deleterious to women who work in the same corporate institution.

A Pyramid Is a Phallic Symbol

All hierarchies are pyramidal in shape, and a pyramid (visualize it) is a perfect phallic symbol. Whether you're looking at it from the outside, or climbing it from the inside, the stamp of the phallus is inescapable—dominant, controlling, and overpowering. No matter what job you hold, you are looked upon first as a woman (the possessor of a vagina) and secondly as a contributor to the significant "work" of the hierarchy. It doesn't matter if you are single, married, divorced, widowed, young, middle-aged, beautiful, or slightly imperfect in physical charms, you are first and foremost a checker in a game—a female object to be manipulated in the interests of maintaining phallic supremacy in the pyramid.

Once a woman travels into the world of big business she is in an all-male preserve. She is judged according to the customs and standards of that male society, not by those she was taught to apply to a different society. No longer is her anatomy her destiny; now male anatomy is her destiny. And male anatomy has a single-minded focus which was vividly described by psychiatrist David Reuben in *Everything You Always Wanted to Know About Sex:*

> *Whenever two nude men encounter each other for the first time in a public shower, a country club locker room, a YMCA swimming pool, their eyes go first to each other's penises. . . . In more than one private club the management has thoughtfully installed large magnifying mirrors over the urinals so that each gentleman who avails himself of their facilities can feast his eyes on the reflection of a phallus which would do credit to a bull elephant.*

It is against this backdrop that women are collectively perceived by those in a male-bonding community such as a business enterprise. The female physical presence is tolerated as a primal adjunct to glorification of the phallic symbolism which represents power, virility, strength, and domination. In the deep recesses of the male-conditioned unconscious, male-female relationships are dictated like moves in a checker game. The conquest of a woman's anatomy, by whatever seductive or commanding means, is a jump-over which gives the male player possession of the captured playing piece. Any temporary gains the female may be allowed are inevitably used to crown her partner's "kings" and make him undisputed lord of the playing board.

To call this game sexual attraction or office love affairs is to use euphemistic expressions to prettify the true nature of the activity. In coldly realistic terms, this is a male-female genital-contact game within a localized setting and it makes no difference what the ostensible motivations, intentions, or emotional needs of the participants are. The strict rules of this game were established millennia ago and adapted by profit organizations centuries ago. The rules never envisioned women as independent, decisive movemakers, so the scoring system rewards only males. *Women can't win this game.* They must not play this game with any male member of their particular business community if they want to remain viable activists in the impersonal master game of corporate politics where the goal is money, success, and independent power.

No individual man can change the rules because the mores of his tribe are all-controlling. No individual woman can change the rules because she is powerless against the entrenched establishment of a male-created business society. Besides, the minute she starts playing the genital-contact game she is a captured object as far as other participants and nonparticipants are concerned. "Fucking checkers"—a term actually in use by male players or would-be players of this working game—is a public game spread out on a playing board for all to see. Every woman who gets into this game (accidentally or on purpose) becomes tagged (unbeknownst to her perhaps) with a popular designation: "Sleep with one, fair game for all."

There's one way for a male-female combination to remove themselves as two individuals from the unvarying formula of the intercourse game; that is marriage to each other. This pits them as a couple into an unrelated and entirely different intracorporate game where the local firm's rules are generally definite and quite often written. That game is called nepotism and is not germane to sex checkers.

351

You won't find them listed in any personnel manual but all companies abide by implicit canons of sexual conduct which apply to their male employees only. Corporate policy-makers are men (lest you forget!), so there is no question that phallus-glorifying activities are legitimate obligations for promising male pyramid climbers. Male employees are not forced to play this game, but neither are they discouraged. It could not be otherwise because sexual control over women is the glue that binds male commonwealths into cohesive societies. Whether they personally play the game or not, male business associates are forced to support and uphold the rights of their compatriots as long as they do not violate the ethics and etiquette of the game, as defined by men, for men. In different corporations the emphasis on or toleration of male indulgence in intra-office sexual affairs may vary to some minor extent, but the pernicious impact on women is consistent throughout industry.

Company codes (supported by unwritten corporate policy) that I've been able to discern include the following points. After the code for male game players I've added its impact on women.

1. Publicly we must maintain that no corporate policy on this volatile issue exists; officially we are always "agin' sin" in any manifestation. Like CIA operatives, all males are considered to be acting on their own when initiating or consummating coital acts. These are personal, social, voluntary enterprises, *but* it is no secret that the "boys upstairs" welcome any assistance in maintaining phallic dominance of the pyramidal structure. (Women who interpret this free and easy, noncritical attitude toward sexual intimacy as if it applies to them neglect to notice that *they are the quarry*; by giving themselves up—or "giving

themselves"—they strengthen the very system which is holding them back economically.)

2. In the interest of our corporate public image, all affairs, regardless of length, must be conducted with discretion and decorum. Any taint of scandal, notoriety, or loss of emotional control will be harshly penalized as anathema to the purpose of the game. (Women who become emotionally involved or fall in love are risks under this rule and are subject to ruthless discard at any moment.)

3. The objective is philandering as one more evidence of your growing ability to take charge in tricky and variable circumstances. (The female partner must be dominated and rigidly controlled under this canon.)

4. Since this is an exhibition in asserting superiority, performance ratings rise according to the status of the female who is conquered and subjugated. (A commercial prostitute is a minimal challenge in this context, just as a receptionist or secretary is less prestigious a conquest than a female publicity director or department manager. A woman client or job competitor is the ultimate prize. But no matter who the woman, it is worth special note that the man who gets the woman is instantly superior in game terms and the woman has been downgraded to inferior status.)

5. All female employees are fair game to all male employees; establishing territorial rights, if desired, is up to each man. Drawing corporate wives into the game is verboten as they are not employees and this is an internal, classified, quasi-business activity. For the same reason, wives of important customers or industry associates are not counted as scoring pieces in the game. (Any and all sexual activity outside the parameters of the immediate corporate business circle is beyond the pale of corporate policy or concern. A woman's sexuality or sexual expression is free and unfettered as long as she selects no partners from the enjoined players, namely employees or

customers of her own corporation to whom the game rules apply.)

6. As a general rule, no scores are totted when sexual activities take place on foreign soil (outside the United States), even though partners are corporate employees at home. (Remember these are male rules. Very few women accompany male associates in international travel, but some of those who do are highly skeptical that this "anything goes" canon would actually "go" for women.)

7. This "unofficial" game and the scoring procedure are classified information under all circumstances. Players' wives must be kept in the dark, and female employees who are too knowledgeable to be trusted must be judiciously removed from the game premises. An innocuous pretext to eliminate unwanted females will be understood and accepted. When such action is deemed warranted, any delay will incur a black mark for the superior. (Women employees are put on somebody's "unwanted" list whenever they succumb to any male co-worker's blandishments, or to their own voluntary sexual feelings, and sleep with a fellow employee or superior. If they are not eliminated from the corporate premises by quitting or being fired, they are automatically excluded from the advancement game because they are branded as an unqualified player or inferior teammate.)

8. Top-level officers, having proven their prowess at voluntary "affairs" within game etiquette terms shall be eligible to hire high-quality professionals (high-priced call girls) for themselves and customers at their level. All such business expenses shall be transacted in untraceable cash and, of course, are subject to all the rules of propriety and decorum. (One reason women are believed "unqualified" to function at very top management levels is their presumed unwillingness or inability to act as procurer of prostitutes for customer entertainment, a widespread business practice deemed necessary to main-

tain goodwill and similar to entertaining at restaurants, theaters, or sporting events.)

9. It goes without saying that phallic supremacy is intensified solely by heterosexual relationships; homosexual proclivities are expressly forbidden. (Female homosexuals are the most dangerous threat to phallic supremacy because lesbians discount the penis entirely as having any usefulness to female sexual satisfaction. Such a thought is enough to cause cardiac arrest or uncontrollable rage in the phallic pyramid, so overt lesbians are hunted down and eliminated.)

What this unwritten and unverbalized canon of male ethics adds up to for women is clear: any corporate woman employee who engages in intercourse (or attempted intercourse, given the potency problems of many hard-driving business executives) has jeopardized her chances of significant advancement within that particular corporate structure. She is irrevocably labeled "inferior" and must go elsewhere to move upward with a clear path.

Office Affairs—the Male Superior Position

Unquestionably sexual affairs in the business environment are infected with all the hang-ups rampant in the larger society, but the mark of the corporate sex game is its impersonality. The moves and countermoves, the objectives and scoring are constants which apply unilaterally. In sex checkers, for instance, the results are unaffected by your personal attitudes about sexual expression. You can be a rigid follower of fundamentalist religious precepts or you can be an uninhibited practitioner of sensuous exploration to bring your sexual responsiveness to full flowering; you can be straight or gay; you can be horny as hell or placidly celibate—the male-designated rules for corporate sex redound to the female's disad-

355

vantage regardless. Sex objects are playing pieces, not people.

The only objective of the game is to increase men's status in the eyes of superiors and colleagues to prove that they "fit into" the elite male camaraderie group which makes decisions about job promotion and salary improvement. A woman increases the status of any and every man she sleeps with, while decreasing her own. There is mighty little equality in sexual entanglements outside the office; there is none possible inside the office. Michael Korda, with his devastating gift for exposing his male colleagues' underlying motivations, explains how the system is manipulated by men in *Male Chauvinism! How It Works* (New York, Random House, 1973):

> *On a basic male chauvinist level an office affair is a* badge of status, *always provided that it's handled well; that is, with the minimal amount of emotional disturbance and with its course and direction firmly controlled (or thought to be firmly controlled) by the male partner. Any display of emotion on the part of the man, or suggestion that the woman either initiated the affair or decides when and how it will end,* loses the man his status in his peer group [*Emphasis mine.*]

No man, if he can help it, is going to let an office sex partner deprive him of peer status. This can happen, for example, if the man has decided to cut the affair off and the woman objects or tries to interfere with his decision and delay the day of reckoning. Her usefulness as a trophy has long since passed and now she becomes an encumbrance. He will find a way to get rid of her and the entire male club will assist him (even though they may like and respect the woman) because "there, but for the immediate grace of God, go I."

Women reveal their game naïveté most painfully when they simple-mindedly repeat rumors that suggest another

356

woman "slept her way to the top." A real-life appreciation of male-superior/female-inferior sex checkers should explode that irrational myth for all time. True, some women have been able to improve their job title or pay *over other women* by begging for a small crumb of reward from a male sex-partner, but that crumb is recognized for what it's worth by male peers—a temporary payment for sexual favors, not a true appraisal of merit or ability in the productive work of the business organism. Nobody's fooled but other women. A payroll pay-off for sexual servicing does not start a woman on the road to merited job recognition nor improve her chances of moving ahead on her own. It marks her as the first to be gotten rid of at the most expeditious moment.

To be fair to countless numbers of decent, well-meaning, nonmalicious men who work in the corporate structure, it must be admitted that a great many do not have any idea how badly they've compromised the future of a woman colleague with whom they've had an affair. *They* may never use the mutually happy alliance against her, but unfortunately they do not control the system nor the attitudes of their men colleagues. They might be as innocent as the woman in believing that one pleasant night's encounter is but an enjoyable personal interlude in a frantic work schedule. But want it or not, *he* will be credited with the pluses and she will get stuck with all the minuses—as long as they both work for the same employer.

If a powerful man deliberately does promote a woman whom he got to know intimately through a sexual alliance, she will not be able to function in the job. Both subordinates and superiors, male and female, will sabotage her work and undermine her authority. She may hold the position as long as her powerful male protector can intimidate the rapacious wolves, but the minute he leaves or loses his clout, she will be eaten alive. Everyone else will assume she is in the job by his sufferance and not her independent ability, and she will never be able to get control of the operation or the people she must work with. Inevitably the actual output of the department or operation will go downhill and even the president cannot justify declining production just because "he once slept with the dame." One way or another, she will be out. For a woman, "sleeping your way to the top" is the fastest road to the bottom. Any woman who envies another who makes such a gross error in gamesmanship merely reveals her own ignorance.

Sleeping with Your Boss

Once you've slept with your boss, you've ended your upward mobility in that company—and the reason has nothing to do with sex. *That* particular career path is closed because you violated the chain-of-command relationship. I've even seen this happen to men who were close friends when the subordinate man failed to observe the mandated deference and distance required once his friend became his boss. And, of course, a social intimacy between two men can't hold a candle to a man-woman sexual entanglement, so the physical proximity of intercourse is beyond the most elastic bounds of boss-subordinate propriety.

Corporations may bend slightly some of the obedience discipline enforced by the military, but the steely inflexibility of the chain-of-command is preserved pretty much intact. The links in this chain are not interlocked circlets; they are like separate and distinct beads strung together with wire or knotted rope so that superior and subordinate positions can never physically or socially touch. The superior can set the distance comparatively close or relatively remote but the subordinate cannot impinge on the deferential space. A superior who has exposed himself to a subordinate in sexual nakedness is vulnerable thereafter in the working situation. He cannot feel comfortable or safe in the circumstances, and his instinctive reaction will be to get rid of the discomfort. He will actually fire the subordinate sex partner at the first opportunity or will make the working situation so unbearable she will quit.

A prior or current sexual affair between a male boss and female subordinate also carries horrendous complications into the functioning of the rest of the team. Male subordinates who are equal colleagues of the offending woman will hate her for taking "unfair advantage" of her sexual attraction. Other women will also hate her for much the same reasons. Her boss's superiors will automatically classify her as a sex-servicing instrument, not a candidate for recognition on her own merits. If the upset in the working team becomes too obvious, the boss's superiors may *order* him to fire her—or leave himself. When the choice is his job or disposal of an illicit sex partner, guess what he chooses? You don't have to guess; you've probably seen the cold-blooded dismissal of the woman partner enacted on more than one occasion.

Everybody knows that long-time affairs between secretaries and their bosses can go on without repercussions, always providing the woman remains in her subservient, noncomplaining role of the dutiful doormat. Those sexual relationships are possible because secretarial jobs have no place in the hierarchy; as presently constituted, they are extraneous servant positions. A secretary has no upward mobility and the job is not a team position. A secretary-boss sexual liaison is degrading to the woman, but it affects nobody else in the hierarchy so nobody really cares—as long as she "behaves herself" and is completely under the man's controlling thumb. Certain other dead-end, nonactive female jobs may also fall into this category.

Talking about It Is Part of the Game

In male-bonding communities such as military barracks or sports locker rooms, it has been estimated that 80 percent of the conversation is about sex, specifically the availability of women and the sexual prowess of the men in "making" those women. Male business communities are duplicate offsprings of their parents; to women it often seems that 80 percent of the conversation that is directed at them or that they overhear is sexually stimulating, teasing, flirtatious, or spicy gossip about proliferating affairs of others.

It stands to reason that as long as sexual conquests of female employees are male status symbols, the trophies must be publicized. Male-initiated propositions and consummations would have no status value if nobody knew about them, so office affairs are the most public personal relationships there are. Even if the two partners try to keep the liaison secret, there's an electricity about sexual attraction that is communicated rapidly to observers. Scarcely any office affairs go undetected, mainly because nobody wants them to be secret. Men obviously have nothing to gain by secrecy, and many women think they gain favor by attachment to a powerful figure, but even fantasy power is pointless unless it is public. Women who are hopelessly in love tell the whole world about it, and women who are being discarded fight recklessly to turn local office opinion in their favor. The whole sexy scenario is custom-tailored to jazz up the office grapevine with titillating tidbits.

Not only does the whole office know who's sleeping with whom, but so does anyone interested in the rest of the company—and in small industries, so does everybody in other companies. A woman who sleeps with a fellow employee is a fool to think the affair will be personal and secret. The "news" gets out and is bruited far and wide; and her job future drains steadily away. In small industries, it is probably wise for a woman to include all companies in her industry as part of her sex checkerboard and build her sex life with men in some other field entirely. Technically the sex game board is circumscribed to employees of your own company plus clients, customers, or suppliers who are financially connected to your job in the company, but specialized circumstances must be taken into account.

Talk about office affairs is not restricted to true facts or incidents. A great deal of the sexy gossip is inaugurated by men trophy-hunters who try to suggest that they have made conquests that never occurred. The woman who rejects advances may find herself talked about in far more disparaging terms than if she put out on demand. Many men are genuinely scared to work with women equals because they know how easy—and common—it is for every female-male work relationship to be viewed in sexual terms. A man who invites a woman for an after-work drink will probably face the urinal inquisitors the next morning: "Well? Did you score?" To uphold his peer status he may describe a passionate movie idyll he dreamed about or he might smile and leer to insinuate that he's now one-up on them, although the facts are that the woman's husband picked her up in the car and her drinking companion also went straight home.

Male sex game ethics *require* that the competitive cocksman lie, deceive, exaggerate, dissemble, and otherwise fabricate a counterfeit front for his sexual athletics. Boasting, bragging, and bombast are what cocks-of-the-walk are made of. Women must be aware of these male preening techniques for two good reasons. First, so they're not surprised or stupefied when they become victims of untrue braggadocio; that's an inevitability that ambitious businesswomen take in stride and ignore. Untrue rumors will die out fairly quickly. Second, so *naïve* women do not

361

believe everything they hear on the office grapevine and pass it along as unvarnished truth. Women who work together needn't love each other, but they should refuse to talk about another woman disparagingly. By so doing they play right into the men's hands and help reduce all women (including themselves) to the contemptible level of cunts.

What If They Call You a Castrating Bitch or a Lez?

Cultural brainwashing is hard to eradicate without strenuous cleansing efforts. Aspiring businesswomen are often more afraid of being called "dirty names" than they are of surrendering their self-respect, an absurdity that can frequently be neutralized by resort to a good dictionary. Women who are demoralized by being aggressive, competitive, pushy, overbearing, castrating, or lesbian need to scrub the stereotype graffiti off their psyche. When normal, healthy, goal-directed, success-oriented attributes are perceived as "dirty" appellations when applied to her, a woman is obstructing her own self-development because of childhood brainwashing.

What's wrong with "pushy"? The dictionary defines it as "possessing business enterprise and energy; an active, energetic person." No ambitious woman will get far without those qualities, yet many women allow themselves to be pushed around or become push-overs ("an easy mark") to avoid the positive label. Considering that a large proportion of working women were English majors, this language confusion should be easier to clean up than seems to be the case. Take "castrating." This word isn't limited to removal of male organs or emasculation; it also applies to desexing females or spaying. Yet many women are ready to be deformed by men and made into what Germaine Greer called "female eunuchs" rather than force men to take responsibility for their own psycho-sexual development.

Homophobia—fear of homosexuality—is like an invisible spirit that hovers over the business landscape. Sexologists and psychiatrists are beginning to concede that the glue in male bonding contains a heavy percentage of latent homosexuality which accounts for the strong taboos against overt male homosexual behavior in all-male groups. But men's fascination with the forbidden subject makes homosexuality a hot topic in male business circles. The Nixon tapes revealed how powerful men derogate other men by calling them queers, fags, fairies, or homos.

With the same evil twist of mind, businessmen (and others) are fast to denounce women who act independently as lezzes or lesbians, insinuating that this is the worst epithet in their dictionary of dirty words. Unfortunately a lot of women who are extremely uncomfortable with their own sexuality are ready to agree. They let themselves be raped rather than be called lesbian. To get along with the least trouble in the salacious atmosphere of the businessmen's milieu, a woman must learn to be unflappable when confronted with sexual innuendoes. If you blush, get upset, become embarrassed, snap back in anger, or let yourself be intimidated, unscrupulous men will tease you unmercifully and make you a laughing stock. If you show that you're terrified of the word "lesbian," you will never hear the end of it—the epithet will be used as a club by some men to beat you into submission. Much better to smile enigmatically and say, "Some of my best friends are." Unknown to you, some of your best friends probably are!

Strangely enough, fear and confusion about their own female sexuality is often the biggest handicap to ambitious women who want to progress in the corporate hierarchy. They are too easily distracted from the main economic political game by the pervasive challenges to play fucking

363

checkers. In this connection, the single most important business textbook for women may turn out to be Shere Hite's myth-shattering revelations in *The Hite Report* (New York: Macmillan, 1976), the first woman-defined study of female sexuality in existence. After reading it, when your male business colleagues *tell* you how you ought to feel about them and their sexual advances, you will be secure enough with your own female sexuality to stick by your guns and make decisions that will benefit your career plans instead of theirs.

What If You Are a Lesbian?

Practicing lesbians have always lived with the fear that their sexual preference will become known to work colleagues and they'll be fired. That was, and is, a realistic concern given the deep-seated homophobia in business organizations. For the present, lesbians cannot flaunt their male-threatening life-style and expect to be promoted very far in the corporate hierarchy. They will have to support and financially subsidize the civil rights activities of gay rights and lesbian feminist groups from the background except for legal reform movements which are backed by straights and gays. Enough societal breakthroughs have occurred to considerably lighten the traditional guilt load on closet lesbians, but private industry may well be the last bastion of anti-lesbianism.

That's the bad news, but it is far outweighed by the positive benefits that a clear understanding of corporate politics games offers lesbians. It is not necessary, for instance, to construct a phony heterosexual "feminine" stereotype role as a work façade; that will only weaken your professional stance. Many lesbians find it easier than straight women to establish comfortable work relations with male bosses and co-workers precisely because they are not sexually attracted to the men. They can use the

364

same excuse as straight women to deflect unwelcome advances—that their career comes before personal gratification. Certainly nothing is gained on the sexual harassment front by letting male pests know you are lesbian. A few young lesbians who inadvertently, or deliberately, tried that method of discouraging male flirtation in the office found that it backfired. The news spread like wildfire and challenged all "redblooded" men to prove that they could "change" the deprived young women into raving heterosexuals.

It is important for lesbians who are newcomers to the business world to remember that homosexual talk and accusations of lesbianism are prevalent gossip items and it *does not mean* that anyone suspects or knows you are a lesbian. Nobody knows your sexual preference unless you tell them. But what can be sensed (by female colleagues at least) is a sexual attraction behavior toward another woman. The advice against sexual entanglements with another employee of the same corporation applies equally to straight and gay women. Sleeping with a lesbian boss is just as much a violation of the chain-of-command distance as when the superior-subordinate links are male/female. All the hierarchical and team rules of play apply whether a man or a woman holds the position. A woman who is moving up the ladder must associate with peers on her level and not ally herself too closely with subordinate ranks or she will symbolically demote herself, or ignore the rank emblems which give her authority. So homosexual relationships as well as heterosexual relationships are equally enjoined when playing around in a hierarchical pyramid. The love life of all women workers belongs outside the working environment.

Sexual Harassment—"Put Out or Get Out"

Sexual harassment—or sexual molestation—or sexual

365

exploitation—or civil rape—is women's most dangerous occupational hazard. It is especially insidious because management denies it exists. When confronted with proof, the male establishment blames the woman, saying that some female subordinates are willing to engage in minor forms of prostitution to advance their position or income; it's the same perverted mind-set of rape psychology— the innocent victim becomes the criminal, and the perpetrator is absolved of responsibility for his acts.

How common is sexual molestation? My own feeling is that more women are refused employment, fired, or forced to quit salaried jobs as the result of sexual demands and the ramifications thereof than for any other single cause. The most common victim is the woman who is financially vulnerable, and the perpetrator is necessarily a male boss who wields economic power over her. She needs the job to feed herself (and often dependent children), and the boss makes it plain that she gets or can keep the job if she submits to his sexual overtures. In many cases the lure is a better-paying job or promotion, in return for being submissive and sexually cooperative with the man in charge. If the woman refuses, she is fired by the man she rejected or her performance evaluations suddenly show her to be incompetent and unsatisfactory as a worker, and somebody else fires her. Most typically, the harassment is verbal, making lewd and lascivious comments about the woman's breasts or ass or legs, or her "bedroom eyes," or her probable performance in bed. Physical molestation runs all the way from male hands squeezing your breast or thigh, pinching and goosing, cruelly assaultive hugs and kisses behind office doors, bellies pressing against you in narrow hallways, orders to work overtime to get you alone in some vacant office, feet in hotel-room doors on business trips, insistent invitations for drinks and demands to take you home afterward (hoping you're too drugged with alcohol to continue resisting). The list goes on ad nauseam, and the practice goes on ad nauseam in every business office in this country.

Lin Farley, whose forthcoming book *Sexual Shakedown: Sexual Harassment of Women at Work*, will be published by McGraw-Hill, tells me the situation has reached epidemic proportions. A couple of years ago she testified before the New York City Commission on Human Rights that in any random group of ten working women, five to seven have had one or more experiences with unwelcome sexual advances on the job and that the longer a woman is in the workforce and the more jobs she holds, the higher the number of experiences. As her national statistical data comes in that estimate is proving to be very conservative; fully one half to two-thirds of *all the women in the workforce* suffer or have been damaged by some form of sexual assault or sexual molestation on the job.

In corporate game terms, women have got to come up with some monumentally effective strategy to counteract the vicious players of sex checkers who abuse those women who beat the game by refusing to become performing sex objects. The only weapon women have is a flashlight to turn the glare of publicity on every corporation which publicly avows it is agin' sin *but* privately allows its salary funds, job performance policies, and premises to be used freely by male supervisors who practice sexual exploitation on company time, with company money. Blowing the whistle on sexual molesters is the only way to get them out of the hierarchy. But since the most dangerous offenders are bosses—and you can't go over their head within the chain-of-command rules—the only recourse is the president or chief executive officer of the company. He's not going to be sympathetic to some babe's complaints about low-echelon sex checkers because he plays that game regularly himself. But he *must* pay attention if the complaint is couched in terms of how much the work production of certain departments is being curtailed by on-the-job sexual shenanigans of specifically named supervisors, or how much of the company's money is being dissipated to satisfy the sexual perversions of named supervisors.

A few stalwart women (bless their souls) are lighting the way with federal court suits against on-the-job sexual molesters. So far, the weight of judicial opinion (all male judges) is running against the women. Two clerical employees took Bausch & Lomb, Inc. to court in Arizona. They claimed they had to leave their job because working conditions were untenable due to "the verbal and physical sexual advances" made to them and other women by the male supervisor of an all-woman department. In March, 1975, the verdict was handed down. They lost because their charge that their boss "persistently takes unsolicited and unwelcome sexual liberties" was judged to be "nothing more than a personal proclivity, peculiarity or mannerism" of the supervisor and not a company policy; hence, not considered sex discrimination under Title VII. In *Miller* v. *Bank of America* (August, 1976), a black California woman testified that she was promised a better job if she would be sexually "cooperative" with her white male supervisor but was terminated when she refused. Not surprisingly, she lost her case. The court decided that "the attraction of males to females and females to males is a natural sex phenomenon" and the woman didn't prove that the employer had a personal policy requiring sex favors as a condition of employment; thus, Title VII did not apply.

But things are picking up. In April, 1976, a woman finally won a sexual harassment case. In *Williams* v. *Saxbe*, Diane Williams took on, of all things, the U.S. Department of Justice! She claimed she was terminated from her job as a public information aide because she refused her supervisor's sexual advances; he said she was fired because her work was unsatisfactory. She was divorced, age twenty-three, with an infant son when she took the job in 1972; her supervisor began making advances soon after she was hired. For the first six months, she got good work ratings, but as the advances escalated and she still refused, her job ratings began to plummet. She was reprimanded; her supervisor withheld information she needed to perform her job; he refused to recognize her as a competent professional; three months later he fired her. In defense, the government argued that whatever happened between Ms. Williams and her supervisor was a private matter that did not reflect employment practices of the Justice Department. But the district court ruled that the sexual advances were imposed as a "condition of employment by the supervisor of an office of the agency," a distinction that brings the incident out of social life and into the realm of sex discrimination under Title VII.

In November, 1976, Adrienne Tompkins won a very significant ruling for women in the federal district court in Newark, N.J. Although the judge ruled that sexual assault cannot be viewed as sex discrimination under Title VII, he ordered a trial to prove her charge that she was *fired because she complained*—a retaliation which would make the company vulnerable to sex discrimination laws. Ms. Tompkins says that her boss at Public Service Electric & Gas Co. pressured her to have sex to keep her job. She complained about him and asked for a transfer to another department, which she got. When she was fired a year later, she contends it was because she complained about the previous sexual advances; the company says she was fired for excessive absences. The decision on this case could be very important for the future of sexual harassment cases.

It's noteworthy that the four sexual harassment cases brought to court are from different places throughout the country. Sexual molesters are everywhere. Two important judicial precedents (Ms. Williams' and Ms. Tompkins' cases) have been set to give women some weapons to use in the battle against corporate rape artists. The spotlights are turning on this pernicious practice condoned by most corporations, and it's high time. Women must clean these vermin from the hierarchy if they are to play the game successfully; no woman can concentrate on doing a competent job if her boss is pushing his penis in her face. To stop this sort of thing, a direct head-on confrontation is necessary. But remember: complain in a detailed written memo sent directly to the chief executive officer of the firm —with copies to no one else in the company. Do keep extra copies in reserve for the local newspapers if your complaint is not satisfactorily acted upon; it's only fair to let other women in your community know which companies consider sex-servicing of their male supervisors a condition of female employment.

Fending Off Outrageous Interview Questions

One of the first obnoxious practices women have to tackle head-on is unwarranted invasion of personal and sexual privacy. This invariably takes place on job interviews either with personnel screeners or with supervisors for whom you'll work if you get the job. I am infuriated every time I hear that interviewers still think they can ask women about their menstrual history, their contraceptive usage, their family plans, their reproductive background, their housekeeping practices, or what their husband does (or if they don't have a husband, why not?). But I am more appalled to hear that women answer these questions without challenging their validity or appropriateness.

The game of corporate politics starts at the interview door. You are entering into a very preliminary bargaining session. If this session and subsequent ones progress smoothly, you will end up with a tacit contract or trading agreement. You agree to devote a specified amount of your time, talent, and energy to the company in return for a stipulated salary, fringe benefits, and working conditions. At the first preliminary meeting, you don't know what the company has to offer, and the interviewer doesn't know what qualifications you have to offer. But there is a definite piece of merchandise under consideration: the job. Every time you let the discussion get off the point of the job specifications and your job qualifications, you have lost a point in the game, and the interviewer has racked one up. A heavy minus-score either loses you the job or insures that you get a lousy job—which is why it's crazy for women to believe that they must answer sexual questions to get a "chance" at a job.

One interesting experiment was reported by Betsy Hogan in *Womanpower*, May, 1976. A male manager agreed to ask the same questions of all female and male applicants when he next had a job opening. The questions included a number of queries worked out by him and a member of Boston NOW (National Organization for Women) that represented the most out-of-bounds inquiries routinely posed to female job applicants. The businessman was astounded at the results of his research project. He reported that *women answered all the questions* having to do with marital status, family planning, contraception, child care, and spouse's future plans. Sometimes they stared at the desk, studied their shoes, or in some way indicated that they resented the line of questioning—but they answered. "Why," the manager asked, "will women answer those outrageous questions?" Because, as he must certainly have known beforehand but proved in his experiment, *male candidates won't!*

Men are instinctive players of corporate politics, even when they don't know all the explicit rules. They prevented the exploratory interview from getting off the track by laughing and treating the impertinent questions as a joke, or by changing the subject of the conversation. When pressed for answers on contraceptive methods or "feeling out of kilter" one or two days a month, men told the

371

interviewer it was none of his business or flatly said, "You got to be kidding. Listen, if this is what it's like to work for your company . . ." and ended the interview.

A woman must learn to differentiate legitimate job information from voyeuristic peering into her vaginal orifice. If the question has a genital focus or obliquely refers to your sexual-reproductive organs, don't answer it. It's a move in the game to degrade women's professional or occupational competence. If it helps you to maintain your balance when thrown these questions, sit there in silence until you can pretend you are a man and anticipate how he might answer such an insult to his occupational qualifications. When it comes to men, management has a rule for all its supervisors to follow: never get involved in an employee's personal affairs; your sole concern is the context of the job and whether or not the work is performed satisfactorily. Women are justified in insisting that the same rules apply to all potentially active team members. In general, here are some moves for women:

1. Never answer out-of-bounds, irrelevant questions on written application forms. The blank spaces force the interviewer to invade your privacy face to face so at least you have a chance to play the game one-to-one.

2. Use "Ms." as a title to correspond to the innocuous "Mr." If pressed to reveal your marital status, answer "single" because you are looking for a single job and you will be singly responsible for your performance. This answer also deflects further unwarranted delving into your private social-sexual relationships.

3. Questions about children are pertinent only if you will be bringing your children to work with you. Respond to such questions by asking about their on-premise childcare facilities. When you find out none exist (as you inevitably will), answer "no" or "zero" to the question since its relevance to your possible job is exactly zero.

4. To lightly parry malicious questions about contraceptives, reproductive plans, cohabitation arrangements, or

living style, fall back on the legal validation for such intrusive, non-job-related questions. A company can ask any pre-employment questions it wants, providing every applicant is similarly queried and evaluated. That would mean that every interviewer who poses the question to you has amassed a pile of statistics on the topic. This could be mighty interesting information, so respond to such questions by professing interest in the topic and the patterns or trends noticed by the interviewer. The nature of your reply might be:

"How interesting that you asked about contraceptives. I've been doing some research myself. What form do you find most popular with employees of this company?"

"I confess I'm interested in the marital status (or child-spacing or whatever) of your employees, but I didn't think it appropriate to bring up. However, as long as you have, what percentage of your workforce is single?" (or "average years between children" or whatever).

"I've noticed that five of your questions have had a direct or indirect sexual focus. Would you mind reviewing the prerequisites of the job you have in mind for me. I'm wondering if there's more here than meets the eye about the proposed job duties."

If these calculated moves to maintain proper direction of the job interview don't do the trick, get out of there fast and not necessarily politely. If you are certain at the beginning that a company is a bad place for women to work, you can be sure you'll have no future there anyway. Incidentally, if you get the job, you *then* fill out the tax, insurance, and medical forms correctly and accurately as to your family circumstances. Once you are on the payroll, such information *is* pertinent to your legal obligations.

Throughout her business career, a woman will have a dual job. Her primary concern will always be that of the work itself, keeping on top or ahead of her job responsibilities or her managerial duties. Her shadow occupation will entail a never-ending alertness to sexual overtures by male business associates. The real key to her continued success may be her expertise in blocking these passes while maintaining a pleasant, friendly, unsullied work relationship with the man (men) involved. As women move up into responsible, well-paying positions, successful executives will become more and more attracted to these interesting, challenging women. Women's success can become an aphrodisiac to male colleagues because major league all-stars are stimulated by playing against other pros. Winning, as we saw in Chapter 3, is only satisfying when the competition is keen; beating amateurs or minor leaguers is no big deal for a skilled professional sportsman.

Underneath this male bravado, as every woman knows, is a frail and fragile male ego. A woman's supreme expertise at playing corporate politics to the top of the pyramid will involve her ability to avoid sexual contact while never casting any disparaging allusions on a male associate's attractiveness, desirability, or sexual competence. Tact and diplomacy are the skills required. Absolute female control of the business interrelationship is the touchdown.

Every relationship between any two people is unique. It's supreme arrogance to suggest that any "rules" or "tips" will have value when the action and reaction is underway; the personality, emotions, and neuroses of the two actors create new dynamics with each experience. Given these caveats, there are some amber warning signals that other women have observed while driving through these tricky traffic circles. Maybe one or more will aid you at some time or another.

* Never turn a male business associate down flat or reject his overtures without a firm, calm explanation of your motives and a sop to his ego. "I'm flattered by your invitation, but I don't date married men." "I'm sure I'd enjoy an evening with you, but I never go out socially with my business friends." "I really regret that I can't join you on your boat, but my husband would be hurt if I didn't share such a lovely trip with him." The thrust of the unequivocal turn-down is "I like you as a person but that's as far as it goes—the answer is no and will always be no." Except for creeps of the sexual molester variety, most men will honor and respect genuine conviction as long as they think you are telling the truth, namely, that you tell other colleagues the same thing and mean it.

* Don't vary your response according to status level or job title of the man. In sex checkers all men are equal and you don't want to be vulnerable to the pettish charge, "I bet you wouldn't say that if I was a senior V-P." You want to stay in position to say, "Oh yes I would—I never mix business and pleasure, no matter how important the man or how much I like him." On a realistic basis, you never know when a man at your level or below today might not turn up as your boss in the future. In business, you never burn bridges, and you pave every road you travel because pyramids narrow as you move closer to the top and your business world shrinks with each increase in your status.

* Squelch the use of terms of endearment. The casual address of Honey, Dear, Darling, Sweetheart, Doll is considered friendly and inoffensive by some men, especially those in creative or entertainment industries. In effect, these terms are far from innocent in a business setting. Such salutations intimate a personal rela-

tionship in the background and indicate possessiveness. Take the offender aside and explain that such words have bad associations for you, that you think of over-eager clerks in a cheap store, and of course you wouldn't want to identify him with such unsophisticated people.

* If you are an only woman in an extrovertive, high-pressure male gang—very likely a sales operation—and can't seem to discourage the wolves whose professional training is "never take no for an answer," sign up for a karate course. Make sure the word gets around the office and every so often talk about a fabulous trick you learned to disable a 300-pound mugger. Your avowed purpose in learning the martial art of self-defense is to protect yourself in bad neighborhoods on your sales rounds or to feel safe when going home alone late at night—never to threaten your male cohorts. But they'll get the idea, if you dramatize it right, that you aren't the type to play around with, and going too far with you may be unhealthy.

* When dinner meetings, convention socializing, out-of-town evening entertainments and similar required business get-togethers with a boss or higher superior take a personal turn ("We're away from the office now. Let's forget about business for a few hours. Tell me about you.")—tell him all about your career plans for yourself. Suggest that business is your vocation, your avocation, your favorite mystery novel, or crossword puzzle. You've probably heard that successful corporate officers claim business is their whole life; well, swallow that hook-line-and-sinker when superiors try to un-cover your private life or turn to amorous subjects. Get all your kicks out of business intricacies, and maybe bring up the matter of your salary and whether you're making as much as men in your same position or at your level. If your companion is getting loosened up from all the drinks you might wheedle a few oddments

of information about coming changes, corporate plans, executive shifts, etc.

* Speaking of drinking. Liquor is the lubricant that keeps the wheels of commerce running. As an executive, you can't escape the drinking circuit because if you do you are being ostracized from the communications hub of business activity. But there are tricks to business drinking like everything else and these I learned through observation and experience over twenty years in hard-drinking industries:

—*Never* get drunk. Just *once*, even mildly, even if most of the men are passed out in drunken stupors, is enough to kill a woman's reputation in business for all time. It's unfair, a double standard, the pot calling the kettle black and all that, but believe me you will never live it down. Silently disappear, but never be caught drunk.

—Act like an enthusiastic drinker. Offer drinks to guests and customers, order refills, suggest stopping for a drink, get familiar with bars and cocktail lounges, join in with the social drinking customs of your business associates, be ready to follow the crowd when the drinking milieu has a quasi-social but definitely insider-business air. If you behave like the group, you can drink plain club soda or tonic water and nobody will notice or care. The glass is the secret; keep a glass in your hand like everybody else, but it can be filled with ice and water if you want. Don't order coffee, milk, or cola in sophisticated drinking circles; it's gauche, it doesn't look right, and it labels you an outsider.

—If you like to drink and can handle your liquor, great, but don't overestimate your capacity compared to men. Women *do* get drunk easier and faster than men for imperfectly understood chemical or psychological reasons, so expert women drinkers watch their intake. Stay away from martinis, manhattans, and similar mixtures. Wines are fine for some, deadly for others; it depends on the length of the cocktail party or drinking bout. The most successful women drinkers I've known stick to Scotch or whiskey diluted with loads of water and chilled with excessive amounts of ice, preferably in huge glasses. As the ice melts, they have it replenished—and their drink always looks fresh and new. Pretty soon the men start reordering rounds for themselves to "keep up."

—When your male associates get drunk and make fools of themselves in your presence, make believe you never noticed. Men can kid around with each other the next day, but women don't dare trespass in that inner core of the men-only club; just the way they try to apologize the next day tells you that. Don't accept any apologies. Pretend you weren't there: "I must have been out of the room then, I didn't see anything." Or, "Gee, you looked fine the last time I saw you, don't know what you're talking about."

* Handling a superior, a customer, a client, or an important business contact who gets too drunk to reason with and insists on sleeping with you poses a delicate problem for the woman executive. If you see such a situation developing, get away before it's too late. But most such problems arise unexpectedly when that one drink too many causes a change in the man's personality or lets him lose his usual control over his feelings or attitude toward you, you as a gender female. You have to get rid of him, but he may be aggressive, nasty, and physical. When it occurs at a convention site, try to solicit help from any available male executives (who may not be willing to get involved). Usually it happens when you're alone and he's forced his way into your apartment or hotel room. The conflict is your job

future vs. "being nice" in letting him stay, letting him sleep it off on the couch while you lock yourself in another room. You can't be "nice." If the man's important and you'll be working with him later, you must get him out of your room because he'll hate you forever after for seeing him in a state of drunken helplessness. His sexual misbehavior won't concern him, but losing power and control over his locomotion will devastate him. Tell him that. Keep reminding him that he'll feel very uncomfortable when he sees you tomorrow. Be ruthless and cruel while he's drunk because tomorrow is what counts. Physically drive him out with some kind of club. Threaten to call the cops. Call male friends, neighbors, a cab driver, or the hotel security guard to remove him. If all fails and he passes out cold, you leave. Do not come back till you're positive he's gone. When he comes to and realizes he has made a fool of himself, you must not be near because he will attach his self-hate to you and your work relationship will not survive—his instinct thereafter will be to avoid the sight of you. Alcohol is a mysterious drug in its own right, but the combination with powerful men, competitive women, business, and sex is a combustible chemical compound with atomic potential. It's a lethal mixture that rising ambitious women must be sure to control.

The Winners' Circle

Women have been victimized for so long because of their sexuality it is not surprising that the rise from oppression in the economic sphere must be fueled by a driving reassertion of sexual autonomy. A woman who assumes command of her body is a formidable foe on the pyramidal ladder. She is perceived as a threat because she is breaking the mold of traditional sex roles which had rigidly defined how she must think, talk about, clothe, exercise, and utilize her body and sexual organs—always in the service of men. Many men feel deprived when their usual succorers don't respond as expected, and many are infuriated because they have been taught that they have an inalienable "right" to the bodies of the female half of the population.

But there are other men—still a small minority, but growing—who welcome the overthrow of the infamous sex stereotypes which force them as well as women to dance to the drum and bugle of a tinny toy soldier brigade. Competing with other men to collect female sex trophies which they don't want and reacting like wind-up toys at the sight or sound of a female whom they don't even know is just as much a form of enslavement as being the object of vulgarity and hypocrisy. For stable, non-neurotic, self-confident men it comes as a great relief to be unburdened of the forced sham and deceit of sex-role play-acting. They no more want to clutter up their lives with unsatisfying office philandering than do intelligent women.

Unfortunately the corporate corridors are not yet over-flowing with an adequate supply of such men. But they do exist, and confident, self-assured, ambitious women can establish honest human relationships with equally confi-dent, self-assured, ambitious men. As one woman execu-tive put it, "My best friends are men I've met in business. They are men I really like, you might even say love, because I can be honest and natural with them. They know I will never sleep with them and they know why, and accept that. If a man is genuinely interested in you, he will not want to destroy your self-esteem or your career. He will be the first to know that an office affair will debase you and he'd never have any part of that any more than you would."

These men are called mentors. If you can find one of

them, you are very lucky. Your chance of winning the game of corporate politics has just multiplied one-hundredfold.

End Zone
The Beauty of Games
—Equality

Books usually end on the last page, but this one begins here. Because this is not a book—it's a game plan. And a pretty rudimentary one at that. It's not meant to be definitive. It is uncontaminated by academic theory, behavorial psychology, management techniques, personnel pabulum, or the latest brand of sexism—that patronizing cliché that "a woman, just because she is a woman, has something special to give to business and to society at large."

The beauty of games is that they are fun to play. They challenge your imagination, your wits, your physical dexterity. They relieve tension and bottled-up anxieties and fears. Serious games, silly games, indoor games, ball games, board games, card games, any games absorb us and provide a stimulating excitement to new learning experiences. Games are immensely challenging to expanding personalities, and one reason many women are immobilized at some pre-pubertal point of personal growth is that they were never taught to play the rough-and-tumble, competitive, active, spirited games that develop confidence, lead to positive self-appraisal, and create a healthy respect for winning. Now working women have a chance to experience the excitement and satisfaction of pitting their wits and abilities against others in the economic games of business.

Women make up a fresh, new, untried team. Their potential as players staggers the imagination. That's because business games, like other games, are eventually the meeting of *equals*. The rules of a structured game give everyone an equal chance. Brains can overcome brawn; planning can outwit experience; foresight and knowledge of the fine points can capitalize on opponents' weaknesses and exploit or magnify your own strengths. New systems, unexpected formations, and clever signals can take rival teams by surprise. Regular practice and correction of faulty techniques can overcome bad habit patterns of the past, but it takes perseverance and concentration on the task.

The game plan of this book is heavily weighted toward correction of bad form and elimination of losing attitudes. The emphasis is less on how-to-do-it than how-to-think-about-it. The most important element in learning a new game is having perspective, being able to judge what is important to the ultimate outcome, and then directing your efforts and energies toward significant ends.

A game plan is not concerned with "how it ought to be" or "how we wish it were." A game plan is a diagram of *how it is!* You can't change a game until you can play by the rules that exist. You can't develop a useful strategy or capitalize on a skill until you know what you're up against. You can't calculate your moves until you are knowledge-able enough to predict countermoves and defensive tactics of rival teams. You can't be part of a winning team until you know what a team is, what cooperation entails, what position you can play best, and what you can expect of other teammates. You can't practice skills unless you know what skills are important. You can't play a game if you approach it like an unpleasant chore. You can't win if you don't make an effort to outplay your challengers. You can't enjoy the encounters if you don't understand that the game of corporate politics is to see who can win the most money. (Those who win the money decide how to spend it, so if you want to change the things money is spent on, you first have to win it.)

A game plan is not an answer or an accomplishment; it simply lays out the problem and points out the variables that can influence the players and change the outcome. It describes the limits within which free choice, bargaining, and negotiating are possible. A game plan defines the rules. The *game* is what the players do within the rules. You are the player. You can choose to play the game any way you like—or not play it if you prefer. But since you're already milling around the fringes of the gridiron, it makes sense to join with all other women like yourself and form a team that can challenge the men's leagues on the basis of equal ability and equal facility.

In every game, luck plays a part. The outcome of a game is never predictable, but a realistic game plan gives you a sporting chance. You take it from here. We are just beginning!

INDEX

388

rules of, 22, 26, 32, 35–36,
  82–83, 93
  see also specific topics
Game plan, this book as a,
  382–384
Games
  beauty of, 381
  girls', 72, 73
  as meeting of equals, 383
  social graces (etiquette) in,
    384
  women's inexperience with,
    282, 380–381
  see also Baseball; Basketball;
    Chess; Football; Poker;
    Team sports
Gaming table
  office as seat at, 283
  popularity at, 282
"General," meaning of, 101
Girls
  bodily expression discouraged
    in, 69, 70
  cooperation and, 80
  meaning of word, in business
    jargon, 115
  as protected, 225
  rules and, 71–72
  team sports and, 75–77
Girl's games, 71–72
Goal
  in career planning, 146
  of chief-executive-officer
    position, 147–174 (*see also*
    Career planning)
  making a profit (winning)
    as, 68–69
"Gold-plating" a task, 154
Government, political activity
  as preparation for business
    relations with, 225
Government bureaucracy, 54
Graduate education
  (graduate degrees), sub-
    sidization of, 218–220
Graham, Katherine, 212
Greer, Germaine, 362
Gropper, Nancy B., 43
Gross income of employer
  company, 233
Gross profit of employer
  company, 233
Group spirit, 70. *See also* "Team
  spirit," appeals to

Hairstyles, 346
Handbag, doing without, 343–345
Harvard Graduate School of
  Business Administration, 99,
  101, 220
Head-hunters (executive search
  firms), 198, 205
  feminist-owned and run, 200,
    201
"Hell," men's apologies for use
  of word, 111
Heller, Joseph, 58–59
Heller, Robert, 152
"Helmsman," meaning of, 114
Henning, Margaret, 165
Hierarchical organization
  (hierarchical structure),
  45–51
  building as representation of,
    262
  chain-of-command in (*see*
    Chain-of-command)
  impersonal quality of, 49–50
  intent of, 48
  novels dealing with, 57–59
  power in, 47–48
  rank system in (*see* Rank)
  see also Military organization
    of business; Pyramid
Hite Report, The, 364
Hockey, ice, 105
Hogan, Betsy, 217, 371
Homophobia, 363, 364
Homosexuality
  fear of (homophobia),
    363, 364
  female (*see* Lesbians)
  latent, 363
Hostility, male, 112, 123, 124
Hotel arrangements, 223
Hourly wage, 264
"Huddle," meaning of, 109
Humorlessness of male
  business language, 98
"Hunch," 134

Ice hockey, 105
Immediate supervisor (boss),
  54–59
  authority of, 54–62
  as coach, 93, 94
  complaints about, 56
  criticism of, 55, 91
  dependency position in
    relation to, 320–321

390

391

394

398

By the year 2000, 2 out of 3 Americans could be illiterate.

It's true.

Today, 75 million adults… about one American in three, can't read adequately. And by the year 2000, U.S. News & World Report envisions an America with a literacy rate of only 30%.

Before that America comes to be, you can stop it… by joining the fight against illiteracy today.

Call the Coalition for Literacy at toll-free **1-800-228-8813** and volunteer.

Volunteer Against Illiteracy. The only degree you need is a degree of caring.

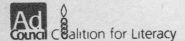

Ad Council Coalition for Literacy